Project Management

Project Management

Ruth Penn

STATES
ACADEMIC PRESS
www.statesacademicpress.com

States Academic Press,
109 South 5th Street,
Brooklyn, NY 11249, USA

ISBN: 978-1-63989-446-8

Cataloging-in-Publication Data

Project management / Ruth Penn
p. cm.
Includes bibliographical references and index.
ISBN 978-1-63989-446-8
1. Project management. 2. Management. I. Penn, Ruth.

HD69.P75 I58 2021

658.404--dc23

For information on all States Academic Press publications visit our website at www.statesacademicpress.com

STATES
ACADEMIC PRESS

TABLE OF CONTENTS

PREFACE

This book is a culmination of my many years of practice in this field. I attribute the success of this book to my support group. I would like to thank my parents who have showered me with unconditional love and support and my peers and professors for their constant guidance.

Project management is the process of initiating, planning, controlling, executing and closing the work of a team to meet certain goals or specific success criteria in a pre-determined period of time. It focuses on completion of a project which complies with the client's needs. The primary constraints of this field are scope, quality, budget and time. It is also concerned with the allocation of necessary resources to obtain defined goals. There are many types of project management such as construction project management, IT project management, biotechnology project management, localization project management, etc. The four key components of this field are planning, processing, power and people. There are various approaches to project management. Some of these are phased approach, benefits realization management, earned value management and product based planning. The book aims to shed light on some of the unexplored aspects of this field. It has been compiled in such a manner that it will provide an in-depth knowledge about the theory and practice of this discipline. This book will provide comprehensive knowledge to the readers.

The details of chapters are provided below for a progressive learning:

Chapter - Introduction

A project is a series of tasks that is concerned with the development of a unique product or service that adds value to an organization. Controlling, initiating, executing, planning and closing the operations of a team for the attainment of goals and objectives specified under a project is an important aspect of project management. This is an introductory chapter which will briefly introduce about project management.

Chapter - Approaches of Project Management

There are certain approaches that are used in project management such as critical chain project management, earned value management, lean project management, agile project management, waterfall methodology, event chain methodology, etc. This chapter has been carefully written to provide an easy understanding of these approaches used in project management.

Chapter – Processes and Phases

Aggregate planning, work breakdown structure, project monitoring, project communication management, project documentation, project networks, project quality management, project cost management, etc. are some of the processes and phases that are studied under the domain of project management. This chapter discusses the different processes and phases of project management.

Chapter – Tools and Techniques

There are various tools and techniques that are used for project management such as schedule compression, phase-gate model, value breakdown structure, graphical path method, critical path method, SWOT analysis, integrated master plan, etc. The topics elaborated in this chapter will help in gaining a better perspective of various tools and techniques used in project management.

Chapter – Project Management Software

Project management software helps project managers and teams to manage and meet goals on time while managing resources and cost. Its functions include task distribution, time tracking, budgeting, resource planning, team collaboration, etc. This chapter delves into the subject of project management software for a thorough understanding of it.

Ruth Penn

Introduction 1

- **Project**
- **Project Management**
- **Organizational Project Management**
- **Project Portfolio Management**
- **Extreme Project Management**

A project is a series of tasks that is concerned with the development of a unique product or service that adds value to an organization. Controlling, initiating, executing, planning and closing the operations of a team for the attainment of goals and objectives specified under a project is an important aspect of project management. This is an introductory chapter which will briefly introduce about project management.

Project

Project in general refers to a new endeavor with specific objective and varies so widely that it is very difficult to precisely define it. Project is a temporary endeavor undertaken to create a unique product or service or result.

Project is a unique process, consist of a set of coordinated and controlled activities with start and finish dates, undertaken to achieve an objective confirming to specific requirements, including the constraints of time cost and resource.

Examples of project include developing a watershed, creating irrigation facility, developing new variety of a crop, developing new breed of an animal, developing agro-processing centre, construction of farm building, sting of a concentrated feed plant etc. It may be noted that each of these projects differ in composition, type, scope, size and time.

Project Characteristics

Despite above diversities, projects share the following common characteristics:

- Unique in nature.

- Have definite objectives (goals) to achieve.
- Requires set of resources.
- Have a specific time frame for completion with a definite start and finish.
- Involves risk and uncertainty.
- Requires cross-functional teams and interdisciplinary approach.

Project Performance Dimensions

Three major dimensions that define the project performance are scope, time, and resource. These parameters are interrelated and interactive. The relationship generally represented as an equilateral triangle. The relationship is shown in figure below.

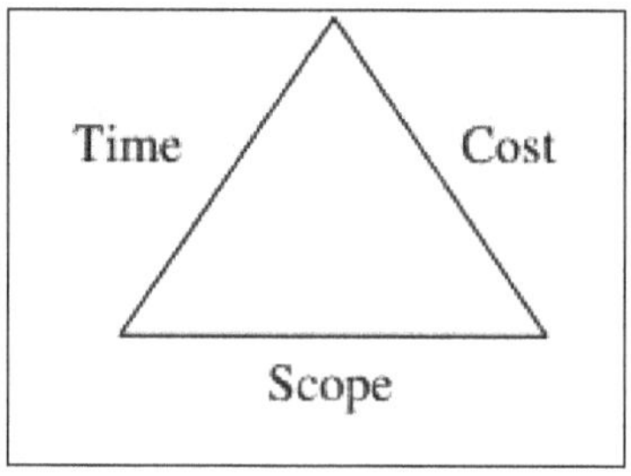

Project performance dimensions.

It is evident that any change in any one of dimensions would affect the other. For example, if the scope is enlarged, project would require more time for completion and the cost would also go up. If time is reduced the scope and cost would also be required to be reduced. Similarly any change in cost would be reflected in scope and time. Successful completion of the project would require accomplishment of specified goals within scheduled time and budget. In recent years a fourth dimension, stakeholder satisfaction, is added to the project. However, the other school of management argues that this dimension is an inherent part of the scope of the project that defines the specifications to which the project is required to be implemented. Thus the performance of a project is measured by the degree to which these three parameters (scope, time and cost) are achieved.

Performance = f (Scope, Cost, Time)

In management literature, this equilateral triangle is also referred as the "Quality triangle" of the project.

Project Life Cycle

Every project, from conception to completion, passes through various phases of a life cycle synonym to life cycle of living beings. There is no universal consensus on the number of phases in a project cycle. An understanding of the life cycle is important to successful completion of the project as it facilitates to understand the logical sequence of events in the continuum of progress from start to finish. Typical project consists of four phases- conceptualization, planning, execution and termination. Each phase is marked by one or more deliverables such as concept note, feasibility report, implementation plan, HRD plan, resource allocation plan, evaluation report etc.

Conceptualization Phase

Conception phase, starting with the seed of an idea, it covers identification of the product/service, pre-feasibility, feasibility studies and appraisal and approval. The project idea is conceptualized with initial considerations of all possible alternatives for achieving the project objectives. As the idea becomes established a proposal is developed setting out rationale, method, estimated costs, benefits and other details for appraisal of the stakeholders. After reaching a broad consensus on the proposal the feasibility dimensions are analyzed in detail.

Planning Phase

In this phase the project structure is planned based on project appraisal and approvals. Detailed plans for activity, finance, and resources are developed and integrated to the quality parameters. In the process major tasks need to be performed in this phase are:

- Identification of activities and their sequencing.
- Time frame for execution.
- Estimation and budgeting.
- Staffing.

A Detailed Project Report (DPR) specifying various aspects of the project is finalized to facilitate execution in this phase.

Execution Phase

This phase of the project witnesses the concentrated activity where the plans are put into operation. Each activity is monitored, controlled and coordinated to achieve project objectives. Important activities in this phase are:

- Communicating with stakeholders.
- Reviewing progress.
- Monitoring cost and time.
- Controlling quality.
- Managing changes.

Termination Phase

This phase marks the completion of the project wherein the agreed deliverables are installed and project is put in to operation with arrangements for follow-up and evaluation.

Life Cycle path

The life cycle of a project from start to completion follows either a "S" shaped path or a "J" shaped path. In "S" shape path the progress is slow at the starting and terminal phase and is fast in the implementation phase. For example, implementation of watershed project. At the beginning detailed sectoral planning and coordination among various implementing agencies etc. makes progress slow and similarly towards termination, creating institutional arrangement for transfer and maintenance of assets to the stakeholders progresses slowly.

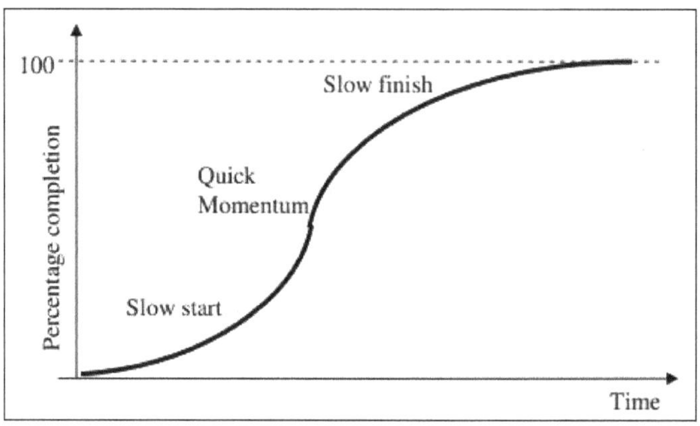

Project life path –"S" shape.

In "J" type cycle path the progress in beginning is slow and as the time moves on the progress of the project improves at fast rate. Example, in a developing an energy plantation. In this the land preparation progresses slowly and as soon as the land and seedling are transplantation is under taken. This is shown in figure.

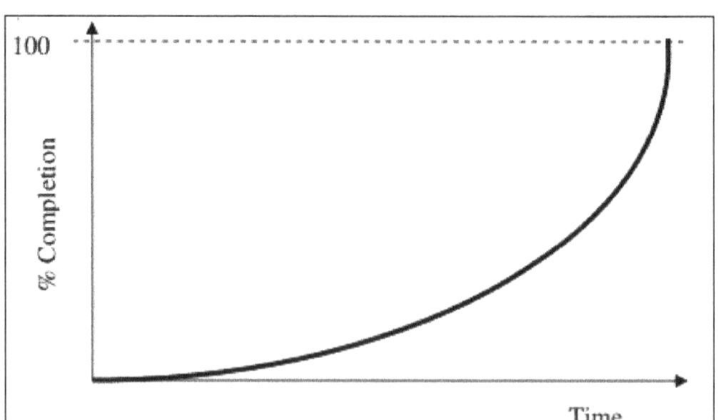

Project life cycle path - "J" Shape.

Project Classification

There is no standard classification of the projects. However considering project goals, these can be classified into two broad groups, industrial and developmental. Each of these groups can be further classified considering nature of work (repetitive, non-repetitive), completion time (long term, shot term etc), cost (large, small, etc.), level of risk (high, low, no-risk), mode of operation (build, build-operate-transfer etc).

Industrial projects also referred as commercial projects, which are undertaken to provide goods or services for meeting the growing needs of the customers and providing attractive returns to the investors/stake holders. Following the background, these projects are further grouped into two categories i.e., demand based and resource / supply based. The demand based projects are designed to satisfy the customers' felt as well the latent needs such as complex fertilizers, agro-processing infrastructure etc. The resource/supply based projects are those which take advantage of the available resources like land, water, agricultural produce, raw material, minerals and even human resource. Projects triggered by successful R&D are also considered as supply based. Examples of resource based projects include food product units, metallurgical industries, oil refineries etc. Examples of projects based on human resource (skilled) availability include projects in IT sector, Clinical Research projects in bio services and others.

Development projects are undertaken to facilitate the promotion and acceleration of overall economic development. These projects act as catalysts for economic development providing a cascading effect. Development projects cover sectors like irrigation, agriculture, infrastructure health and education.

Table: Difference between Industrial and Developmental Projects.

Dimension	Industrial Project	Developmental Project
Scale of project	Limited	Large
Promoters	Entrepreneurs or corporates	Government, public sectors, NGOs.
Investment	---	High
Gestation period	---	High
Profitabilty	High, considered on IRR (Internal Rate of Return)	Modest, Considered on ERR (Economic Rate of Return).
Finance	Stringent debt equity norms	Operates on higher debt equity norms.
Source of fund	National stock markets and from domestic financial institutions	International organizations like World Bank, IMF, ADB, DFID and others mostly as loan, yet times providing for some grants.
Interest rates and repayment period:	Market rate and the repayment period is generally 7 to 10 years	Very low for borrowed funds and the repayment period extends up to 25 years and even beyond.

Project Management

Project management is a distinct area of management that helps in handling projects. It has three key features to distinguish it from other forms of management and they include: A project manager, the project team and the project management system. The project management system comprises organization structure, information processing and decision making and the procedures that facilitate integration of horizontal and vertical elements of the project organization. The project management system focuses on integrated planning and control.

Benefits of Project Management Approach

The rationale for following project management approach is as follows:

- Project management approach will help in handling complex, costly and risky assignments by providing interdisciplinary approach in handling the assignments. Example: R&D organizations.
- Project management approaches help in handling assignments in a specified time frame with definite start and completion points. Example handling customer orders by Industries involved in production of capital goods.
- Project management approaches provide task orientation to personnel in an Organization in handling assignments. Example: Organizations in IT sector handling software development assignments for clients.

Project Identification and Formulation

A project in the economic sense directly or indirectly adds to the economy of the Nation. However an introspection of the project performance clearly indicates that the situation is far from satisfactory. Most of the major and critical projects in public sector that too in crucial sectors like irrigation, agriculture, and infrastructure are plagued by tremendous time and cost overruns. Even in the private sector the performance is not all that satisfactory as is evident from the growing sickness in industry and rapid increase in non-performing assets (NPAS) of Banks and Financial Institutions. The reasons for time and cost over runs are several and they can be broadly classified under-technical, financial, procedural and managerial. Most of these problems mainly stem from inadequate project formulation and haphazard implementation.

Project Identification

Project identification is an important step in project formulation. These are conceived with the objective of meeting the market demand, exploiting natural resources or creating wealth. The project ideas for developmental projects come mainly from the national planning process, where as industrial projects usually stem from identification of commercial prospects and profit potential.

As projects are a means to achieving certain objectives, there may be several alternative projects that will meet these objectives. It is important to indicate all the other alternatives considered with justification in favour of the specific project proposed for consideration.

Sectoral studies, opportunity studies, support studies, project identification essentially focuses on screening the number of project ideas that come up based on information and data available and based on expert opinions and to come up with a limited number of project options which are promising.

Project Formulation

"Project Formulation" is the processes of presenting a project idea in a form in which it can be subjected to comparative appraisals for the purpose of determining in definitive terms the priority that should be attached to a project under sever resource constraints. Project Formulation involves the following steps.

PROJECT FORMULATION
↓
OPPORTUNITY STUDIES/Support Studies
↓
IDENTIFICATION OF PRODUCT/SERVICE
↓
PREFEASIBILITY STUDY
↓
FEASIBILITY STUDY
(TECHNO ECONOMIC FEASIBILITY)
↓
PROJECT APPRAISAL
↓
DETAILED PROJECT REPORT

Project Formulation –Schematic view.

Opportunity Studies

An opportunity study identifies investment opportunities and is normally undertaken at macro level by agencies involved in economic planning and development. In general opportunity studies there are three types of study: Area Study, sectoral and Sub-sectoral Studies and Resource Based Studies. Opportunity Studies and Support studies provide sound basis for project identification.

Pre-feasibility Studies/Opportunity Studies

A pre-feasibility study should be viewed as an intermediate stage between a project opportunity study and a detailed feasibility study, the difference being primarily the extent of details of the information obtained. It is the process of gathering facts and opinions pertaining to the project. This information is then vetted for the purpose of tentatively determining whether the project idea is worth pursuing furthering. Pre-feasibility study lays stress on assessing market potential, magnitude of investment, technical feasibility, financial analysis, risk analysis etc. The breadth and depth of pre -feasibility depend upon the time available and the confidence of the decision maker. Pre-feasibility studies help in preparing a project profile for presentation to various stakeholders including funding agencies to solicit their support to the project. It also throws light on aspects of the project that are critical in nature and necessitate further investigation through functional support studies.

Support studies are carried out before commissioning pre-feasibility or a feasibility study of projects requiring large-scale investments. These studies also form an integral part of the feasibility studies. They cover one or more critical aspects of project in detail. The contents of the Support Study vary depending on the nature of the study and the project contemplated. Since it relates to a vital aspect of the project the conclusions should be clear enough to give a direction to the subsequent stage of project preparation.

Feasibility Study

Feasibility Study forms the backbone of Project Formulation and presents a balanced picture incorporating all aspects of possible concern. The study investigates practicalities, ways of achieving objectives, strategy options, methodology, and predict likely outcome, risk and the consequences of each course of action. It becomes the foundation on which project definition and rationale will be based so that the quality is reflected in subsequent project activity. A well conducted study provides a sound base for decisions, clarifications of objectives, logical planning, minimal risk, and a successful cost effective project. Assessing feasibility of a proposal requires understanding of the STEEP factors. These are as under Social, Technological, Ecological, Economic, and Political.

A feasibility study is not an end in itself but only a means to arrive at an investment decision. The preparation of a feasibility study report is often made difficulty by the number of alternatives (regarding the choice of technology, plant capacity, location, financing etc.) and assumptions on which the decisions are made. The project feasibility studies focus on:

- Economic and Market Analysis.
- Technical Analysis.
- Market Analysis.
- Financial Analysis.
- Economic Benefits.

- Project Risk and Uncertainty.
- Management Aspects.

Economic and Market Analysis

In the recent years the market analysis has undergone a paradigm shift. The demand forecast and projection of demand supply gap for products/ services can no longer be based on extrapolation of past trends using statistical tools and techniques. One has to look at multiple parameters that influence the market. Demand projections are to be made keeping in view all possible developments. Review of the projects executed over the years suggests that many projects have failed not because of technological and financial problems but mainly because of the fact that the projects ignored customer requirements and market forces.

In market analysis a number of factors need to be considered covering – product specifications, pricing, channels of distribution, trade practices, threat of substitutes, domestic and international competition, opportunities for exports etc. It should aim at providing analysis of future market scenario so that the decision on project investment can be taken in an objective manner keeping in view the market risk and uncertainty.

Technical Analysis

Technical analysis is based on the description of the product and specifications and also the requirements of quality standards. The analysis encompasses available alternative technologies, selection of the most appropriate technology in terms of optimum combination of project components, implications of the acquisition of technology, and contractual aspects of licensing. Special attention is given to technical dimensions such as in project selection. The technology chosen should also keep in view the requirements of raw materials and other inputs in terms of quality and should ensure that the cost of production would be competitive. In brief the technical analysis included the following aspects:

Technology

- Availability.
- Alternatives.
- Latest/state-of-art.
- Other implications.

Plant Capacity

- Market demand.

- Technological parameters.

Inputs

- Raw materials.
- Components.
- Power.
- Water.
- Fuel.
- Others.

Environmental Impact Studies

All most all projects have some impact on environment. Current concern of environmental quality requires the environmental clearance for all projects. Therefore environ impact analysis needs to be undertaken before commencement of feasibility study.

Objectives of Environmental Impact Studies

- To identify and describe the environmental resources/values (ER/Vs) or the environmental attributes (EA) which will be affected by the project (in a quantified manner as far as possible).
- To describe, measure and assess the environmental effects that the proposed project will have on the ER/Vs.
- To describe the alternatives to the proposed project this could accomplish the same results but with a different set of environmental effects.

The environmental impact studies would facilitate providing necessary remedial measures in terms of the equipments and facilities to be provided in the project to comply with the environmental regulation specifications.

Financial Analysis

The Financial Analysis, examines the viability of the project from financial or commercial considerations and indicates the return on the investments. Some of the commonly used techniques for financial analysis are as follows:

- Pay-back period.
- Return on Investment (ROI).
- Net Present Value (NPV).

- Profitability Index (PI)/Benefit Cost Ratio.
- Internal Rate of Return (IRR).

Pay-back Period

This is the simplest of all methods and calculates the time required to recover the initial project investment out of the subsequent cash flow. It is computed by dividing the investment amount by the sum of the annual returns (income – expenditure) until it is equal to the capital cost.

Example of Uniform Annual Return

A farmer has invested about Rs. 20000/- in constructing a fish pond and gets annual net return of Rs.5000/- (difference between annual income and expenditure). The pay-back period for the project is 4 years (20000/ 5000).

Example of Varying Annual Return

In a project Rs.1,00,000/- an initial investment of establishing a horticultural orchard. The annual cash flow is as under.

Time	Annual Income	Annual Expenditure	Annual Return	Cumulative Return
1 st Year	60,000	30,000	30,000	30,000
2 nd Year	70,000	30,000	40,000	70,000
3 rd Year	85,000	25,000	60,000	1,30,000
Pay-back period = Two and half years				

The drawback in this method is that it ignores any return received after the payback period and assumes equal value for the income and expenditure irrespective of the time.

It is also possible that projects with high return on investments beyond the pay-back period may not get the deserved importance i.e., two projects having same pay-back period – one giving no return and the other providing large return after pay-back period will be treated equally, which is logically not correct.

Return on Investment (ROI)

The ROI is the annual return as percentage of the initial investment and is computed by dividing the annual return with investment. It is calculation is simple when the return is uniform. For example the ROI of the fish ponds is (5000/10000) X 100 = 50%. When the return is not uniform the average of annual returns over a period is used. For horticultural orchard average return is (1,30,000/3) = 43333. ROI = (43333/100000) X 100 = 43.3 %.

Computation of ROI also suffers from similar limitation as of pay-back period. It does not differentiate between two projects one yielding immediate return (lift irrigation project) and another project where return is received after some gestation period say about 2-3 years (developing new variety of crop).

Both the pay-back period and ROI are simple ones and more suited for quick analysis of the projects and sometimes provide inadequate measures of project viability. It is desirable to use these methods in conjunction with other discounted cash flow methods such as Net Present Value (NPV), Internal Rate of Return (IRR) and Benefit-Cost ratio.

Discounted Cash Flow Analysis

The principle of discounting is the reverse of compounding and takes the value of money over time. To understand his let us take an example of compounding first. Assuming return of 10 %, Rs.100 would grow to Rs.110/- in the first year and Rs.121 in the second year. In a reverse statement, at a discount rate of 10% the return of Rs.110 in the next year is equivalent to Rs100 at present. In other words the present worth of next years return at a discount rate 10 % is only Rs.90.91 i.e., (100/110). Similarly Rs.121 in the second year worth Rs.100/- at present or the present value of a return after two years is Rs.82.64 (100/121). These values Rs.90.91 and Rs.82.64 are known as present value of of future annual return of Rs.100 in first and second year respectively. Mathematically, the formula for computing present value (PV) of a cash flow "Cn" in "nth" year at a discount rate of "d" is as follows:

$$PV= C_n/(1+d)^n$$

The computed discount factor tables are also available for ready reference. In the financial analysis the present value is computed for both investment and returns. The results are presented in three different measures ie. NPV, B-C Ratio, and IRR.

Net Present Value (NPV)

Net Present Value is considered as one of the important measure for deciding the financial viability of a project. The sum of discounted values of the stream of investments in different years of project implementation gives present value of the cost (say C). Similarly sum of discounted returns yields the present value of benefits (say B). The net present value (NPV) of the project is the difference between these two values (B- C). Higher the value of NPV is always desirable for a project.

Benefit-Cost Ratio (B-C Ratio) or Profitability Index (PI)

The B-C Ratio also referred as Profitability Index (PI), reflects the profitability of a project and computed as the ratio of total present value of the returns to the total present value of the investments (B/C). Higher the ratio better is the return.

Internal Rate of Return (IRR)

Internal Rate of Return (IRR) indicates the limit or the rate of discount at which the project total present value of return (B) equals to total present value of investments (C) i.e. B-C = Zero. In other words it is the discount rate at which the NPV of the project is zero. The IRR is computed by iteration i.e. computing NPV at different discount rate till the value is nearly zero. It is desirable to have projects with higher IRR.

Risk and Uncertainty

Risk and Uncertainty are associated with every project. Risk is related to occurrence of adverse consequences and is quantifiable. It is analysed through probability of occurrences. Where as uncertainty refers to inherently unpredictable dimensions and is assessed through sensitivity analysis. It is therefore necessary to analyse these dimensions during formulation and appraisal phase of the programme. Factors attributing to risk and uncertainties of a project are grouped under the following:

- Technical: Relates to project scope, change in technology, quality and quantity of inputs, activity times, estimation errors etc.
- Economical: Pertains to market, cost, competitive environment, change in policy, exchange rate etc.
- Socio-political: Includes dimensions such as labour, stakeholders etc.
- Environmental: Factors could be level of pollution, environmental degradation etc.

Economic Benefits

Apart from the financial benefits (in terms of Return on Investment) the economic benefits of the project are also analyzed in the feasibility study. The economic benefits include employment generation, economic development of the area where the project is located, foreign exchange savings in case of import substitutes or earning of foreign exchange in case of export oriented projects and others.

Management Aspects

Management aspects are becoming very important in project feasibility studies. The management aspects cover the background of promoters, management philosophy, the organization set up and staffing for project implementation phase as well as operational phase, the aspects of decentralization and delegation, systems and procedures, the method of execution and finally the accountability.

Time Frame for Project Implementation

The feasibility study also presents a broad time frame for project implementation. The time frame influences preoperative expenses and cost escalations which will impact the profitability and viability of the project.

Feasibility Report

Based on the feasibility studies the Techno economic feasibility report or the project report is prepared to facilitate project evaluation and appraisal and investment decisions.

Project Appraisal

The project appraisal is the process of critical examination and analysis of the proposal in totality. The appraisal goes beyond the analysis presented in the feasibility report. At this stage, if required compilation of additional information and further analysis of project dimensions are 17 undertaken. At the end of the process an appraisal note is prepared for facilitating decision on the project implementation. The appraisal process generally concentrates on the following aspects:

- Market Appraisal: Focusing on demand projections, adequacy of marketing infrastructure and competence of the key marketing personnel.
- Technical Appraisal: Covering product mix, capacity, process of manufacture engineering know-how and technical collaboration, raw materials and consumables, location and site, building, plant and equipments, manpower requirements and breakeven point.
- Environmental Appraisal: Impact on land use and micro-environment, commitment of natural resources, and Government policy.
- Financial Appraisal: Capital, rate of return, specifications, contingencies, cost projection, capacity utilization, and financing pattern.
- Economic Appraisal: Considered as a supportive appraisal it reviews economic rate of return, effective rate of protection and domestic resource cost.
- Managerial Appraisal: Focuses on promoters, organization structure, managerial personnel, and HR management.
- Social Cost Benefit Analysis (SCBA): Social Cost Benefit Analysis is a methodology for evaluating projects from the social point of view and focuses on social cost and benefits of a project. There often tend to differ from the costs incurred in monetary terms and benefits earned in monetary terms by the project SCBA may be based on UNIDO method or the Little-Mirriles (L-M) approach. Under UNIDO method the net benefits of the project are considered in terms of economic (efficiency) prices also referred to as shadow prices. As per the L-M approach the outputs and inputs of a project are classified into (1) traded goods and services (2) Non-traded goods and services; and (3) Labor. All over the world including

India currently the focus is on Economic Rate of Return (ERR) based on SCBA assume importance in project formulation and investment decisions.

Detailed Project Report (DPR)

Once the projects are appraised and the investment decisions are made a Detailed Project Report (DPR) is prepared. It provides all the relevant details including design drawings, specifications, detailed cost estimates etc. and this would act as a blue print for project implementation.

Project Management Techniques

Project management involves decision making for the planning, organizing, coordination, monitoring and control of a number of interrelated time bound activities. Project Manager therefore, often depends on tools and techniques that are effective enough not only for drawing up the best possible initial plan but also capable of projecting instantaneously the impact of deviations so as to initiate necessary corrective measures. The search for an effective tool has resulted in development of a variety of techniques. These project management techniques can be classified under two broad categories i.e., Bar Charts and Networks.

Bar Charts

Bar charts are the pictorial representation of various tasks required to be performed for accomplishment of the project objectives. These charts have formed the basis of development of many other project management techniques.

Gantt Chart

Henry L Gantt around 1917 developed a system of bar charts for scheduling and reporting progress of a project. These charts latter were known as Gantt Charts. It is a pictorial representation specifying the start and finish time for various tasks to be performed in a project on a horizontal time-scale. Each project is broken down to physically identifiable and controllable units, called the Tasks. These tasks are indicated by means of a bar, preferably at equi-distance in the vertical axis and time is plotted in the horizontal axis. In this figure "Task A" is land preparation, "Task B" is procurement of inputs etc. Land preparation (Task A) takes five days starting from day one. However in practice the time scale is superimposed on a calendar i.e., if land preparation starts on 1st June it would be completed by 5th June.

Length of the bar indicates required time for the task whereas the width has no significance. Though the bar chart is comprehensive, convenient, and very effective, it has the following limitations:

- Like many other graphical techniques are often difficult to handle large number of tasks in other words a complex project.

- Does not indicate the inter relationship between the tasks i.e., if one activity overruns time what would be the impact on project completion.

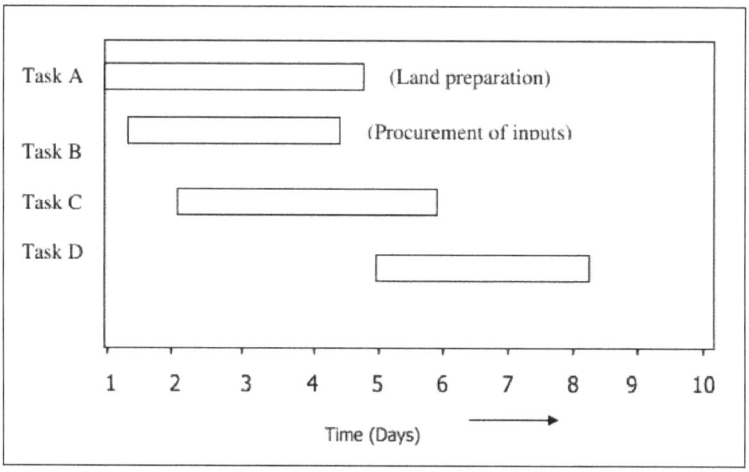

Bar chart.

Milestone Chart

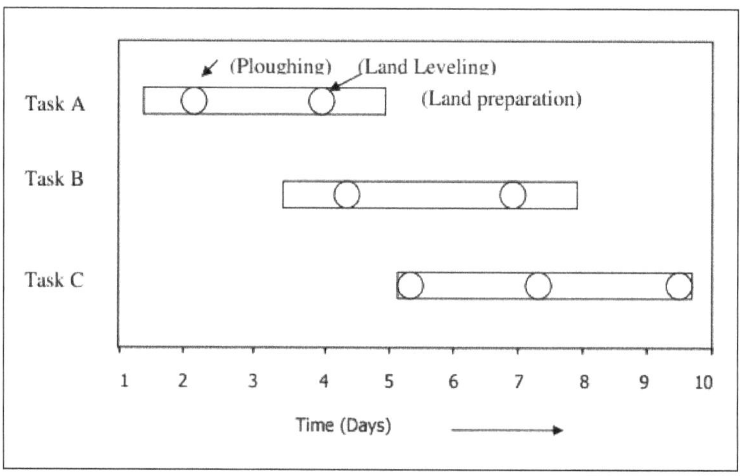

Milestone chart.

Milestone chart is an improvement over the bar chart (Gantt chart) by introducing the concept of milestone. The milestone, represented by a circle over a task in the bar chart indicates completion of a specific phase of the task figure. For example land preparation (Task A) includes ploughing and leveling. From the simple bar chart it is difficult to monitor progress of the ploughing. Introduction of a milestone on day 3 would specify that the ploughing would be completed by day 3 of the project i.e. 3rd June. In a milestone chart a task is broken down in to specific phases (activities) and after accomplishment of each of the specific activity a milestone is reached or in other words an event occurs. The chart also shows the sequential relationship among the milestones or events within the same task but not the relationship among milestones contained in different tasks. For example in figure, the milestone 2 of task A cannot be reached until the milestone 1 is crossed and the activity between milestone 1 and 2 is over. Similarly, in task B the milestone 4 can begin only after completion of milestone 3. But the relationship between the milestone of task A and task B is not indicated in the milestone chart. Other weaknesses of this chart are as follows:

- Does not show interdependence between tasks.
- Does not indicate critical activities.
- Does not consider the concept of uncertainty in accomplishing the task.
- Very cumbersome to draw the chart for large projects.

Networks

The network is a logical extension of Gantt's milestone chart incorporating the modifications so as to illustrate interrelationship between and among all the milestones in an entire project. The two best-known techniques for network analysis are Programme Evaluation and review Technique (PERT) and Critical Path Method (CPM). These two techniques were developed almost simultaneously during 1956-1958. PERT was developed for US navy for scheduling the research and development activities for Polaris missiles programme. CPM was developed by E.I. du Pont de Nemours & Company as an application to construction project. Though these two methods were developed simultaneously they have striking similarity and the significant difference is that the time estimates for activities is assumed deterministic in CPM and probabilistic in PERT. There is also little distinction in terms of application of these concepts. PERT is used where emphasis is on scheduling and monitoring the project and CPM is used where emphasis is on optimizing resource allocation. However, now-a-days the two techniques are used synonymously in network analysis and the differences are considered to be historical.

Both CPM and PERT describe the work plan of project where arrows and circles respectively indicate the activities and events in the project. This arrow or network diagram includes all the activities and events that should be completed to reach the project objectives. The activities and events are laid in a planned sequence of their accomplishments. However, there are two types of notations used in the network diagram. They are as under:

1. Activity-on-Arrow (AOA).
2. Activity-on-Node (AON).

In AOA notation, the arrow represents the work to be done and the circle represents an event – either the beginning of another activity or completion of previous one.

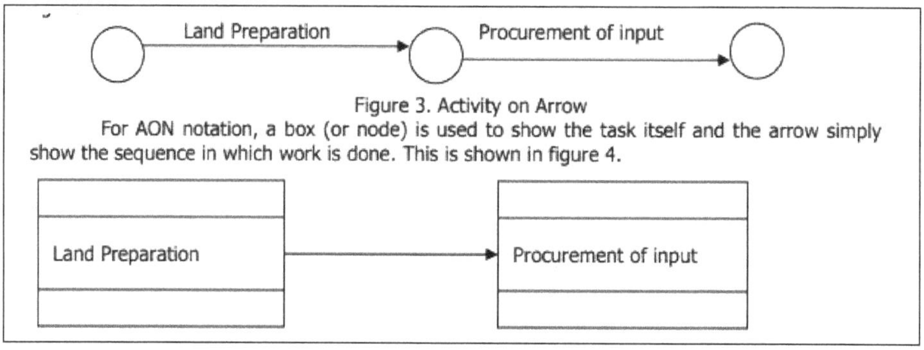

AON diagram.

Most project management software usually uses AON diagram. AOA network diagram are usually associated with the PERT diagram.

Programme Evaluation and Review Technique (PERT)

The PERT technique is a method of minimizing trouble spots, programme bottlenecks, delays and interruptions by determining critical activities before they occur so that various activities in the project can be coordinated.

PERT Terminology

Some of the terms frequently used in PERT are as follows:

- Activity: A recognizable work item of a project requiring time and resource for its completion.
- Dummy Activity: An activity that indicates precedence relationship and requires neither time nor resource.
- Critical Activity: Activities on the critical path having zero slack/float time.
- Critical Path: The longest time path connecting the critical activities in the project network. The total time on this path is the shortest duration of the project.
- Event: An instantaneous point in time signifying completion or beginning of an activity.
- Burst Event: An event which gives rise to more than one activity.
- Merge Event: The event which occurs only when more than one activity are accomplished.
- Expected Time: The weighted average of the estimated optimistic, most likely and pessimistic time duration of a project activity:

Expected Time (T_E) = $\frac{T_o + 4T_M + T_P}{6}$

where,

T_o is the Optimistic time.

T_M is the Most likely time.

T_P is the Pessimistic time.

- Earliest Start Time (EST): The earliest possible time at which the event can occur. The EST also denotes the Earliest Start Time (EST) of an activity as activities emanate from events. The EST of an activity is the time before which it cannot commence without affecting the immediate preceding activity.
- Latest Start Time (LST): The latest time at which the event can take place. Also referred as the Latest Start Time (LST) indicating the latest time at which an activity can begin without delaying the project completion time.
- Slack: The amount of spare time available between completion of an activity and beginning of next activity.

Steps for Network Analysis

The six steps of network analysis are as follows:

- Prepare the list of activities.
- Define the inter relationship among the activities.
- Estimate the activity duration.
- Assemble the activities in the form of a flow diagram.
- Draw the network.
- Analyze the network i.e. compute EST and LST; identify critical events, critical path and critical activities.

Prepare the List of Activities

An activity in a project is the lowest level of resource consuming, time-bound work having a specified beginning and endpoint. It should be quantifiable, measurable, costable, and discrete. The total project is subdivided into activities and each activity is given an alphabetical symbol / code. When the number of activities is more than 26, alphanumeric or multi -alphabet codes can be used. This involves a detailed delineation of the activities to be performed to complete the project. There is no limit to the number of activities to which the project should be splitted. However, it is advisable to limit the number to the minimum required from managerial consideration for avoiding unnecessary complexity. In a simple project it may be easier to identify the activity. In complex projects project activities are identified by splitting it into different hierarchical levels (sub-projects). For example in the activities of a watershed project could be broken down in to sub-projects such as agricultural sub-projects, Soil & water conservation sub-projects, Aforestation sub-project etc. For each of these subprojects the activities could be identified. Depending on the size and nature of the project sub-projects could be further divided into sub-sub project.

For illustration of the process, a simple example of creating facility for lift irrigation in a farm would be used in the following text. Some of the assumptions are as under:

- It is assumed that the competent authority has approved the project and the project scheduling starts with the activity of "Site selection".
- Irrigation would be provided from a newly dug well.
- Field channels from the well would be laid after its digging.
- Suitable pump would be procured and installed for lifting water.
- Specification for the pump is finalized based on the groundwater prospecting data before digging.
- Pump and other inputs would not be procured until the site is selected.
- Pump would be installed after digging the well.

With above assumptions, the activities of the project are listed in table. It may be noted the list is not exhaustive. The list would be different with different set of assumption or the perception of the project manager. More activities could be added to the list or some of the activities could be further subdivided. The number of activities in this example has been delineated and limited to only six numbers with objective of simplicity and to demonstrate the process of networking.

Table: List of activity.

Sr. No	Activity	Symbol/Code
1.	Site selection	A
2.	Digging well	B
3.	Laying field channels	C
4.	Procurement of pump	D
5.	Installation of pump	E
6.	Test run	F

Define the Inter Relationship among the Activities

The relationship among the activities could be defined by specifying the preceding and succeeding activity. Preceding activity for an activity is its immediate predecessor, i.e. the activity that needs to be completed before the start of the new activity. In the given example, selection of the site precedes digging of well. In other words the site needs to be selected before digging of the well. Thus the activity “Selection of site” becomes proceeding activity to the activity of “Digging the well” Succeeding activity is the one that immediately starts after completion of the activity. “Digging well” is the succeeding activity to “Selection of site”.

In PERT the interrelationship is generally defined using the preceding activity. Only the terminating activities will not have any preceding activity. And all other activities must appear at least once as a preceding activity in the table. The inter relationship among the activities listed in the example is as in table below.

Table: Interrelationship of activities.

Sr. No	Activity	Symbol	Preceding activity
1.	Site selection	A	----
2.	Digging well	B	A
3.	Laying field channels	C	B
4.	Procurement of pump	D	A
5.	Installation of pump	E	B, D
6.	Test run	F	C, E

Estimation of Activity Time

The activity time is the time, which is actually expected to be expended in carrying out the activity. In deterministic cases as in CPM one time estimate is used. In probabilistic cases as in PERT, the activity time has some kind of probabilistic distribution and is the weighted average of three time estimates (Optimistic time, Pessimistic time and Most likely time) for each activity. The expected time for each activity is computed as following:

$$\text{Expected Time } (T_E) = \frac{T_o + 4T_M + T_P}{6}$$

where,

T_o is the Optimistic time, (minimum time assuming everything goes well).

T_M is the Most likely time, (modal time required under normal circumstances).

T_P is the Pessimistic time, (maximum time assuming everything goes wrong).

Example: Estimation of estimated time for the activity "Site selection". For this activity the tree time estimates i.e., Optimistic, Most likely and Pessimistic times are 4, 6 and 14 days respectively, i.e. $T_O = 4$, $T_M = 6$, and $T_P = 14$.

$$T_E = \frac{4+4*6+14}{6} = \frac{4+24+14}{6} = \frac{42}{6} = 7 \textit{ days}$$

Three time estimates, optimistic, pessimistic and most likely, could the decided on past experiences in execution of similar activities or from the feedback from individuals with relevance experience. The three time estimates and computed estimated time for the project activities are given in table below.

Table: Activity time estimates.

Sr. No	Activity	Symbol	Precedin g activity	Optimis tic Time T_O	Most likely time T_M	Pessimis tic time T_P	Estimate d time T_E
1.	Site selec- tion	A	----	4	6	14	7
2.	Digging well	B	A	2	3	4	3
3.	Laying field channels	C	B	7	16	19	15
4.	Procure- ment of pump	D	A	4	7	10	7
5.	Installation of pump	E	D, B	3	4	11	3
6.	Test run	F	C, E	1	2	3	2

Network Diagram

Having decided on activities, their relationship and duration (estimated time of the activity), next step is to draw the network diagram of the project. PERT network is a schematic model that depicts the sequential relationship among the activities that must be completed to accomplish the project.

Assemble the Activities in the form of a Flow Chart

In a flow chart the activity and its duration is shown in a box. The boxes are connected with lines according to the preceding and succeeding activity relationship. The flow charts do not give details like start and completion time of each activity until unless it is super imposed on a calendar. It also does not facilitate computation of various slacks. However, the critical path for the project can be identified by comparing the various path lengths (sum of activity time, from start to finish, on any path). The longest path in the chart is the critical path.

The flow diagram for the project considered for illustration is as in figure below.

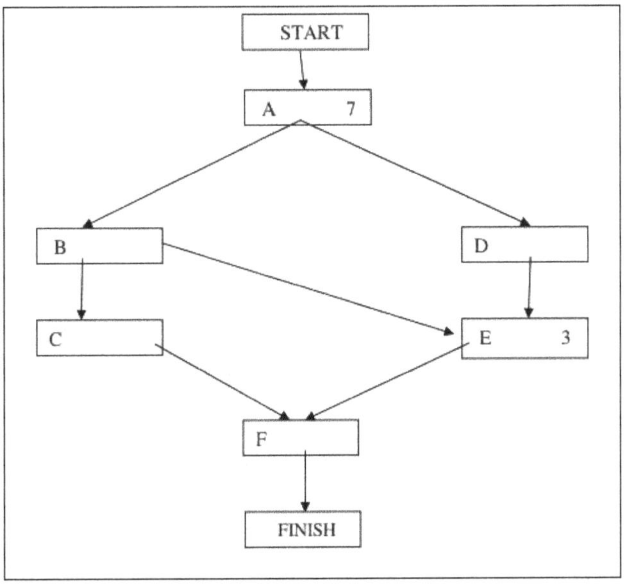

The flow diagram.

Path I A-B-E-F 7+3+3+2 = 15

Path II A-B-C-F 7+3+15+2 = 27

Path III A-D-E-F 7+7+3+2 = 19

Path II i.e., A-B-C-F being the longest path (27 days) is the Critical path.

Draw the Network

This graphical representation of the project shows the precedence relationship among the activities. An arrow generally represents activities in the diagram while a circle represents event. Each activity starts with an event and end in an event. Activities in a project are performed either sequentially i.e. one after another or they are undertaken concurrently i.e. simultaneously. To draw the network it requires the knowledge of specifying which activities must be completed before other activities can be started, which activities can be performed in parallel, and which activities immediately succeed other activities. Some of the common combination of activity in a project is as follows:

Sl No	Diagram	Logic
1	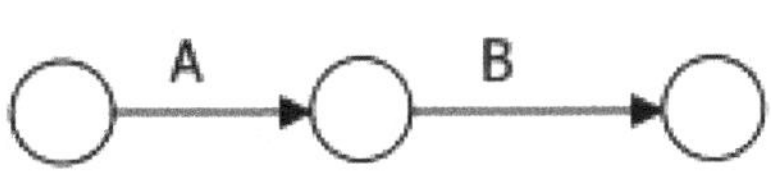	Activity "A" is preceding activity of "B". i.e. activity "A" need to be completed before start of activity "B". In other words "B" starts after "A" is finished.

<table>
<tr><td>2</td><td>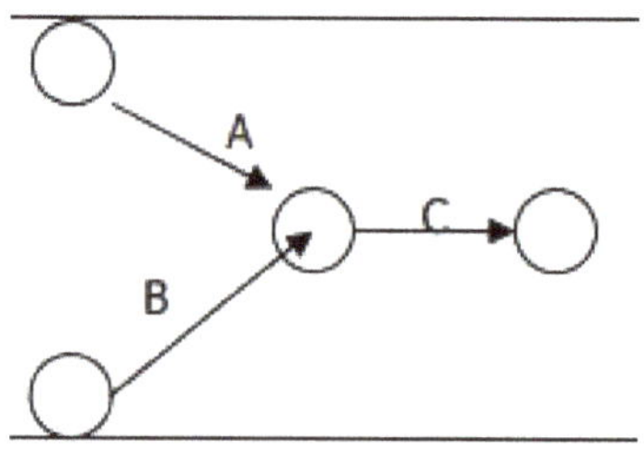</td><td>Activity "A" and "B" are concurrent. Activity "C" cannot start until both the activities "A" and "B" are completed.</td></tr>
<tr><td>3</td><td>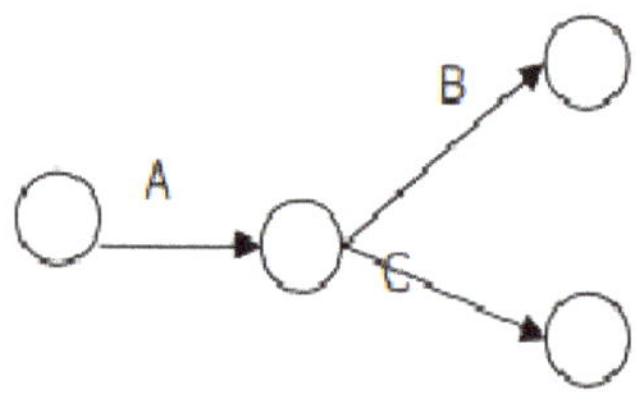</td><td>Activity "B" and "C" are concurrent activities. Any one of these cannot start until activity "A" is completed.</td></tr>
<tr><td>4</td><td>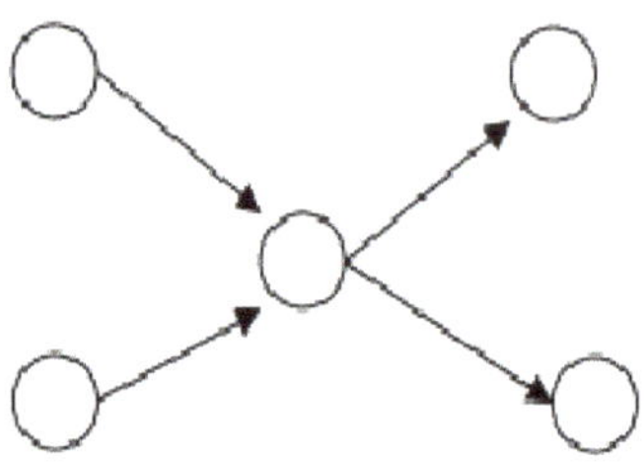</td><td>Neither activity C nor D can start until both the activities A and B arc completed. But C and D can start independently.</td></tr>
<tr><td>5</td><td>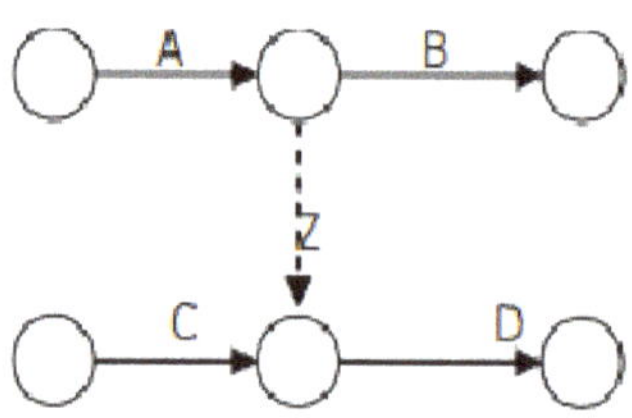</td><td>Activity D cannot begin until both A & C are completed. But B can start after A is complete. The activity Z, represented by dashed arrow, is a dummy activity. It specifies the inter relationship.</td></tr>
</table>

Dummy Activity

For example in a project Crop 2 is to be raised in same plot of land after harvesting of Crop 1. The activities and there inter relation could be as under:

Sl No	Activity	Code	Preceding activity
1	Harvesting of Crop-1	A	-
2	Sale of Crop – 1	B	A
3	Raising nursery of Crop-2	C	-
4	Transplanting Crop-2	D	A, C

The network diagram of the above project would be as follows:

The activity "Z", represented by dashed arrow in the diagram, is a dummy activity. This does not consume any resource i.e. have zero time and zero cost. This only represents the logical relation among the activities.

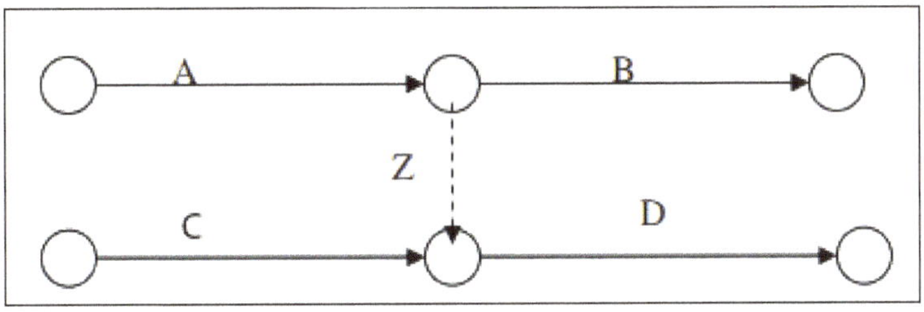

Rules for Drawing the Network

- Each activity is represented by one and only one arrow in the network.
- All the arrows must run from left to right.
- Dotted line arrows represent dummy activities.
- A circle represents an event.
- Every activity starts and ends with an event.
- No two activities can be identified by the same head and tail event.
- Do not use dummy activity unless required to reflect the logic.
- Avoid Looping and crossing of activity arrows by repositioning.
- Every Activity, except the first and the last, must have at least one preceding and one succeeding activity.
- Danglers, isolated activities must be avoided.
- For coding use alphabets for all activities including the dummy activity and numbers for events.
- Standard representation of the event.

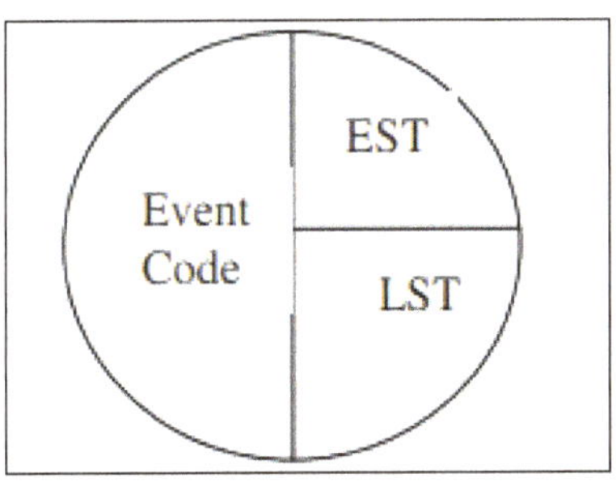

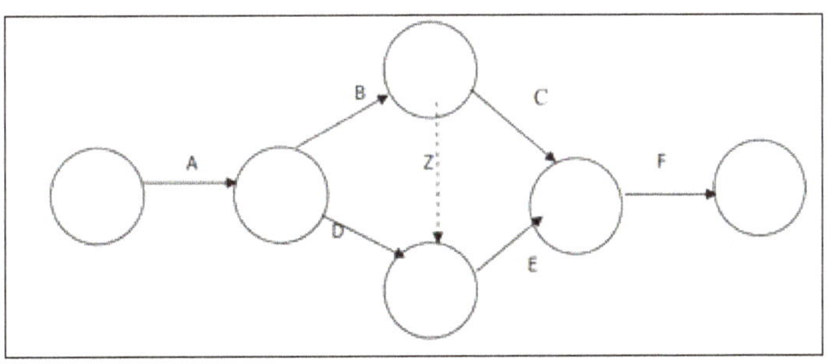

Activity inter-relationship.

Project Team

A project team is a team whose members usually belong to different groups, have different functions and are assigned by the project manager to activities for the same project. A team can be divided into sub-teams according to need. Usually project teams are only used for a defined period of time. They are disbanded after the project is deemed complete. Due to the nature of the specific formation and disbandment, project teams are usually in organizations.

A team in this context is defined as “an interdependent collection of individuals who work together towards a common goal and who share responsibility for specific outcomes of their organizations”. An additional requirement to the original definition is that “the team is identified as such by those within and outside of the team”. As project teams work on specific projects, the first requirement is usually met. In the early stages of a project, the project team may not be recognized as a team, leading to some confusion within the organization. The central characteristic of project teams in modern organizations is the autonomy and flexibility availed in the process or method undertaken to meet their goals.

Most project teams require involvement from more than one department, therefore most project teams can be classified as cross-functional teams. The project team usually consists of a variety of members often working under the direction of a project manager or of a senior member of the organization. Projects that may not receive strong support initially often have the backing of a project champion. Individual team-members can either be involved on a part-time or full-time basis. Their time commitment can change throughout the project depending on the project development stage.

Project teams need to have the right combination of skills, abilities and personality types to achieve collaborative tension. Teams can be formulated in a variety of ways. The most common method is at the discretion of a senior member of the organization.

There are many components to becoming a top-performing team, but the key is working on highly cooperative relationship. The job of management is to foster a relaxed and comfortable atmosphere where members can be themselves and are engaged and invested in the project work. All team members are encouraged for relationship building. Each member is responsible to give constructive feedback, recognize,value and utilize unique strengths of each other. The whole team is tunedon trust and cooperation.

Organizational Project Management

Organizational project management is a strategy execution framework utilizing project, program, and portfolio management as well as organizational enabling practices to consistently and predictably deliver organizational strategy producing better performance, better results, and sustainable competitive advantage.” OPM joins the knowledge, processes, tools, and techniques to create a platform from which an organization can flexibly fit these proven capabilities to the unique needs and circumstances of its strategy.

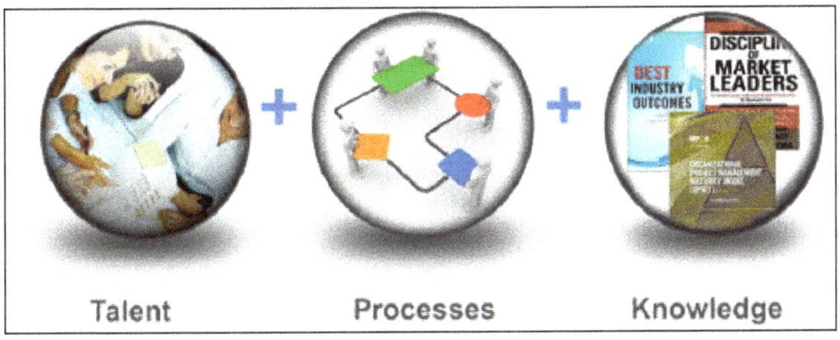

Strategy Execution Framework – Integration.

First, OPM integrates talent, process, and knowledge resources across the organization to ensure the engagement of all functions and stakeholders in the delivery of its strategy. Regardless of its market discipline, every organization delivers its strategy through the projects that represent priority changes to operations and the products and/or services it delivers to its customers. It is only through change that an organization grows and achieves a competitive advantage. Projects are the means by which change is delivered. Integrating the resources of the organization across functions and stakeholders is essential to ensure that "the right combination of the right projects is done right" to deliver the value embedded in its strategy. OPM does not replace the management systems necessary to effectively lead and manage the business; rather, it ensures their effective integration to maximize their engagement and contribution to the delivery of its strategy.

Completing the "strategy execution framework," OPM aligns the organization to maximize its delivery of strategy. As figure illustrates, OPM aligns the development of strategy with implementation through the deployment of its portfolio of programs and projects for the creation and delivery of strategic business results. Alignment also harmonizes the strategic goals of the organization with operations or business-as-usual to ensure optimum assignment of talent, knowledge, and capital resources.

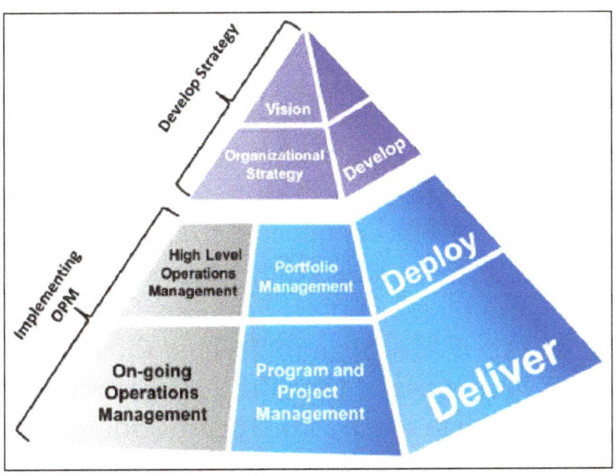

Strategy Execution Framework – Alignment.

Again, OPM is a business approach to the deployment and delivery of organizational strategy through the effective implementation of project, program, and portfolio management. It must be stressed that OPM is an adaptive approach for fitting the capabilities of project, program, and portfolio management to the unique circumstances and needs of the organization. Process improvement principles, such as those documented in The Guide to Lean Enablers for Managing Engineering Programs and other sources already referenced, can be applied to all of the disciplines of OPM to achieve the benefits of fit.

The Role of a Strategic PMO

The key to effectively fitting and maturing the capabilities of OPM is a strategically positioned and practicing Project Management Office (PMO) that can utilize all the described resources to bridge the gap that exists between having knowledge of OPM and realization of the potential it offers an organization.

The Strategic PMO does not have to be a formal institution, department, or entity within an organization nor does it have to be called a PMO. What it must have at minimum is the authority to:

- Align the portfolio of programs and projects to business strategy.
- Customize program and project management practices.
- Enhance governance and accountability.
- Optimize the investment of the portfolio of programs and projects.
- Manage talent.
- Ensure stakeholder buy-in.
- Drive needed change.
- Proactively navigate risk.

Without the executive-level support to accomplish the above, organizations will see the PMO at best as a functional support that follows up on the use of methodology and provides as-needed resources, or worse yet, will eliminate it all together. In order to avoid this travesty, much research has been conducted to demonstrate the value of the role of the Strategic PMO. Most notably, Price water house Coopers (PwC) has published a third global survey of more than 1,500 participants, from more than 30 industries and almost 40 countries, called Insights and Trends: Current Portfolio, Programme, and Project Management Processes; in addition, PMI has released its annual Pulse of the Profession 2011, an annual survey of more than 1,000 project, program, and portfolio managers around the world. Both surveys unequivocally validate what has long been anecdotally reported: Strategic PMOs can be the vehicle organizations count on to move from business as usual, to making program and project management a central component of their strategy.

Aligning the Portfolio to the Business Strategy

The very first responsibility of a Strategic PMO is to ensure that all programs and projects are aligned with the strategic direction of the company. This step sets the stage and then carries through the entire process, because after selecting the right portfolio of programs and projects, the Strategic PMO must vigilantly monitor and continually adjust the portfolio as risks escalate, opportunities arise, and change occurs.

Customizing Program and Project Management Practices

Another critically important role of the Strategic PMO is to ensure the value of OPM is fully realized through a customized approach to implementation that takes into consideration the underlying drivers of an organization's strategy. But at a high-level the Strategic PMO can accomplish this critical first step of implementing OPM by taking into consideration the internal and external contexts of an organization when defining a configuration of OPM or methodology that will deliver the most strategic value. "Organizations adopting the surface appearances of implementation that worked for others, hoping that they will realize the same results, appear destined for disappointment".

Enhancing Governance and Accountability

The Strategic PMO is tasked with ensuring that all of the programs and projects are carried out in an effective and efficient manner. Confusion, caused by ambiguity, lack of accountability, and poor coordination are prevented when the Strategic PMO is accountable for the governance and leadership of the practices, roles, and responsibilities, as well as driving integration of talent, processes, and knowledge. An undeniable positive correlation between having a Strategic PMO in place and better performance. The higher the alignment between organizational and business needs, the higher the overall project performance.

Optimizing the Investment of Portfolio of Programs and Projects:

In order to optimize the efficiency and effectiveness of the portfolio of programs and projects, the Strategic PMO must be involved in the following:

- Business decisions that result in new programs and projects.
- Strategic program and project planning.
- Setting of portfolio priorities.
- Periodic program and project reviews that result in decisions to discontinue programs and projects (The PwC survey results highlight that program and project selection was one of the most critical capabilities of the Strategic PMO).

The Strategic PMO must also be committed to the continuous improvement in the practices of program and project management, optimizing the utilization of resources, and guaranteeing the delivery of the anticipated business results to maximize the organization's investment in its portfolio of programs and projects. The more mature the organization's program and project management processes are, the better the results. "When an organization has a methodology in place to improve program and project performance and management and focuses on continuous improvement, it will have a competitive advantage strategy in place to remain successful in the marketplace."

Managing Talent

Strategic PMOs recognized that engaged, experienced key staff leads to program and project success. After all, "Methodologies and processes don't deliver programs and projects; people do." (PwC) and, "if an organization is to undertake all the programs and projects necessary to implement the chosen organizational strategy, there must be sufficient people with the right competences, skills, attitudes, and know-how to deliver the full portfolio". This is why Strategic PMOs are investing in the development of their program and project management competencies, providing access to training for their talent, and identifying opportunities for career advancement within the organization for those who want to grow.

Ensuring Stakeholder Buy-in

Much has been written on the topic of why programs and projects fail. At the top of every list is the lack of stakeholder buy-in, followed closely by any one and usually all of the following: hidden agendas, unmanaged expectations, and/or ineffective communication. The Strategic PMO is tasked with ensuring that the organization is aware of program and project management; identifying and supporting stakeholders (either positively or negatively) impacted by the programs and projects in the portfolio to help them understand that the change is necessary; and contributing to the creation of sustained long-term value for the organization. Evidence shows that the use of efficient and effective communication methodologies have a positive effect on the success of programs and projects (projects with efficient and effective communication methods were 17% more likely to finish within budget).

Driving needed Change

There is a complexity to internal organizational dynamics, such as shared understanding of the strategy and how staff roles support its achievement; shifting priorities among and within the portfolio of programs and projects require an organization to evolve. The Strategic PMO is at the heart of driving and managing that organizational change through the portfolio of programs and projects—ensuring that organizational change management becomes a critical organizational enabling practice within OPM, and helping organizations adapt to change, uncertainty, and complexity so that strategy is effectively implemented and the expected benefits and changes are realized.

Proactively Navigating Risk

Last, but not least, the Strategic PMO creates a culture of proactive risk management by the identification and navigation of threats as well as opportunities—as supported by Global Risk Management Study of almost 400 executives from 10 major industries: "To achieve effective enterprise risk management, organizations must focus on being proactive, rather than merely reactive." The role of the Strategic PMO is to establish an integrated approach to risk management throughout the portfolio in order to support the organization in delivering value and differentiation from competition.

OPM and the Strategic PMO are inexorably linked. OPM gives the organization the capabilities to effectively implement the delivery of its strategy, and a Strategic PMO moves beyond the traditional functions of a PMO with executive-level support to effectively fit and successfully implement OPM.

Operationalizing OPM

OPM is a strategy execution framework that positions an organization to achieve better performance, better results, and a sustainable competitive advantage in the delivery of its strategy. "The degree of value that organizations realize is determined by how well what is implemented meets the needs of the organization." The Value Chain of Strategy (VCS) as a business model for the implementation of OPM, fitting and maturing the capabilities of PMI's foundational standards to the needs and circumstances of the organization. For a greater understanding of the capabilities applied in the VCS, please refer to the current version of PMI's standards for portfolio, program, and project management as well as OPM3.

The development of strategy serves as input to the processes of OPM; however, Figure reveals the transformational gap that exists between strategy and the realization of intended business results. It is this gap that a strategic PMO fills by using the VCS to operationalize the organization's delivery of strategy.

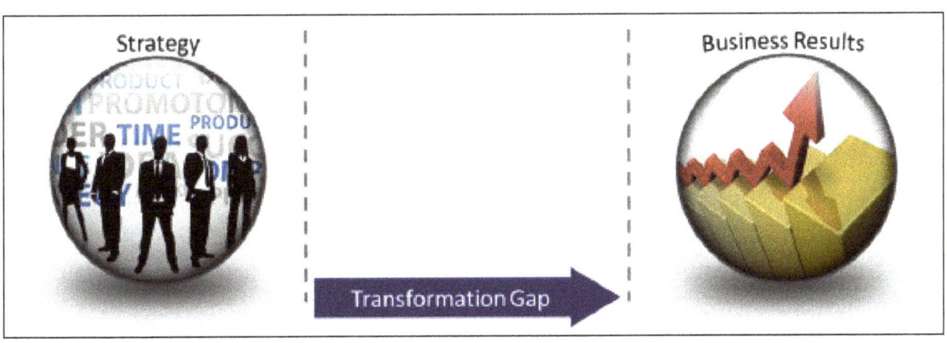

Implementing the Delivery of Strategy with OPM.

An organization's portfolio of programs and projects represents those investments in change that leadership believes to be most significant and necessary to succeed in its chosen market(s). Therefore, deployment of strategy into a balanced mix of priority initiatives is the first and most crucial step in the successful implementation of strategy. It doesn't matter how well an organization manages its programs or executes its projects; if they are the wrong initiatives, the entire effort will amount to a lost opportunity. Not only is the deployment of strategy into a balanced portfolio crucial, it is also the most leveraging step in the allocation of scarce organizational resources to ensure maintenance of efficient and effective operations or business-as-usual.

Strategy and deployment of the portfolio is not a once-and-done activity. Although a portfolio is typically deployed to represent a specific planning period, it must be reviewed periodically in the context of a rapidly changing global environment to ensure its continued relevance and ability to deliver intended business results. Accordingly, the mix of initiatives represented in the portfolio may undergo change during both the short- and long-term horizons. The ongoing monitoring and management of this important facet of OPM will be addressed shortly.

Before proceeding with the description of the VCS, it is important to understand the distinction between project management success and project success in the delivery of organizational strategy. Project management success focuses on the delivery of the result or product of a project and is most typically measured by performance against time, cost, and scope. Although these are very important measures, they do not represent project success, which measures the outcomes and benefits of the project in relation to those specified in the business case justifying its inclusion in the portfolio of strategic investments. Together, project management and project success comprise the business life cycle of a project. Knowing this distinction will help in understanding the roles and relationships of program and project management in the VCS.

An important element of each investment in an organization's portfolio is the change and resulting benefits each project is expected to deliver to its respective stakeholders. It is the role of program management to map out and manage project results to ensure maximum realization of intended strategic outcomes and benefits. Although more comprehensive than this simple description, it must be understood that effective program management establishes the governance and processes needed to fulfill this role for the organization and should be measured by the achievement of strategic business results.

Projects deliver the results or products that must be integrated into operations to achieve intended business results. Although project management is focused on project execution, typically measured against time, cost, and the scope of project results, it is important for project managers to evaluate proposed adjustments in these measures relative to their impact on project success. To fulfill this role, project management must integrate with operations in the analysis of changes impacting project results and the full business life cycle for the project. Figure illustrates the ongoing interaction between project, program, and portfolio management that focuses attention on the alignment with strategy and the delivery of optimum business results.

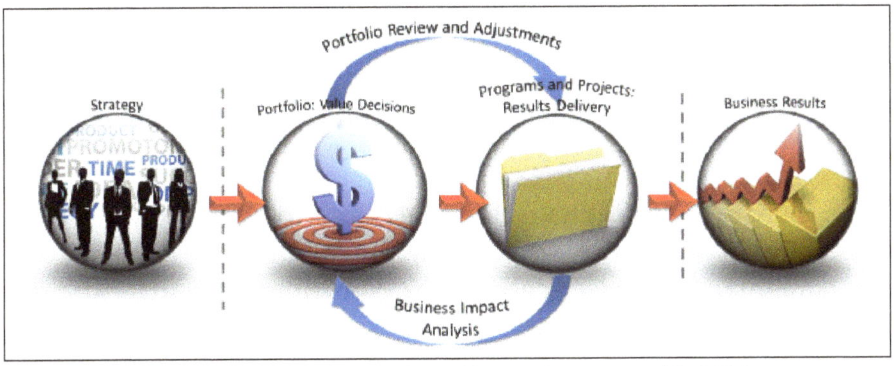

Managing and Adapting the Delivery of Strategy with OPM.

The final step in the VCS is a value performance analysis, returning actual versus planned outcome and benefit performance information, as well as lessons learned, to strategy development for evaluation and adjustment if needed. If an adjustment in strategy is indicated, it can be accommodated in a timely manner; however, information returned through this process will most likely signal adjustments in the portfolio or some other aspect of the business model to continuously improve organizational performance. As Will Rogers once said, "Even if you're on the right track, you'll get run over if you just sit still." For this reason, continuous improvement in both the fit and maturity of the capabilities of OPM is crucial to achieving differentiated implementation and delivery of organizational strategy.

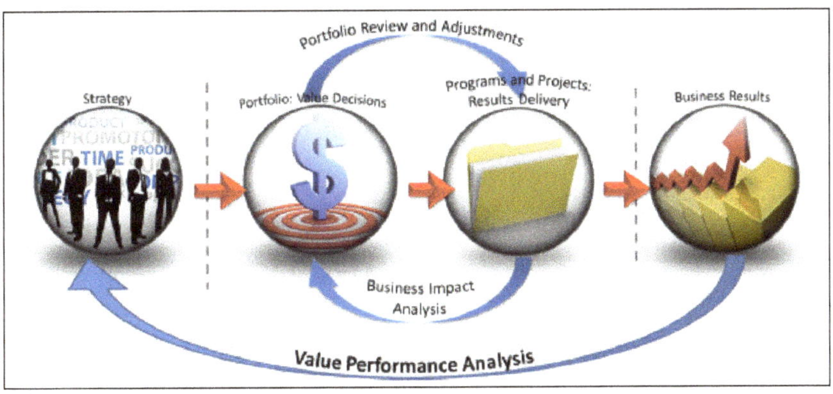

Results Analysis and Learning with OPM.

Who should be Interested in OPM

So, when all is said and done, who in the organization should be interested in OPM? First, senior leadership should be interested, because OPM cuts across the organization to provide a flexible, yet disciplined and systematic means of delivering strategy. It signals leadership's commitment to the process and establishes a business focus for integrating and aligning the organization to its purpose, fostering a culture of engagement and continuous improvement.

A strategically positioned and practicing PMO should be interested because OPM provides it with the relationships and tools to help the organization realize its full performance improvement potential. By fitting and maturing the capabilities of project, program, and portfolio management to the unique circumstances and needs of the organization, the PMO can ensure the goal of OPM of better performance, better results, and sustainable competitive advantage through continuous improvement in the delivery of its strategy.

For portfolio managers, OPM provides a framework to align the work and resources of the organization to strategy while giving program managers greater visibility of the short and long-term strategic goals. The VCS provides the PMO with the means to better define and manage the business of delivering intended outcomes and business results.

For project managers, OPM opens a path for professional development and career advancement through greater involvement in the organization's strategy through control of the full business life cycle of the project. Rather than being viewed purely as technical experts, they are recognized because of their role in the business decision-making process as having influence on both project management and project success.

Finally, the other management functions within the organization should be interested because of the positive ancillary effects OPM can bring to their operation. For human resources, the approach opens a powerful opportunity for talent development and a career path for building and retaining skills and knowledge essential to growth and a sustainable competitive advantage. For finance, OPM provides access to the critical business-focused measures and data that align the organization to meaningful performance, while giving operations the type of predictive view to be more proactive with conditions impacting the delivery of strategic value to stakeholders.

Project Portfolio Management

Project portfolio management (PPfM) is fundamentally different from project and program management. Project and program management are about execution and delivery doing projects right. In contrast, PPfM focuses on doing the right projects at the right time by selecting and managing projects as a portfolio of investments. It requires completely different techniques and perspectives.

Good portfolio management increases business value by aligning projects with an organization's strategic direction, making the best use of limited resources, and building synergies between projects. Unfortunately, organizations often do portfolio management poorly. As a result, they fail to deliver strategic results because they attempt the wrong projects or can't say "no" to too many projects.

The Business Problem

Nearly all organizations have more project work to do than people and money to do the work. Often the management team has difficulty saying "no." Instead, they try to do everything by cramming more work onto the calendars of already overworked project teams or by cutting corners during the project.

Despite a heavy investment of people and money in projects, the organization still gets poor results because people are working on the wrong projects or on too many projects. Trying to do too much causes all projects to suffer from delays, cost overruns, or poor quality.

Effective project organizations focus their limited resources on the best projects, declining to do projects that are good but not good enough. PPfM enables them to make and implement these tough project selection decisions.

PPfM is a funnel that connects strategic planning to the execution of projects, making the strategic objectives executable.

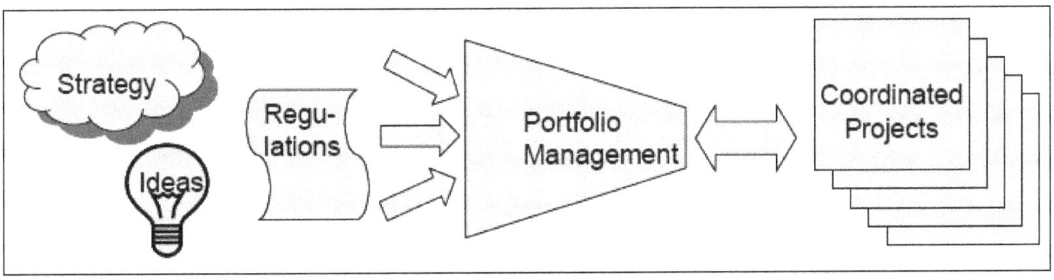

Portfolio Management Connects Strategy with Execution.

The mouth of the funnel takes in all of the ideas for projects that the organization might do. These ideas may come from strategy, customer requests, regulatory requirements, or ideas from individual contributors. The purpose of the funnel is to select only those projects that meet certain criteria and to say "no" to the others. The resulting collection of projects is a focused, coordinated, and executable portfolio of projects that will achieve the goals of the organization.

PPfM complements project and program management. It aims the organization in the right direction by selecting the best projects to do. The selected projects are turned over to program and project management, which is the engine that initiates and completes them successfully. Doing projects right, doing projects together, and doing the right projects: Project organizations must excel at all three to have long-term success.

Project Management	Do project Light
Program Management	Do Project Together
Portfolio Management	Do the right projects

The Portfolio Management Process

- Clarify business objectives.
- Capture and research requests and ideas.
- Select the best projects using defined differentiators that align, maximize, and balance.
- Validate portfolio feasibility and initiate projects.
- Manage and monitor the portfolio.

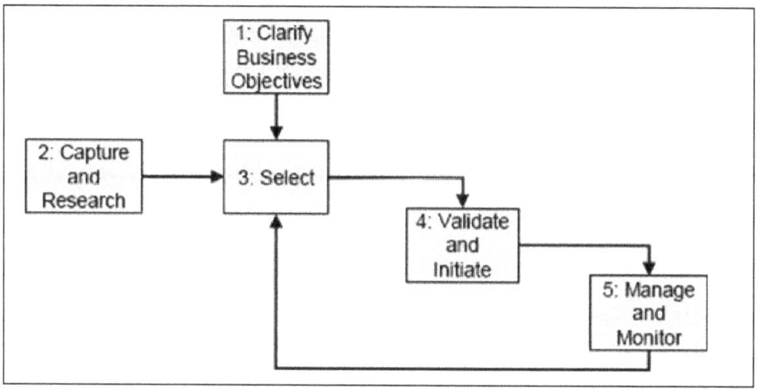

Portfolio Management Process.

This process identifies the most important differentiators between projects, such as Return on Investment, risk, efficiency, or strategic alignment. Then it uses these differentiators to select the high impact projects, clear out the clutter, and set priorities. Tradeoffs is made in a disciplined way, rather than by allowing the loudest voice to win.

The PPfM process accomplishes three things:

- Aligns execution with strategy. Each selected project must play a role in carrying out the strategy of the organization. No more pet projects.
- Maximizes the value of the entire portfolio of projects to get the "most bang for the buck." Taken together, the projects must have a high return on the organization's investment. This may be in terms of dollars or other measures that are important to the organization.
- Balances the portfolio. Makes sure that it is not lopsided for example, by being too risky or too focused on short-term results.

Clarify Business Objectives

First, aim the in the right direction: You must be able to clearly state your organization's strategic objectives before starting portfolio management. This is often the first obstacle people run into when trying to implement PPfM. If you can't determine the strategic objectives, stop working on portfolio management and fix that problem first.

As an example, a very popular framework for strategic planning is the strategy map, based on the strategic perspectives developed by Kaplan and Norton. A strategy map derives and links initiatives in a cause and effect hierarchy so that they support each other. The top level of the hierarchy is financial objectives, because creating financial returns for shareholders and owners is a priority at for-profit companies. The supporting levels of the hierarchy are:

- Customer value: What value can the company create for the customer that will translate into financial results?
- Processes: What internal processes will generate that customer value?
- Learning and growth: What capabilities and internal learning must the company have to make the processes work effectively?

Decide what Value Means

Portfolio management requires a systematic method of differentiating between candidate projects to determine which ones are "best." What does "best" mean? The definition is unique to every organization. For example, one company might value environmental stewardship most highly, while another places top priority on ROI. Select a critical few criteria that will measure each project's true value to your unique organization. Rigorously limit the number of criteria to four to ten to keep the amount of data manageable.

The right criteria are critical, because poor criteria will cause you to select the wrong projects. There are two primary approaches to defining valuation criteria: financial and scoring.

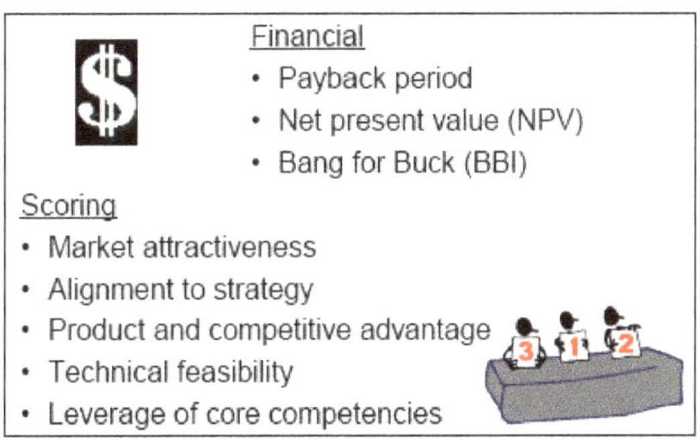

Valuation Criteria Divides into Two Approaches

The financial approach to valuation uses quantitative monetary measures, such as net present value, to define the differences between projects. Unfortunately, a financial approach may mislead portfolio managers to mistake precision for accuracy. Robert Cooper says:

> "In spite of the fact that financial methods are theoretically correct, the most rigorous of all methods, and the most popular of all tools, of all the methods we studied in a large sample survey of practices versus results, they yielded the poorest results on just about every portfolio performance metric. The sophistication of these methods far exceeds the quality of the data."

Valuation by scoring takes a different approach. In many fields, researchers understand which characteristics of projects correlate with success. Scoring uses these predicting factors as the criteria for differentiating between candidate projects. For example, Cooper lists three factors in new product development that correlate well with eventual product success:

- Unique, differentiated product that offers superior value to customers.
- Product is targeted at an attractive market.
- Product and project leverages internal company strengths.

Regardless of theoretical superiority, use a valuation method that fits with the executive decision making style in your organization. Some companies are more comfortable with financial analysis, while others prefer the framework for voting and discussion that scoring brings. Yet others combine financial and scoring criteria into a single system.

Capture and Research

Step 1 of the PPfM process builds a foundation for creating a portfolio. It requires all of the decision makers to agree on strategic objectives and the vital few valuation criteria, so initially it can be difficult and time consuming. Fortunately, only periodic review and update is needed after that.

Step 2 builds on this foundation by starting to build a specific portfolio. Exhibit 5 shows the steps for constructing a tentative portfolio. The first two steps are research:

- Create an inventory of candidate projects for the portfolio. Include in-progress projects as well as ideas for new projects. Sources can include customer requests, initiatives from strategic planning, regulatory requirements, and good ideas from employees and project managers.
- Gather data for each candidate project on the inventory. These include data that will allow you to rate the projects against the criteria that you have developed. It may also include early estimates of dependencies and high-level resource requirements.

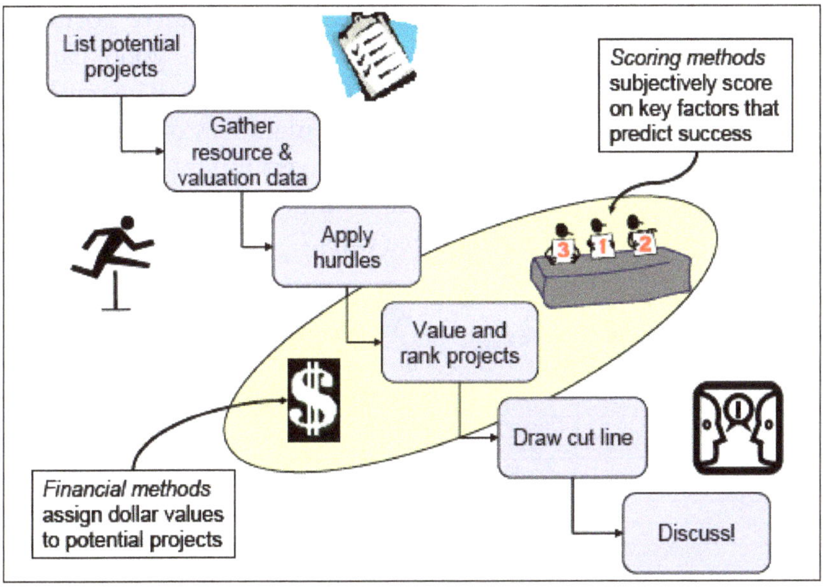

Constructing a tentative portfolio leads to valuable.

At first, identifying and gathering data on all of the candidate projects may be a major challenge, requiring much investigation and interviewing. As your organization matures at PPfM, this step will get faster and easier.

Select the best Projects

Maximize the Portfolio's Value

With project data from Step 2 in hand, determine which combination of projects creates the highest total value for the portfolio, given high-level resource constraints. This is called portfolio maximization.

First, rate each candidate project against the valuation criteria to compute the value of each project. This will be either a weighted score or a financial value. Next, rank the candidates from highest to lowest value.

		Scores on Criteria						
		1	2	1	1	0	0	< Weight
Project Code	Short Name	Resolve	Prevent	Guide	Grow	Skills	Tools	Score
AP01	Project 1	H	H	H	H	Y	Y	15
AM01	Project 2	H	H	H	H	N	N	15
AP09	Project 3	H	H	H	M	Y	Y	14
TK04	Project 4	H	H	H	M	Y	Y	14
AP02	Project 5	H	H	H	L	Y	Y	13

Use Scoring Criteria to Rank Candidate Projects

Starting with the highest value projects, allocate available resources until they are exhausted. Draw the "cut line" at this point, creating a tentative portfolio. The portfolio is tentative because no valuation criteria, no matter how good, can capture all of the subtleties that must go into real-world funding decisions. The cut line becomes a starting point for vigorous discussion among the members of the portfolio management team, as they use their real-world experience and judgment to tune the tentative portfolio. The process, criteria, and data form a framework that guides this discussion, instead of selecting projects by "loudest voice wins."

Tentative "go"

Code	Project	Product Line	Project Type	Months to FCS	Payback Period (months)	NPV ($M)	Resource Requirements (total remain)	Resource Requirements (next quarter)
InterK	Internet Kitchen Control Center	GourmetChef	Transform	11	15	$40.0	$2.0	$0.5
BBQ	Premium BBQ Smoker	GourmetChef	Transform	2	8	$35.0	$5.0	$5.0
Stove	Stove	ValueChef	Upgrade	8	9	$29.5	$8.3	$3.8
BotRef	Bottom Freezer Refrigerator	GourmetChef	New	5	8	$25.2	$4.2	$2.0
ComFrz	Commercial Freezer	ProChef	Upgrade	8	11	$21.1	$2.6	$0.8
Chill	Chiller Oven	GourmetChef	New	15	17	$18.7	$3.8	$0.8
SSRef	Side by Side Refrigerator	GourmetChef	Upgrade	5	6	$18.0	$2.0	$1.5
Fryer	High Efficiency Deep Fryer	ProChef	Upgrade	2	4	$15.4	$0.7	$0.6
BIRef	Built In Refrigerator	GourmetChef	Upgrade	1	2	$13.3	$0.5	$0.5
Tando	Tandoori Oven	ProChef	Transform	13	23	$12.0	$6.2	$1.2
VMicro	Microwave	ValueChef	Upgrade	12	17	$10.1	$4.3	$1.1
Dish	Dishwasher	ValueChef	Upgrade	6	9	$8.6	$2.1	$1.4
Grido	Griddle / Oven	ProChef	New	7	16	$8.4	$1.5	$0.6
Ctop	Cooktop	GourmetChef	Upgrade	4	15	$5.2	$1.4	$1.2
Amicro	Automated Microwave	ProChef	New	10	20	$5.1	$2.7	$0.5
Cmicro	Microwave + Convection Oven	GourmetChef	New	17	25	$12.7	$5.7	$1.1
SSDish	Super Silent Dishwasher	GourmetChef	New	4	37	$1.6	$1.0	$0.8
TopRef	Top Freezer Refrigerator	ValueChef	Upgrade	24	30	$30.0	$3.1	$0.3
	Total Requested					$309.9	$57.1	$23.7
	Total Available							$15
	Actual					$202.9		$15.0

Missed hurdles

Hold for resources

Use NPV and resource data to draw a cut line.

Balance the Portfolio

A maximized portfolio may be out of balance in important ways. For example, it may have an inappropriate risk profile, subjecting the organization to either too much or too little risk. According to Cooper, balance is the second weakest element in portfolio construction, after "too many projects."

Use balance displays to check the balance of a tentative portfolio across important dimensions. Figure shows a bubble chart that displays risk versus reward in a small portfolio, where each bubble represents a project. Some popular balance displays are:

- Risk versus reward.
- Strategy tactical range.
- Market or product-line segmentation.
- Distribution of time to completion or time to profit.

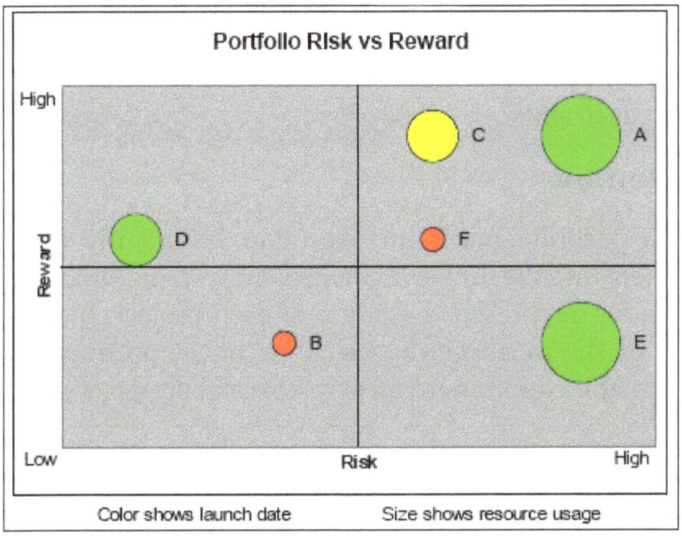

Balance display compares portfolio risk and reward.

Validate and Initiate

To keep the amount of data manageable, a portfolio is initially constructed at high level of abstraction. The resulting portfolio ignores some important constraints and details about its projects. For example, a portfolio's demand for resources often appears feasible when analyzed at the FTE (full-time equivalents) level. However, this masks bottlenecks caused by limited availability of certain skill sets. Thus, a portfolio may not be feasible to execute even though it is maximized and balanced.

Before starting execution, validate that a tentative portfolio appears to be feasible. Team up with the people who will run the projects and thus know them best generally line and project managers, perhaps coordinated by the project management office (PMO).

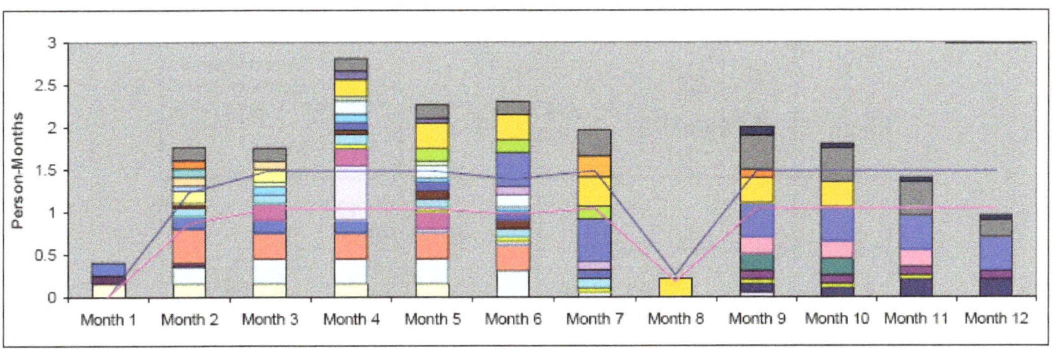

When looking at portfolio feasibility, consider the following:

- Interproject dependencies.
- Knowledge and capabilities of the performing organizations.

- Time-phased resource demand and availability, including considerations of key skill sets.
- Budgetary constraints.

Manage and Monitor

After validating the portfolio, put it into execution. Initiate the new projects and programs, inserting them into the project management system. Although the project manager is responsible for day-to-day execution of each project, the portfolio manager's job continues. He or she monitors the execution of the portfolio and its component projects, ensuring that it continues to meet its original design objectives.

In this step, the portfolio manager works closely with the project managers or the PMO to:

- Gather information to monitor the performance of the portfolio.
- Identify and resolve issues within the portfolio, including reallocating resources.
- Steer the portfolio, making changes when necessary to rescue, re-scope, cancel, or introduce new projects.
- Manage escalations and midcycle requests for changes to portfolio composition for example, adding new projects.
- Initiate a full portfolio review and reconstruction on a scheduled basis, such as quarterly or annually.

Portfolio Governance

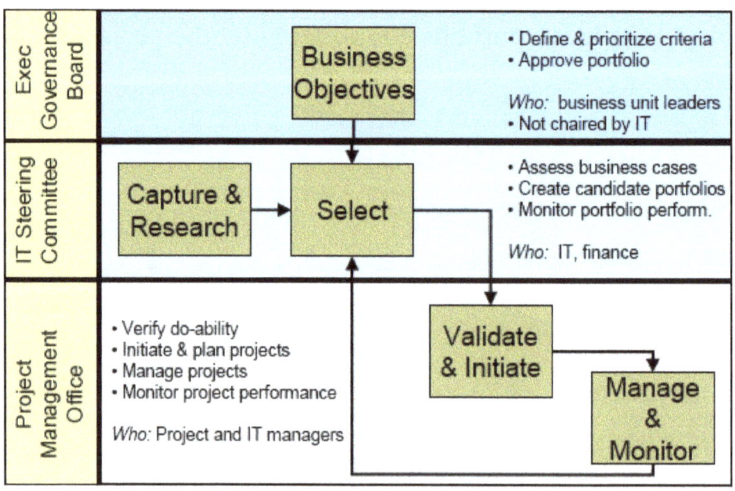

Portfolio Governance and Process Work Together.

Just having knowledge regarding the PPfM process and tools is not enough. PPfM must have a governance framework. Governance specifies who has responsibilities in each process step and how these individuals will work together to make good decisions about projects. PPfM is about sharing power and decision making at very senior management levels, so clear governance is vital. As an example, figure shows an IT organization's governance structure for implementing the PPfM process.

Extreme Project Management

Extreme project management is the art and science of facilitating and managing the flow of thoughts, emotions, and interactions in a way that produces valued outcomes under turbulent and complex conditions: those that feature high speed, high change, high uncertainty, and high stress.

From development of new technologies and shift in customer needs, to economic conditions or some new ground breaking ideas, a number of project requirements can change every day due to a variety of circumstances. This is where extreme project management enters the game.

Extreme projects are carried out in turbulent environments where it's difficult to estimate the speed of the project and obstacles you will encounter. On extreme projects, things are unpredictable, planning is chaotic and just-in-time, and the entire project development is messy.

Despite their extreme nature, extreme projects can still contribute to success and extreme project management allows you to manage the unknown and unpredictable by self-correcting along the way.

Traditional vs. Extreme Project Management

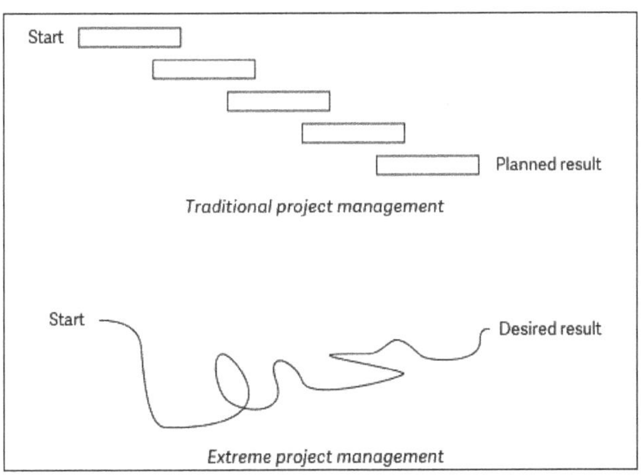

Traditional project management is a perfect solution for managing engineering and construction projects because they have a specific goal and a well-defined path on how to get there. But today, many projects don't have a proven path and a predictable life cycle, and requirements are constantly changing.

Unlike traditional management, where circumstances are highly predictable, extreme project management thrives in the chaotic environment where the level of certainty is very low. Also, traditional approach is more streamlined while extreme one is more flexible.

The basic differences between the two approaches:

- Traditional project management is past oriented. Extreme project management is future oriented.
- Traditional project management makes people the servants of the process. Extreme project management makes the process the servant of people.
- Traditional project management is about centralizing control of people, processes, and tools. Extreme project management is about distributing control.
- Traditional project management tries to take charge of the world (things, people, schedule). Extreme project management is about taking charge of yourself, your attitudes, and your approach to the world.
- Traditional project management is about managing. Extreme project management is about leading.

Differences between extreme project management and traditional project management

Traditional Project Management	Extreme Project Management
Manages the known	Manages the unknown
Slow and stable	Chaotic, messy and unpredictable
Aimed at producing the planned result	Self-correcting and making in-the-spot decisions
Focused on efficiency	Focused on effectiveness

Extreme project management characteristics:

- There is a rough idea about the goal but little idea about how to achieve that goal.
- All the standard tools, templates, and processes engineers used to apply in the past don't make much contribution to the extreme project management.
- Instead of following the safe path, in extreme management project managers discuss the best alternative with the client, carry out the experiment, learn from what happens ,and use their knowledge for the next project cycle.

Mindset as an Important Factor

It's obvious that steps you need to take in extreme approach differ significantly from the steps in the traditional approach. The extreme approach requires a particular mindset, that is, a set of beliefs and assumptions of how things function. With this in mind, changing the mindset of your project team and adapting it to extreme circumstances they have to work in is the imperative.

There are a few ground rules and expectations your project team has to adopt to successfully implement extreme approach:

- Requirements and project activities are chaotic and unpredictable.
- Team should rely on uncertainty.
- It's virtually impossible to fully control this kind of projects.
- Change is inevitable.
- Flexibility and openness bring the feeling of security.

Five Steps of Extreme Project Management Life Cycle Model

There are five steps every extreme project management team needs to follow to carry out the project successfully:

- Envision: Define your vision clearly before embarking on extreme project management.
- Speculate: Have your team participate in creative thinking process and brainstorm ideas that will achieve your vision.
- Innovate: Make your team test their speculations by coming up with innovative solutions.
- Re-evaluate: As the cycle approaches its end, your team must re-evaluate their work.
- Disseminate: After going through a learning process, it's essential to spread the knowledge and apply it to future stages of the project as well as future projects in general.

When to use Extreme Project Management

Whether your team will employ a straightforward and well-structured traditional project management or the radical extreme project management approach depends on the project they are involved in. You should use extreme project management when your projects require:

- Fast-paced work.
- Frequent changes as the project progresses due to the dynamic environment.

- A trial-and-error approach to see what works.
- Self-correcting processes when things go wrong.
- People-driven processes instead of process-driven (when people are in control of processes rather than the other way around).

Advantages of Extreme Project Management

Unlike other methodologies that rely on software tools and templates, extreme approach is much more people-centric:

- It's holistic: Although it includes methods, tools, and templates, they only make sense if they refer to the project as the whole. In other words, it allows you to view the project as a single system without analyzing its parts.
- It's people-centric: It puts emphasis on project dynamics, meaning it allows stakeholders to communicate and interact. This helps you reach meaningful solutions and meet your client's needs.
- It's humanistic: One of the principles of this approach is takes into account quality of life of the stakeholder as they are baked into the project. Because people are an integral part of the project, their job satisfaction and the team culture they develop can have a profound effect on the business
- It's business focused: Once you have reached the project's outcome, you can have a clear insight into how the project can benefit your client. The team is constantly focused on delivering value early and often.
- It's reality based: It allows you to work in the highly unpredictable environment that is prone to change and helps you recognize that you cannot change the reality to adapt to your project.

References

- PM: manage.gov.in, Retrieved 12 June, 2020
- Pmo-opm-performance-strategy-6075: pmi.org, Retrieved 21 July, 2020
- Extreme-project-management-xpm, project-management: activecollab.com, Retrieved 25 April, 2020
- Project-portfolio-management-limited-resources-6948: pmi.org, Retrieved 27 August, 2020
- Bond-Barnard, Taryn Jane; Fletcher, Lizelle; Steyn, Herman (2018-05-08). "Linking trust and collaboration in project teams to project management success". International Journal of Managing Projects in Business. 11 (2): 432–457. doi:10.1108/IJMPB-06-2017-0068. ISSN 1753-8378

Approaches of Project Management

2

- Critical Chain Project Management
- Earned Value Management
- Lean Project Management
- Project Production Management
- PRINCE2
- Agile Project Management
- Benefits Realisation Management
- Iterative and Incremental Project Management
- Process-based Management
- Event Chain Methodology
- Waterfall Methodology

There are certain approaches that are used in project management such as critical chain project management, earned value management, lean project management, agile project management, waterfall methodology, event chain methodology, etc. This chapter has been carefully written to provide an easy understanding of these approaches used in project management.

Critical Chain Project Management

Critical Chain Project Management (CCPM) is a project management methodology introduced in 1997 by Eliyahu (Eli) M. Goldratt. It applies Goldratt's Theory of Constraints (TOC) to resolve project task and delivery issues.

CCPM addresses issues related to project timing, increased costs, performance and under-delivery, versus traditional methods, such as critical path, where the emphasis is placed on tight scheduling and ordered tasks.

CCPM approaches projects by applying the following steps:

- Planning: This stage includes defining the critical chain, which is comprised of critical tasks; reducing task estimates and safety.
- Execution: Project resources are prioritized according to determinations defined in the planning stage.
- Review: Buffer management is applied to assess the status of each task. Buffers and their consumption rates serve as excellent touch point indicators for projects and related tasks.

Critical Path Project Management Defines Three Types of Buffers

- Project Buffer: The total pooled buffer depicted in the image above is referred to as the project buffer.
- Feeding Buffer: In a project network, there are path/s which feed into the critical path. The pooled buffer on each such path represents the feeding buffer to the critical path, resulting in providing some slack to the critical path.
- Resource Buffer: This is a virtual task inserted just before critical chain tasks that require critical resources. This acts as a trigger point for the resource, indicating when the critical path is about to begin.

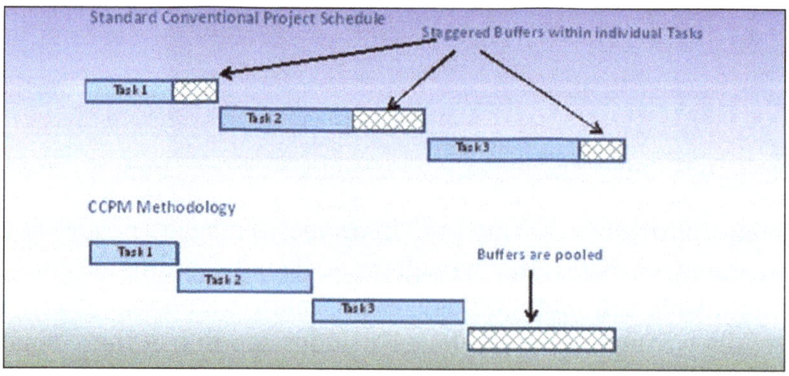

As the progress of the project is reported, the critical chain is recalculated. In fact, monitoring and controlling of the project primarily focused on the utilization of the buffers. As you can see, the critical chain method considers the basic critical path based project network and schedule to derive a completely new schedule.

The critical path project management methodology is very effective in organizations which do not have evolved project management practices.

However, the methodology does not advocate multi-tasking, and in projects with complex schedule networks, the results of implementing the critical path methodology have proven to be a deterrent to the overall project schedule. In addition, there is no standard method for calculating and optimizing the project buffers. The critical path project management methodology has had a fair amount of success in manufacturing; however, it has not achieved any noteworthy success in the IT industry.

Along similar lines, the event chain methodology of project management focuses on determining the uncertain events and the chain reactions they propagate. It is a method of modeling uncertainties and is based on Monte Carlo analysis, Bayesian Belief Network, and other established simulation methodologies. When they occur, events can cause other events, triggering an event chain, which will effectively alter the course of the project. Events and event chains are identified, and quantitative analysis is performed to determine the extent of the uncertainty and the probable impact of the same on the project. From this exercise, critical event chains are derived, which have the potential to impact the project significantly. Event chain diagrams are visual representations of events, event chains, and their impact.

It is clear that neither the critical path project management methodology nor the event chain methodology can be considered alternatives to the standard methodology for project management as advocated by PMBOK. While the critical path project management methodology can be at best used as a tool for deriving project schedule networks, the event chain methodology for project management can be used as a tool for quantitative risk analysis.

Earned Value Management

Earned value management (EVM), earned value project management, or earned value performance management (EVPM) is a project management technique for measuring project performance and progress in an objective manner.

Earned value management is a project management technique for measuring project performance and progress. It has the ability to combine measurements of the project management triangle: scope, time, and costs.

In a single integrated system, earned value management is able to provide accurate forecasts of project performance problems, which is an important contribution for project management.

Early EVM research showed that the areas of planning and control are significantly impacted by its use; and similarly, using the methodology improves both scope definition as well as the analysis of overall project performance. More recent research studies have shown that the principles of EVM are positive predictors of project success. Popularity of EVM has grown in recent years beyond government contracting, a sector in which its importance continues to rise (e.g. recent new DFARS rules), in part because EVM can also surface in and help substantiate contract disputes.

Essential features of any EVM implementation include:

- A project plan that identifies work to be accomplished.
- A valuation of planned work, called planned value (PV) or budgeted cost of work scheduled (BCWS).
- Pre-defined "earning rules" (also called metrics) to quantify the accomplishment of work, called earned value (EV) or budgeted cost of work performed (BCWP).

EVM implementations for large or complex projects include many more features, such as indicators and forecasts of cost performance (over budget or under budget) and schedule performance (behind schedule or ahead of schedule). However, the most basic requirement of an EVM system is that it quantifies progress using PV and EV.

Application Example

Project A has been approved for a duration of one year and with the budget of X. It was also planned that the project spends 50% of the approved budget and expects 50% of the work to be complete in the first six months. If now, six months after the start of the project, a project manager would report that he has spent 50% of the budget, one can initially think, that the project is perfectly on plan. However, in reality the provided information is not sufficient to come to such a conclusion. The project can spend 50% of the budget, whilst finishing only 25% of the work, which would mean the project is not doing well; or the project can spend 50% of the budget, whilst completing 75% of the work, which would mean that project is doing better than planned. EVM is meant to address such and similar issues.

Project Tracking

It is helpful to see an example of project tracking that does not include earned value performance management. Consider a project that has been planned in detail, including a time-phased spend plan for all elements of work. Figure shows the cumulative budget (cost) for this project as a function of time (the blue line, labeled PV). It also shows the cumulative actual cost of the project (red line, labeled AC) through week 8. To those unfamiliar with EVM, it might appear that this project was over budget through week 4 and then under budget from week 6 through week 8. However, what is missing from this chart is any understanding of how much work has been accomplished during the project. If the project was actually completed at week 8, then the project would actually be well under budget and well ahead of schedule. If, on the other hand, the project is only 10% complete at week 8, the project is significantly over budget and behind schedule. A method is needed to measure technical performance objectively and quantitatively, and that is what EVM accomplishes.

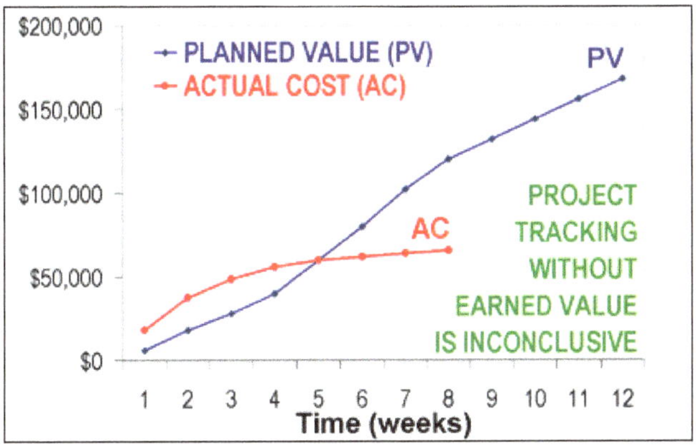

With EVM

Consider the same project, except this time the project plan includes pre-defined methods of quantifying the accomplishment of work. At the end of each week, the project manager identifies every detailed element of work that has been completed, and sums the EV for each of these completed elements. Earned value may be accumulated monthly, weekly, or as progress is made.

Earned Value (EV)

$$EV = \sum_{Start}^{Current} PV(Completed) \quad or \quad EV = BudgetatCompletion\ (BAC) \times Actual\ \%\ Complete$$

EV is calculated by multiplying %complete of each task (completed or in progress) by its planned value

Figure shows the EV curve (in green) along with the PV curve from figure. The chart indicates that technical performance (i.e. progress) started more rapidly than planned, but slowed significantly and fell behind schedule at week 7 and 8. This chart illustrates the schedule performance aspect of EVM. It is complementary to critical path or critical chain schedule management.

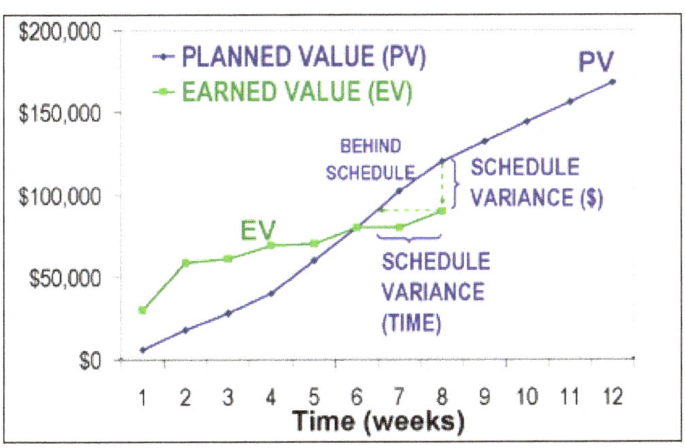

Figure shows the same EV curve (green) with the actual cost data from Figure 1 (in red). It can be seen that the project was actually under budget, relative to the amount of work accomplished, since the start of the project. This is a much better conclusion than might be derived from figure.

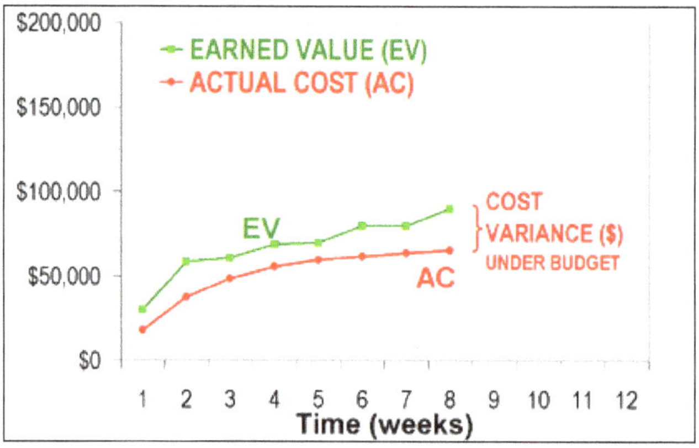

Figure shows all three curves together – which is a typical EVM line chart. The best way to read these three-line charts is to identify the EV curve first, then compare it to PV (for schedule performance) and AC (for cost performance). It can be seen from this illustration that a true understanding of cost performance and schedule performance *relies first on measuring technical performance objectively*. This is the *foundational principle* of EVM.

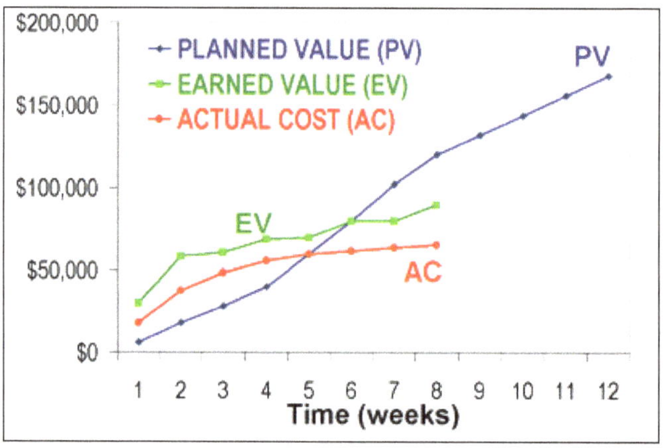

Scaling EVM from Simple to Advanced Implementations

The *foundational principle* of EVM, does not depend on the size or complexity of the project. However, the *implementations* of EVM can vary significantly depending on the circumstances. In many cases, organizations establish an all-or-nothing threshold; projects above the threshold require a full-featured (complex) EVM system and projects below the threshold are exempted. Another approach that is gaining favor is to scale EVM implementation according to the project at hand and skill level of the project team.

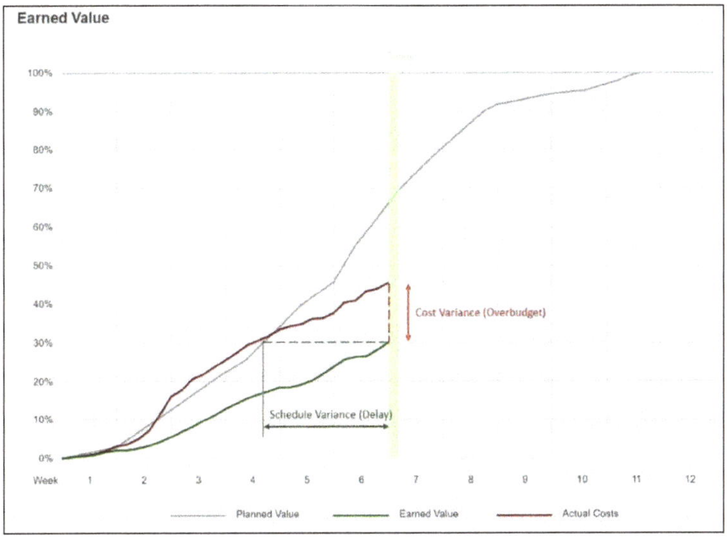

Earned value chart shows planned value, earned value, actual cost, and their variances in percent. The approach is used in project management simulation simultrain.

Simple Implementations (Emphasizing only Technical Performance)

There are many more small and simple projects than there are large and complex ones, yet historically only the largest and most complex have enjoyed the benefits of EVM. Still, lightweight implementations of EVM are achievable by any person who has basic spreadsheet skills. In fact, spreadsheet implementations are an excellent way to learn basic EVM skills.

The *first step* is to define the work. This is typically done in a hierarchical arrangement called a work breakdown structure (WBS) although the simplest projects may use a simple list of tasks. In either case, it is important that the WBS or list be comprehensive. It is also important that the elements be mutually exclusive, so that work is easily categorized in one and only one element of work. The most detailed elements of a WBS hierarchy (or the items in a list) are called activities (or tasks).

The *second step* is to assign a value, called planned value (PV), to each activity. For large projects, PV is almost always an allocation of the total project budget, and may be in units of currency (e.g. dollar, euro or naira) or in labor hours, or both. However, in very simple projects, each activity may be assigned a weighted "point value" which might not be a budget number. Assigning weighted values and achieving consensus on all PV quantities yields an important benefit of EVM, because it exposes misunderstandings and miscommunications about the scope of the project, and resolving these differences should always occur as early as possible. Some terminal elements cannot be known (planned) in great detail in advance, and that is expected, because they can be further refined at a later time.

The *third step* is to define "earning rules" for each activity. The simplest method is to apply just one earning rule, such as the 0/100 rule, to all activities. Using the 0/100 rule, no credit is earned for an element of work until it is finished. A related rule is called the 50/50 rule, which means 50% credit is earned when an element of work is started, and the remaining 50% is earned upon completion. Other fixed earning rules such as a 25/75 rule or 20/80 rule are gaining favor, because they assign more weight to finishing work than for starting it, but they also motivate the project team to identify when an element of work is started, which can improve awareness of work-in-progress. These simple earning rules work well for small or simple projects because generally each activity tends to be fairly short in duration.

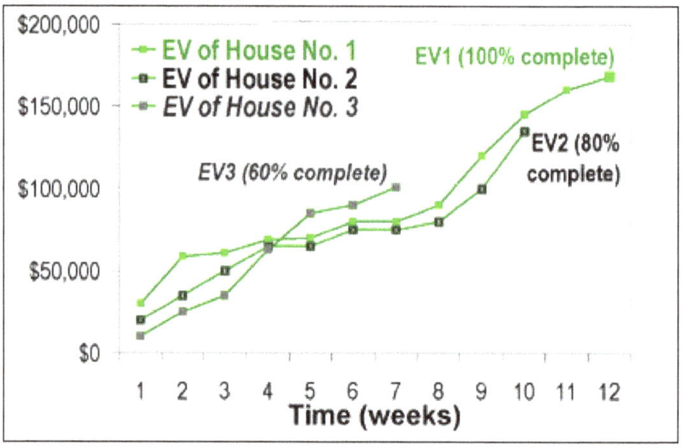

These initial three steps define the minimal amount of planning for simplified EVM. The *final step* is to execute the project according to the plan and measure progress. When activities are started or finished, EV is accumulated according to the earning rule. This is typically done at regular intervals (e.g. weekly or monthly), but there is no reason why EV cannot be accumulated in near real-time, when work elements are started/completed. In fact, waiting to update EV only once per month (simply because that is when cost data are available) only detracts from a primary benefit of using EVM, which is to create a technical performance scoreboard for the project team.

In a lightweight implementation, the project manager has not accumulated cost nor defined a detailed project schedule network (i.e. using a critical path or critical chain methodology). While such omissions are inappropriate for managing large projects, they are a common and reasonable occurrence in many very small or simple projects. Any project can benefit from using EV alone as a real-time score of progress. One useful result of this very simple approach (without schedule models and actual cost accumulation) is to compare EV curves of similar projects, as illustrated in figure. In this example, the progresses of three residential construction projects are compared by aligning the starting dates. If these three home construction projects were measured with the same PV valuations, the *relative* schedule performance of the projects can be easily compared.

Making Earned Value Schedule Metrics Concordant with the CPM Schedule

The actual critical path is ultimately the determining factor of every project's duration. Because earned value schedule metrics take no account of critical path data, big budget activities that are not on the critical path have the potential to dwarf the impact of performing small budget critical path activities. This can lead to "gaming" the SV and Schedule Performance Index or SPI metrics by ignoring critical path activities in favor of big budget activities that may have lots of float. This can sometimes even lead to performing activities out-of-sequence just to improve the schedule tracking metrics, which can cause major problems with quality.

A simple two-step process has been suggested to fix this:

- Create a second earned value baseline strictly for schedule, with the weighted activities and milestones on the as-late-as-possible dates of the backward pass of the critical path algorithm, where there is no float.
- Allow earned value credit for schedule metrics to be taken no earlier than the reporting period during which the activity is scheduled unless it is on the project's current critical path.

In this way, the distorting aspect of float would be eliminated. There would be no benefit to performing a non-critical activity with lots of float until it is due in proper sequence. Also, an activity would not generate a negative schedule variance until it had used up its float. Under this method, one way of gaming the schedule metrics would be eliminated. The only way of generating a positive schedule variance (or SPI over 1.0) would be by completing work on the current critical path ahead of schedule, which is in fact the only way for a project to get ahead of schedule.

Advanced Implementations (Integrating Cost, Schedule and Technical Performance)

In addition to managing technical and schedule performance, large and complex projects require that cost performance be monitored and reviewed at regular intervals. To measure cost performance, planned value (or BCWS - Budgeted Cost of Work Scheduled) and earned value (or BCWP - Budgeted Cost of Work Performed) must be in units of currency (the same units that actual costs are measured).

In large implementations, the planned value curve is commonly called a Performance Measurement Baseline (PMB) and may be arranged in control accounts, summary-level planning packages, planning packages and work packages.

In large projects, establishing control accounts is the primary method of delegating responsibility and authority to various parts of the performing organization. Control accounts are cells of a responsibility assignment (RACI) matrix, which is the intersection of the project WBS and the organizational breakdown structure (OBS). Control accounts are assigned to Control Account Managers (CAMs).

Large projects require more elaborate processes for controlling baseline revisions, more thorough integration with subcontractor EVM systems, and more elaborate management of procured materials.

In the United States, the primary standard for full-featured EVM systems is the ANSI/EIA-748A standard, published in May 1998 and reaffirmed in August 2002. The standard defines 32 criteria for full-featured EVM system compliance. As of the year 2007, a draft of ANSI/EIA-748B, a revision to the original is available from ANSI. Other countries have established similar standards.

In addition to using BCWS and BCWP, prior to 1998 implementations often use the term actual cost of work performed (ACWP) instead of AC. Additional acronyms and formulas include:

1. Budget at completion (BAC): The total planned value (PV or BCWS) at the end of the project. If a project has a management reserve (MR), it is typically *not* included in the BAC, and respectively, in the performance measurement baseline.

2. Cost variance (CV):

$$CV = EV - AC$$

CV greater than 0 is good (under budget).

3. Cost performance index (CPI):

$$CPI = \frac{EV}{AC}$$

CPI greater than 1 is favourable (under budget):

- < 1 means that the cost of completing the work is higher than planned (bad).
- = 1 means that the cost of completing the work is right on plan (good).
- > 1 means that the cost of completing the work is less than planned (good or sometimes bad).

Having a CPI that is very high (in some cases, very high is only 1.2) may mean that the plan was too conservative, and thus a very high number may in fact not be good, as the CPI is being measured against a poor baseline. Management or the customer may be upset with the planners as an overly conservative baseline ties up available funds for other purposes, and the baseline is also used for manpower planning.

4. Estimate at completion (EAC): EAC is the manager's projection of total cost of the project at completion.

$$EAC = AC + \frac{(BAC - EV)}{CPI} = \frac{BAC}{CPI}$$

This formula is based on the assumption that the performance of the project (or rather a deviation of the actual performance from a baseline) to date gives a good indication of what a performance (or rather deviation of a performance from a baseline) will be in the future. In other words this formula is using statistics of the project to date to predict future results. Therefore it has to be used carefully, when the nature of the project in the future is likely to be different from the one to date (e.g. performance of the project compare to baseline at the design phase may not be a good indication of what it will be during a construction phase).

5. Estimate to complete (ETC): ETC is the estimates to complete the remaining work of the project. ETC must be based on objective measures of the outstanding work remaining, typically based on the measures or estimates used to create the original planned value (PV) profile, including any adjustments to predict performance based on historical performance, actions being taken to improve performance, or acknowledgement of degraded performance.

While algebraically, ETC = EAC-AC is correct, ETC should *never* be computed using either EAC or AC. In the following equation,

$$EAC = AC + ETC$$

ETC is the independent variable, EAC is the dependent variable, and AC is fixed based on expenditures to date. ETC should always be reported truthfully to reflect the project team estimate to complete the outstanding work. If ETC pushes EAC to exceed BAC, then project management skills are employed to either recommend performance improvements or scope change, but never force ETC to give the "correct" answer so that EAC=BAC. Managing project activities to keep the project within budget is a human factors activity, not a mathematical function.

6. To-complete performance index (TCPI): The TCPI provides a projection of the anticipated performance required to achieve either the BAC or the EAC. TCPI indicates the future required cost efficiency needed to achieve a target BAC (Budget at Complete) or EAC (Estimate at Complete). Any significant difference between CPI, the cost performance to date, and the TCPI, the cost performance needed to meet the BAC or the EAC, should be accounted for by management in their forecast of the final cost.

For the TCPI based on BAC (describing the performance required to meet the original BAC budgeted total):

$$TCPI_{BAC} = \frac{BAC - EV}{BAC - AC}$$

or for the TCPI based on EAC (describing the performance required to meet a new, revised budget total EAC):

$$TCPI_{EAC} = \frac{BAC - EV}{EAC - AC}$$

This implies, that if revised budget (EAC) is calculated using Earned Value methodology formula (BAC/CPI), then at the moment, when TCPI based on EAC is first time calculated, it will always be equal to CPI of a project at that moment. This happens because when EAC is calculated using formula BAC/CPI it is assumed, that cost performance of the remaining part of the project will be the same as the cost performance of the project to date.

7. Independent estimate at completion (IEAC): The IEAC is a metric to project total cost using the performance to date to project overall performance. This can be compared to the EAC, which is the manager's projection.

$$IEAC = \sum AC + \frac{\left(BAC - \sum EV\right)}{CPI}$$

Limitations

Proponents of EVM note a number of issues with implementing it, and further limitations may be inherent to the concept itself.

Because EVM requires quantification of a project plan, it is often perceived to be inapplicable to discovery-driven or Agile software development projects. For example, it may be impossible to plan certain research projects far in advance, because research itself uncovers some opportunities (research paths) and actively eliminates others. However, another school of thought holds that all work can be planned, even if in weekly timeboxes or other short increments.

Traditional EVM is not intended for non-discrete (continuous) effort. In traditional EVM standards, non-discrete effort is called "level of effort" (LOE). If a project plan contains a significant portion of LOE, and the LOE is intermixed with discrete effort, EVM results will be contaminated. This is another area of EVM research.

Traditional definitions of EVM typically assume that project accounting and project network schedule management are prerequisites to achieving any benefit from EVM. Many small projects don't satisfy either of these prerequisites, but they too can benefit from EVM. Other projects can be planned with a project network, but do not have access to true and timely actual cost data. In practice, the collection of true and timely actual cost data can be the most difficult aspect of EVM. Such projects can benefit from EVM.

As a means of overcoming objections to EVM's lack of connection to qualitative performance issues, the Naval Air Systems Command (NAVAIR) PEO(A) organization initiated a project in the late 1990s to integrate true technical achievement into EVM projections by utilizing risk profiles. These risk profiles anticipate opportunities that may be revealed and possibly be exploited as development and testing proceeds. The published research resulted in a Technical Performance Management (TPM) methodology and software application that is still used by many DoD agencies in informing EVM estimates with technical achievement. The research was peer-reviewed and was the recipient of the Defense Acquisition University Acquisition Research Symposium 1997 Acker Award for excellence in the exchange of information in the field of acquisition research.

There is the difficulty inherent for any periodic monitoring of synchronizing data timing: actual deliveries, actual invoicing, and the date the EVM analysis is done are all independent, so that some items have arrived but their invoicing has not and by the time analysis is delivered the data will likely be weeks behind events. This may limit EVM to a less tactical or less definitive role where use is combined with other forms to explain why or add recent news and manage future expectations.

There is a measurement limitation for how precisely EVM can be used, stemming from classic conflict between accuracy and precision, as the mathematics can calculate deceptively far beyond the precision of the measurements of data and the approximation that is the plan estimation. The limitation on estimation is commonly understood (such as the ninety-ninety rule in software) but is not visible in any margin of error. The limitations on measurement are largely a form of digitization error as EVM measurements ultimately can be no finer than by item, which may be the Work Breakdown Structure terminal element size, to the scale of reporting period, typically end summary of a month, and by the means of delivery measure. (The delivery measure may be actual deliveries, may include estimates of partial work done at the end of month subject to estimation limits, and typically does not include QC check or risk offsets.)

Lean Project Management

Lean project management is the application of lean concepts such as lean construction, lean manufacturing and lean thinking to project management.

Lean project management has many ideas in common with other lean concepts; however, the main principle of lean project management is delivering more value with less waste in a project context.

Lean Project Management applies all five of those principles to project management.

"Lean" is a systematic method for the elimination of waste ("Muda") within a manufacturing system. Lean also takes into account waste created through overburden ("Muri") and waste created through unevenness in work loads ("Mura"). Working from the perspective of the client who consumes a product or service, "value" is any action or process that a customer would be willing to pay for.

Lean approach makes obvious what adds value by reducing everything else which does not add value. This management philosophy is derived mostly from the Toyota Production System (TPS) and identified as "lean" only in the 1990s. TPS is renowned for its focus on reduction of the original Toyota seven wastes to improve overall customer value, but there are varying perspectives on how this is best achieved. The steady growth of Toyota, from a small company to the world's largest automaker, has focused attention on how it has achieved this success.

Types of Lean Project Management

In general, a project can be said to be Lean if it applies the principles of lean thinking. There are, however, different implementations of this idea that don't necessarily apply all of the principles with equal weight.

Two well-known types are "Kanban" and "Last Planner System".

The term Kanban comes from manufacturing but was adapted for software development by David Anderson when he was working at Microsoft in 2005 and inherited an underperforming maintenance team. The success of the approach in that environment, led Anderson to experiment with Kanban in projects, with similarly positive results. As Anderson publicised his findings through talks and his book , software developers began to experiment with Kanban and it is now one of the most widely used methods for managing agile software development projects.

The Last Planner System is used principally in construction and particularly focuses on pull and flow but perhaps more important than those is its emphasis on a collaborative approach in which all trades work together to create a visual representation of the work that needs to be done.

Project Production Management

Project production management (PPM) is the application of operations management to the delivery of capital projects. The PPM framework is based on a project as a production system view, in which a project transforms inputs (raw materials, information, labor, plant & machinery) into outputs (goods and services).

The knowledge that forms the basis of PPM originated in the discipline of industrial engineering during the Industrial Revolution. During this time, industrial engineering matured and then found application in many areas such as military planning and logistics for both the First and Second World Wars and manufacturing systems. As a coherent body of knowledge began to form, industrial engineering evolved into various scientific disciplines including operations research, operations management and queueing theory, amongst other areas of focus. Project Production Management (PPM) is the application of this body of knowledge to the delivery of capital projects.

Project management, as defined by the Project Management Institute, specifically excludes operations management from its body of knowledge, on the basis that projects are temporary endeavors with a beginning and an end, whereas operations refer to activities that are either ongoing or repetitive. However, by looking at a large capital project as a production system, such as what is encountered in construction, it is possible to apply the theory and associated technical frameworks from operations research, industrial engineering and queuing theory to optimize, plan, control and improve project performance.

For example, Project Production Management applies tools and techniques typically used in manufacturing management, such as described by Philip M. Morse in, or in Factory Physics to assess the impact of variability and inventory on project performance. Although any variability in a production system degrades its performance, by understanding which variability is detrimental to the business and which is beneficial, steps can be implemented to reduce detrimental variability. After mitigation steps are put in place, the impact of any residual variability can be addressed by allocating buffers at select points in the project production system – a combination of capacity, inventory and time.

Scientific and Engineering disciplines have contributed to many mathematical methods for the design and planning in project planning and scheduling, most notably linear and dynamic programming yielding techniques such as the critical path method (CPM) and the program evaluation and review technique (PERT). The application of engineering disciplines, particularly the areas of operations research, industrial engineering and queueing theory have found much application in the fields of manufacturing and factory production systems. Factory Physics is an example of where these scientific principles are described as forming a framework for manufacturing and production management. Just as Factory Physics is the application of scientific principles to construct a framework for manufacturing and production management. Project Production Management is the application of the very same operations principles to the activities in a project, covering an area that has been conventionally out of scope for project management.

Modern project management theory and techniques started with Frederick Taylor and Taylorism/scientific management at the beginning of the 20th century, with the advent of mass manufacturing. It was refined further in the 1950s with techniques such as critical path method (CPM) and program evaluation and review technique (PERT). Use of CPM and PERT became more common as the computer revolution progressed. As the field of project management continued to grow, the role of the project manager was created and certifying organizations such as the Project Management Institute (PMI) emerged. Modern project management has evolved into a broad variety of knowledge areas described in the Guide to the Project Management Body of Knowledge (PMBOK).

Operations management (related to the fields of production management, operations research and industrial engineering) is a field of science that emerged from the modern manufacturing industry and focuses on modeling and controlling actual work processes. The practice is based upon defining and controlling production systems, which typically consist of a series of inputs, transformational activities, inventory and outputs. Over the last 50 years, project management and operations management have been considered separate fields of study and practice.

PPM applies the theory and results of the various disciplines known as operations management, operations research, queueing theory and industrial engineering to the management and execution of projects. By viewing a project as a production system, the delivery of capital projects can be analyzed for the impact of variability. The effects of variability can be summarized by VUT equation (specifically Kingman's formula for G/G/1 queue). By using a combination of buffers – capacity, inventory and time – the impact of variability to project execution performance can be minimized.

A set of key results used to analyze and optimize the work in projects were originally articulated by Philip Morse, considered the father of operations research in the U.S. and summarized in his seminal volume. In introducing its framework for manufacturing management, *Factory Physics* summarizes these results:

- A perfect world of maximum profitability and service occurs when demand and transformation (also called supply) are perfectly synchronized: All demand is met instantly at minimum cost.
- Because there is variability, demand and transformation can never be perfectly synchronized. In some cases, detrimental variability can be removed. An example would be the statistical quality control techniques used in manufacturing to control deviations, but even then, there is residual detrimental variability that causes demand and supply never to be perfectly synchronized.
- Buffers are required when synchronizing demand and transformation in the presence of variability.
- There are only three buffers: Capacity, inventory and time.

There are key mathematical models that describe the relationships between buffers and variability. Little's law – named after academic John Little – describes the relationship between throughput, cycle time and work-in-process (WIP) or inventory. The Cycle Time Formula summarizes how much time a set of tasks at a particular point in a project take to execute. Kingman's formula, also known as the VUT equation – summarizing the impact of variability.

PRINCE2

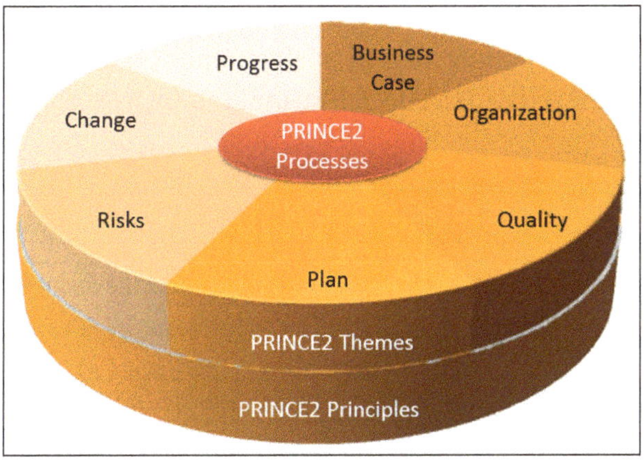

PRINCE2 – Structure.

PRINCE2 (PRojects IN Controlled Environments) is a structured project management method and practitioner certification programme. PRINCE2 emphasises dividing projects into manageable and controllable stages.

It is adopted in many countries worldwide, including the UK, Western European countries, and Australia. PRINCE2 training is available in many languages.

PRINCE2 was developed as a UK government standard for information systems projects. In July 2013, ownership of the rights to PRINCE2 was transferred from HM Cabinet Office to AXELOS Ltd, a joint venture by the Cabinet Office and Capita, with 49% and 51% stakes respectively.

PRINCE was derived from an earlier method called PROMPT II (Project Resource Organisation Management Planning Techniques). In 1989 the Central Computer and Telecommunications Agency (CCTA) adopted a version of PROMPT II as a UK Government standard for information systems (IT) project management. They gave it the name 'PRINCE', which originally stood for "PROMPT II IN the CCTA Environment". PRINCE was renamed in a Civil service competition as an acronym for "PRojects IN Controlled Environments". PRINCE2 is the second edition of the earlier PRINCE method which was initially announced and developed in 1989 by CCTA *(the central computer and Telecommunications Agency)*, a UK government support agency. PRINCE2 was released in 1996 as a generic project management method. PRINCE2 has become increasingly popular and is now a *de facto* standard for project management in many UK government departments and across the United Nations system.

There have been two major revisions of PRINCE2 since its launch in 1996: "PRINCE2:2009 Refresh" in 2009, and "PRINCE2 2017 Update" in 2017. The justification for the 2017 update was the evolutions in practical business practices and feedback from PRINCE2 practitioners in the actual project environment. The second edition was announced and released in 1996 as a generic *PM methodology*.

Six Aspects

These aspects are also called tolerances or performance goals. They quantify the project tolerance and are considered during decision-making processes. In some organizations these can be KPIs.

Tolerance Type	Maintained in the project level	Example
Scope	Project Plan	The printer should print the documents only in black/white.
Timescale	Project Plan	The project/stage/team plan cannot last longer than 3 months.
Risk	Risk Management Approach	Printer might not work if it is in water.
Quality	Project Product Description	Printer should print at least 10 different standard page sizes.
Benefits	Business Case	Printer should be set up by the customer 10% faster than the ones from the competitors, and it must be 10% cheaper.
Cost	Project Plan	The cost of the project should not exceed £100,000.

Benefits can have as target the cost of the benefit, but the cost tolerance above is related to the cost of the project, not the cost of the benefit.

Each management level is checked against these tolerances, coming from the upper level.

Management level	Tolerance type authorized to the lower level	Exception type addressed to upper level	Plan type
Corporate/Programme	Project tolerance	n/a	Programme
Project board	Stage tolerance	Project exception	Project plan
Project manager	Work package tolerance	Stage exception	Stage plan
Team manager	n/a	Issue	Team plan

Seven Principles

PRINCE2 is based on seven principles and these cannot be tailored. The PRINCE2 principles can be described as a mindset that keeps the project aligned with the PRINCE2 methodology. If a project does not adhere to these principles, it is not being managed using PRINCE2.

- Continued Business Justification: The business case is the most important document, and is updated at every stage of the project to ensure that the project is still viable. Early termination can occur if this ceases to be the case.

- Learn From Experience: Each project maintains a lessons log and projects should continually refer to their own and to previous and concurrent projects' lesson logs to avoid reinventing wheels. Unless lessons provoke change, they are only lessons identified (not learned).
- Defined Roles and Responsibilities: Roles are separated from individuals, who may take on multiple roles or share a role. Roles in PRINCE2 are structured in four levels (corporate or programme management, project board, project manager level and team level). Project Management Team contains the last three, where all primary stakeholders (business, user, supplier) need to be presented.
- Manage by Stages: The project is planned and controlled on a stage by stage basis. Moving between stages includes updating the business case, risks, overall plan, and detailed next-stage plan in the light of new evidence.
- Manage by Exception: A PRINCE2 project has defined tolerances (6 aspects above) for each project objective, to establish limits of delegated authority. If a management level forecasts that these tolerances are exceeded (e.g. time of a management stage will be longer than the estimated time in the current management stage). It is escalated to the next management level for a decision how to proceed.
- Focus on Products: A PRINCE2 project focuses on the definition and delivery of the products, in particular their quality requirements.
- Tailor to Suit Project Environment: PRINCE2 is tailored to suit the project environment, size, complexity, importance, time capability and risk. Tailoring is the first activity in the process Initiating A Project and reviewed for each stage.

Not every aspect of PRINCE2 will be applicable to every project, thus every process has a note on scalability. This provides guidance to the project manager (and others involved in the project) as to *how much* of the process to apply. The positive aspect of this is that PRINCE2 can be tailored to the needs of a particular project. The negative aspect is that many of the essential elements of PRINCE2 can be omitted sometimes resulting in a PINO project – Prince in Name Only.

Seven Processes

- Starting Up A Project, in which the project team is appointed including an executive and a project manager, and a project brief is produced.
- Initiating A Project, in which the business case refined and Project Initiation Documentation assembled.
- Directing A Project, which dictates the ways in which the Project Board oversees the project.
- Controlling A Stage, which dictates how each individual stage should be controlled, including the way in which work packages are authorised and distributed.

- Managing Product Delivery, which has the purpose of controlling the link between the Project Manager and the Team Managers by placing formal requirements on accepting, executing and delivering project work.
- Managing Stage Boundaries, which dictates how to transition from one stage to the next.
- Closing A Project, which covers the formal decommissioning of the project, follow-on actions and evaluation of the benefits.

Management Products

The PRINCE2 manual contains 26 suggested templates for documentation associated with the project, which it terms *management products* and which are divided into *baselines*, *records* and *reports*. Some examples of management products are:

- Benefits Management Approach: Defines how and when a measurement of the project's benefits, expected by the Senior User, can be made.
- Business Case: Used to capture financial justification for the project. It is a PRINCE2 principle that a project must have continued business justification. As soon as a Business Case fails to make sense, change or stop that project.
- Checkpoint Report: A progress report created by the Team Manager and sent to the Project Manager on a regular basis to report the status of the Work Package.
- Communications Management Approach: A description of the methods and frequency of communication to stakeholders, covering the flow of information in both directions to and from stakeholders (Information required to be provided from the project and information required to be provided to the project).
- Configuration Item Record: Provides a record of the product History, Status, Version, Variant, Details of any relationships between items/products, and Product owner/Product copy holders.
- Change Control Approach: Used to identify how the project's products will be identified, controlled and protected, this document is created by the Project Manager in the Initiating a Project process.
- Daily Log: Used to record informal issues.
- End Project Report: Reviews how the project performed against the original Project Initiation Documentation (PID).
- Issues Register: An issue log of notes about change requests, problems and complaints sent by all project members.
- Lessons Log: A set of notes of lessons learned which may be useful to future projects.

- Project Brief: Used by the Project Board to authorize the Initiation Stage (1st stage of the project). In the Initiating a Project process, the contents of the Project Brief are extended and refined and the Project Brief evolves to form the Project Initiation Documentation (PID).
- Quality Register: Details of all planned quality control activities, dates, and personnel involved.
- Risk Register: A record of identified risks (threats and opportunities) relating to the project.

Integration with other Techniques

The 26 Management Products described by PRINCE2 are only used for the "high-level" management of the project. Within its tasks, task managers must still decide on their own project management framework. Some suggestions given in the PRINCE2 manual are product based planning, change control, quality review technique, Gantt charts, PERT charts and critical path analysis.

PRINCE2 can also be used to manage projects that use agile software development methods.

Quality Review Technique

The quality review technique ensures a project's products are of the required standard (i.e. meet defined quality criteria). This takes place in a quality review meeting, which identifies errors in the product. The quality review meeting will not attempt to solve the problems it identifies. The meeting brings together people who have an interest in the project's outputs (or products) and people on the project team able to address issues identified.

PRINCE2 Agile

PRINCE2 Agile is an extension to the original PRINCE2 how to adapt PRINCE2 so that it can be deployed when utilised with agile behaviours, frameworks and additional techniques. An agile framework (e.g. Scrum) is a project environment. This way an agile framework is made manageable by a project management method. Agile frameworks define neither decision-making governance, nor risk management. PRINCE2 on top of an agile framework fills this gap.

Basically it uses the following techniques:

- Cynefin framework to understand the complexity of the project to find out whether classical, process-based PRINCE2 or agile framework based PRINCE2 shall be used. It is used during the Starting Up a Project and Initiating a Project process.

- Agilometer as a vehicle to understand how much tailoring and agility to be used in the PRINCE2 project, with focus on estimating the risk response performance of the project. It is reviewed, eventually updated during the Managing Stage Boundary process.
- Scrum for timebox-based, Kanban for flow-based work package management.

Advantages and Criticisms

PRINCE2 provides a method for managing projects within a clearly defined framework, but project management is a complex discipline and using such a framework is no guarantee of a successful project.

Some of the advertised benefits of PRINCE2 are: Increased quality of the finished products, efficient control of resources, avoidance of either "heroic" (under-regulated) or "mechanistic" (over-regulated) working, and increased confidence among the project team.

PRINCE2 is sometimes considered inappropriate for small projects or where requirements are expected to change, due to the work required in creating and maintaining documents, logs and lists. The deliverable structure may also lead to focus on producing deliverables for their own sake, to "tick the boxes" rather than do more useful work.

The general response of PRINCE2's authors to criticism has been to point out that the methodology is scalable and can be tailored to suit the specific requirements and constraints of the project and the environment. This strong emphasis on tailoring has led some users to complain that PRINCE2 is unfalsifiable, i.e. it is impossible to tell whether PRINCE2 "works" or constitutes "best practice" if any problems encountered with a project can be blamed on inappropriate application of PRINCE2 rather than on PRINCE2 itself.

The experiences of the Blair administration in the UK between 1997 and 2007 (and of subsequent UK governments) arguably undermine PRINCE2's claim to be "best practice", given the string of high-profile failed IT projects charged to the taxpayer during that time, and the controversy surrounding the financial relationship between the Blair government and PRINCE2's co-owners Capita. PRINCE2's training material addresses these failures, blaming them on inappropriate tailoring of PRINCE2 to the project environment, and advocating for more PRINCE2 training for government project managers to solve the problem.

Product-based Planning

Product-based planning is a fundamental part of the PRINCE2 approach to project management, and is a method of identifying all of the products (project deliverables) that make up or contribute to delivering the objectives of the project, and the associated work required to deliver them. The documents which define the Project itself are also considered Products.

Product Breakdown Structure

Product-based planning is intended to ensure that all of the necessary products are identified and captured, and begins by identifying a product breakdown structure which is then repeatedly refined until all of the requisite products are identified. The PBS is thus a hierarchical family tree of all the products and sub-products that comprise the final end-product.

It is important to understand that in this context the term 'product' includes intermediate documentary products that are essential to the work of delivering the project. In this sense the product breakdown structure is a great deal *more* than simply an exploded view of the final end-product. Products included might also be products required to manage the project such as paper-based products and quality products such as approvals or quality checks on earlier made products. Examples include such things as requirement specifications, design approvals, test documentation, safety certifications, and so on.

Product Flow Diagram

Once a product breakdown structure has been created, work can then begin on creating a product flow diagram (PFD) (or *product flowchart*) which identifies the order of precedence of products and will typically include multiple and complex parallel paths. For practical purposes this flowchart is essentially the same as the PERT chart used for critical path scheduling and leads naturally to the development of a project schedule.

Work Breakdown Structure

With an understanding of the deliverables required, and the sequence in which they should be produced, work can then begin on defining the tasks required to produce them.

A significant advantage of product-based planning is the ability to surface critical assumptions and constraints. For example, if your project is to build another floor on top of a house a required *product* will be the floor underneath on which to build the one you are commissioned to deliver. As a *product* you hope that it is there and will be fit for purpose but as you are not commissioned to deliver it, it falls outside your scope - and into your assumptions. In this way, by defining the *whole* product set necessary for the project, and not just those that are in your scope, you can surface and document the critical assumptions. Another advantage compared to activity-based planning has to do with reporting. Products are either finished or not, activities can be 90% finished for a long time even though work is taking place. One tends to forget things that have to be done to complete a project. This method captures them all, reducing the chance that any will be overlooked.

This method is used in PRINCE2, the UK's government mandated method for the management of major projects.

Example of Product-based Planning

A refrigerator is a final product with sub-products being door, shelves, heat exchange unit, fans, ice cube dispensers, lights, etc.

Each of the sub-products are made up of smaller products such as door handle, insulation, magnetic closure strip and internal covering.

Product Breakdown Structure

In project management under the PRINCE2 methodology, a product breakdown structure (PBS) is a tool for analysing, documenting and communicating the outcomes of a project, and forms part of the product based planning technique.

The PBS provides "an exhaustive, hierarchical tree structure of deliverables that make up the project, arranged in whole-part relationship".

This diagrammatic representation of project outputs provides a clear and unambiguous statement of what the project is to deliver.

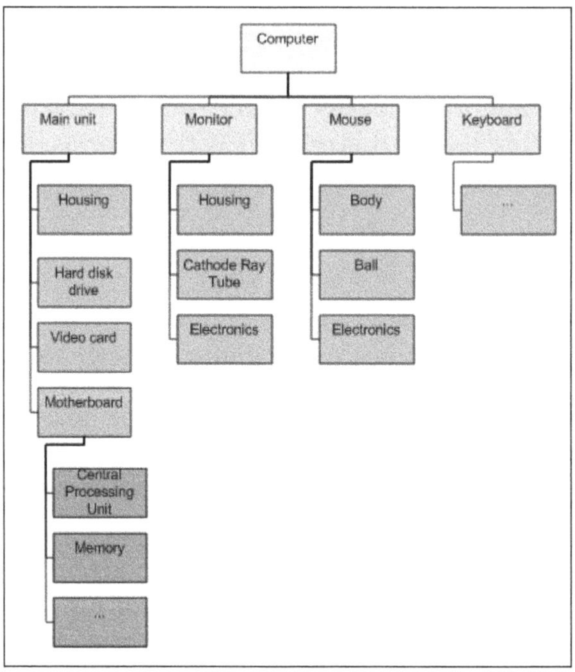

Example of a product breakdown structure of a computer.

The PBS is identical in format to the work breakdown structure (WBS), but is a separate entity and is used at a different step in the planning process. The PBS precedes the WBS and focuses on cataloguing all the desired outputs (products) needed to achieve the goal of the project. This feeds into creation of the WBS, which identifies the tasks and activities required to deliver those outputs. Supporters of product based planning suggest that this overcomes difficulties that arise from assumptions about what to do and how to do it by focusing instead on the goals and objectives of the project – an oft-quoted analogy is that "PBS defines where you want to go, the WBS tells you how to get there".

Agile Project Management

Agile is a project management methodology that uses short development cycles called "sprints" to focus on continuous improvement in the development of a product or service.

Although incremental software development methods go as far back as 1957, agile was first discussed in depth in the 1970s by William Royce who published a paper on the development of large software systems. Later in 2001, the Agile Manifesto, a "formal proclamation of four key values and 12 principles to guide an iterative and people-centric approach to software development," was published by 17 software developers. These developers gathered together to discuss lightweight development methods based on their combined experience.

The Principles of Agile

- Customer satisfaction is always the highest priority and is achieved through rapid and continuous delivery.
- Changing environments are embraced at any stage of the process to provide the customer with a competitive advantage.
- A product or service is delivered with higher frequency.
- Stakeholders and developers collaborate closely on a daily basis.
- All stakeholders and team members remain motivated for optimal project outcomes, while teams are provided with all the necessary tools and support, and are trusted to accomplish project goals.
- Face-to-face meetings are deemed the most efficient and effective format for project success.
- A final working product is the ultimate measure of success.
- Sustainable development is accomplished through agile processes whereby development teams and stakeholders are able to maintain a constant and ongoing pace.
- Agility is enhanced through a continuous focus on technical excellence and proper design.
- Simplicity is an essential element.

- Self-organizing teams are most likely to develop the best architectures and designs and to meet requirements.
- Regular intervals are used by teams to improve efficiency through fine-tuning behaviors.

Agile Methodology Adoption

Although designed originally for the software industry, many industries now use agile when developing products and services because of the highly collaborative and more efficient nature of the methodology. The following table shows adoption rates of the agile methodology in a variety of leading industries, as shown in the 11th Annual State of Agile survey by Version One.

Industry	Agile adoption rate
Software (ISV)	23 percent
Financial services	14 percent
Professional services	12 percent
Insurance	6 percent
Healthcare	6 percent
Government	5 percent
Telecoms	4 percent
Transportation	4 percent
Manufacturing	4 percent

The Benefits of Agile

Agile was originally developed for the software industry to streamline and improve the development process in an effort to rapidly identify and adjust for issues and defects. It provides a way for developers and teams to deliver a better product, in a faster manner, through short, iterative, interactive sessions/sprints. In the era of digital transformation, with many companies migrating to a digital workplace, agile is a perfect fit for organizations looking to transform how they manage projects and operate as a whole. Agile can help ensure company-wide process and methodological alignment. In terms of business benefits, both the digital workplace and agile provide:

- Increased flexibility.
- Increased productivity.
- Increased transparency.
- Higher quality deliverables.

- Decreased risk of missed objectives.
- Increased stakeholder engagement and satisfaction.

Advantages of Agile for Project Management

In the project management field, agile provides project teams, sponsors, project leaders and customers many project-specific benefits, including:

- More rapid deployment of solutions.
- Reduced waste through minimization of resources.
- Increased flexibility and adaptability to change.
- Increased success through more focused efforts.
- Faster turnaround times.
- Faster detection of issues and defects.
- Optimized development processes.
- A lighter weight framework.
- Optimal project control.
- Increased focus on specific customer needs.
- Increased frequency of collaboration and feedback.

The Drawbacks of Agile

As with any other methodology, agile is not well-suited for every project, and sufficient due diligence is always recommended to identify the best methodology for each unique situation. Agile may not work as intended if a customer is not clear on goals, the project manager or team is inexperienced, or if they do not function well under significant pressure. Throughout the development process, agile favors the developers, project teams and customer goals, but not necessarily the end user's experience. Due to its less formal and more flexible processes, agile may not always be easily absorbed within larger more traditional organizations where there are significant amounts of rigidity or flexibility within processes, policies, or teams. It may also face problems being used with customers who similarly have rigid processes or operating methods.

Combining Agile with other Methodologies

The opportunity exists to combine agile with other methodologies such as waterfall to create a hybrid solution. Companies sometimes use waterfall to handle one or more phases — such as planning — where these do not require rapid or repetitive steps. Planning in particular requires a more comprehensive, methodical, often slower approach to defining, analyzing, and documenting aspects of a project. This makes waterfall a better approach. Once a project enters the development phase, rapid and repetitive changes require a different approach and this is where agile kicks in to deliver the best results in the shortest amount of time.

This hybrid approach aids in making agile even more adaptable within various industries or to suit the more unique nature of a project, product, or service. Again, due diligence is required to determine the suitability and capacity of the different methods and processes available.

Popular Agile Methodologies

Within agile there are some frequently used or popular methods, with Scrum, Kanban, and Lean being the most popular. Some agile methods include:

- Scrum.
- Kanban.
- Lean (LN).
- Dynamic System Development Model, (DSDM).
- Extreme Programming (XP).
- Crystal.
- Adaptive software development (ASD).
- Agile Unified Process (AUP).
- Crystal Clear methods.
- Disciplined agile delivery.
- Feature-driven development (FDD).
- Scrumban.
- RAD(Rapid Application Development).

Benefits Realization Management

Benefits Realization Management (BRM) (also benefits management, benefits realisation or project benefits management) is one of the many ways of managing how time and resources are invested into making desirable changes.

Benefits Realization Management has four main definitions. The first definition is to consider benefits management as an organisational change process. It is defined as "the process of organizing and managing, such that the potential benefits arising from the use of IT are actually realized". The second definition perceives it as a process. Benefits management is defined by the Association for Project Management (APM) as the identification, definition, planning, tracking and realization of business benefits. The third definition is to apply this concept on project management level. Project benefits management is defined as "the initiating, planning, organizing, executing, controlling, transitioning and supporting of change in the organisation and its consequences as incurred by project management mechanisms to realize predefined project benefits". Finally, the last definition perceives benefits realization management as a set of processes structured to close the gap between strategy planning and execution by ensuring the implementation of the most valuable initiatives.

The popularity of BRM began in 1995 in the UK, when Scottish Widows created a Benefits Realisation method as part of its Project Management Handbook, and rolled its use out across the entire firm. It grew in the UK with the inclusion of BRM by the UK Government in their standardized approach to programmes, *Managing Successful Programmes (MSP).*

BRM practices aim to ensure the alignment between project outcomes and business strategies and has been shown to increase project success across different countries and industries. The Project Management Institute (PMI) identified that only one in five organizations report high maturity in benefits realization.

If value is to be created and sustained, benefits need to be actively managed through the whole investment lifecycle. From describing and selecting the investment, through programme scoping and design, delivery of the programme to create the capability and execution of the business changes required to utilise that capability, and the operation and eventual retirement of the resulting assets. Unfortunately, this is rarely the case.

As with all project management methodologies, BRM has clear roles and responsibilities, processes, principles and deliverables. The main roles are Business Change Managers (BCMs) who help the Benefits Owners (i.e. the main beneficiaries) identify, plan and review the expected benefits from the change and project managers who deliver the reliable capability on time and within budget. BRM is used to manage the investment by organizations in procurement, projects, programmes and portfolios. BRM is also used to ensure the organization maintains a benefits focus during continuing business operations.

Outcomes are changes identified as important by stakeholders and can be strategic or non-strategic. A benefit is a measurable positive impact of change. A dis-benefit is a measurable negative impact of change. Successful BRM requires accountable people, relevant measures and proactive management.

A generic BRM process is to:

- Identify the investment outcomes.
- Define benefit measures for each outcome.
- Collect current benefit measure data to have a quantitative basis for decision making.
- Agree to a tailored BRM approach for this investment.
- Plan the new or changed capabilities necessary to realize the benefits.
- Plan the investments needed to make the changes necessary to create or change the capabilities.
- Optimize the plan to reduce waste and have acceptable levels of resource, risk, cost, quality and time.
- Implement the plan.
- Review the impact of the plan implementation on the Benefit Measures and use insights to improve.
- On completion of the plan, ensure BRM continues to sustain the capabilities and realisation of benefits.

To identify the investment outcomes, pictorial views of the outcomes of interest on an *outcome map* (also called a *results chain*, *benefits dependency network* or *benefit map*) can be created. This technique supports agreement of the outcomes sought as it shows the outcomes and relationships between them on a single page. They can be agreed upon and communicated clearly as a result.

Data can then be captured either separately or within a suitable modelling tool for each outcome that will include the benefit measures used for each, ownership and accountability information and information to support realisation management.

Mapping Styles

Constructing benefits maps or graphs is usually done from right to left, with what is attempting to be achieved (often called objectives, strategic outcomes etc.) being the start point, then moving through intermediate outcomes to the things required to cause these to happen at the very left.

Benefits Dependency Networks (BDN)

The *benefits dependency network* has five types of object within maps:

- Investment Objectives: A small number of statements that define the focus of the project and how it links to investment drivers.

- Benefits: Advantages to specific individuals or groups of individuals.
- Business Changes: Changes required in the business to hit the Benefits.
- Enabling Changes: Changes required to allow the Business Changes to happen.
- IS/IT enablers: "The information systems and technology required to support the realization of identified benefits and allow the necessary changes to be undertaken."

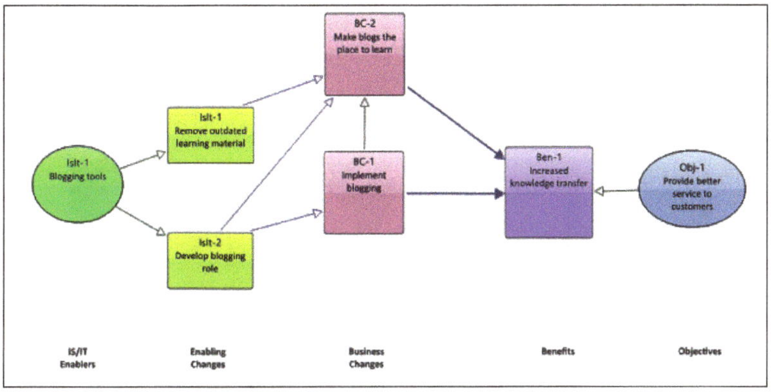

A diagram showing the Benefits Dependency Network Modelling style by John Ward and Elizabeth Daniel.

Benefits Dependency Map (BDM)

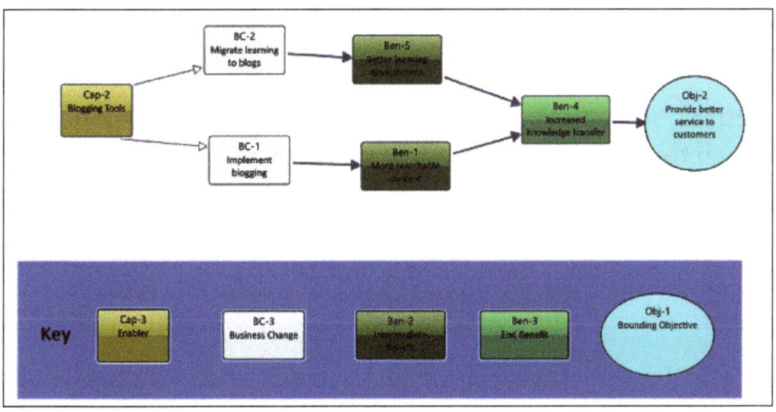

A diagram showing the Benefits Dependency Map Modelling style by Gerald Bradley.

The *benefits dependency map* also has five types of object on the maps:

- Bounding Objective: Measurable end goals which support the vision of what is being attempted.
- End Benefit: Independent Benefits (not interlinked) that achieve the objective.
- Intermediate Benefit: "An outcome of change which is perceived as positive by a stakeholder".

- Business Change: Changes to the business or environment of the business.
- Enabler: Something developed/purchased to enable the realisation of benefit.

Results Chain

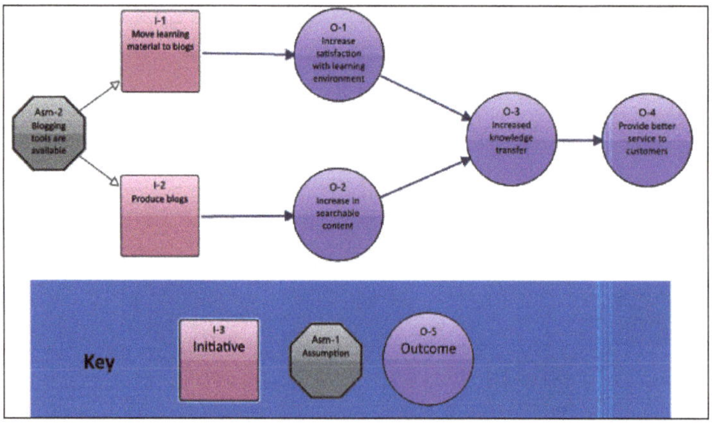

A diagram showing the Results Chain Modelling style by John Thorp.

The *results chain* has four types of object on the maps:

- Outcome: The results being aimed at.
- Initiative: An action or activity that contributes to outcomes.
- Contribution: A measurable description of how an initiative is expected to contribute to an outcome.
- Assumption: Something believed to be required to realize outcomes or initiatives which the organisation has no or little control over.

Iterative and Incremental Project Management

Implementing an ERP solution provides many benefits to an organization, including process efficiencies, improved user interface, technology enhancements, lower maintenance costs and the ability to leverage leading industry practices. Iterative planning on an ERP project provides many benefits: major risks are identified and addressed early in the project; requirement changes are identified and prioritized efficiently; project team utilization is optimized; and progress and quality are continuously monitored and corrected.

Iterative

In an iterative approach such as OUM, the project is divided into periods of time, usually from two to six weeks (in some cases, two to four weeks), called iterations. During each of these periods, the team executes tasks in order to achieve the iteration's goals. Therefore, the term, "iterative" means that work on an ERP project is divided into a series of "iterations" that are essentially run as mini-projects.

Incremental

Incremental means that the system is developed in chunks, iteration by iteration. Each iteration results in an increment, which is a "release" of the system that contains added or improved functionality compared with the previous release. At the end of iteration, the resulting increment of functionality is presented to users, and requirements are re-evaluated so as to plan the next iteration.

Putting this all together, iterative and incremental means that the ERP solution is developed through a series of mini-projects (iterative) and in smaller portions at a time (incremental), allowing the project team to take advantage of what was learned during development of earlier parts or versions of the system and incorporate external feedback from project stakeholders.

Layered Approach to Planning ERP Projects

ERP project plans need to be scalable for different project sizes and complexity and contain the right level of detail for the current planning horizon. Plans that are too detailed are almost instantly inaccurate and obscure key objectives. On the other hand, plans that are too high level will not allow for measurement of project progress nor keep the project team focused on their day-to-day activities.

ERP project plans also need to display the appropriate level of detail and planning horizon for specific audiences. For example, C-level executives, business area managers, and external stakeholders have their focus on the release date, major milestones, business impacts, and points at which major decisions must be made. On the other hand, the project team needs the details on the lower level plans to plan their daily work and measure progress.

There are two plans active in the project at any given time on an ERP project – the implementation and the iteration plan.

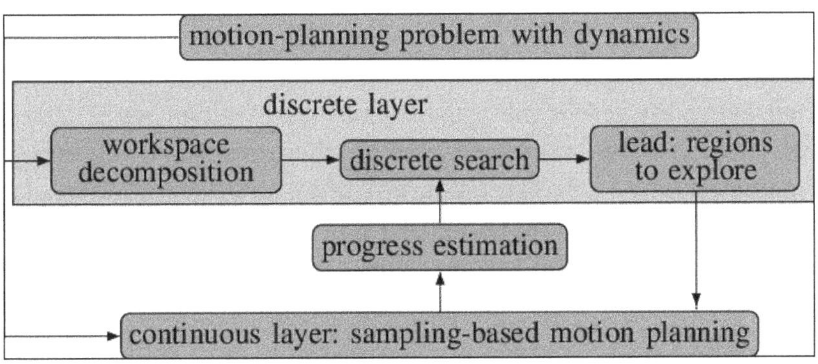

Layered planning approach.

The Implementation Plan

The implementation plan is a brief, coarse-grained outline for the project, which provides a roadmap for achieving the objectives for the project. The implementation plan's purpose is to demonstrate how the project will achieve its objectives and display targeted dates for major achievements and/or decisions in the form of milestones.

The Iteration Plan

The iteration plan represents the lowest and most detailed layer of planning. An individual iteration plan will be created for each iteration in the project. The main purpose of the iteration plan is to lay out how the team will achieve the stated objectives for the given iteration.

Top-Down/Bottom-up Planning

Planning should start early in an ERP project where the focus is on the implementation plan. Also, the initial iteration should be drafted to the degree that the project is able to move into the first phase of the project.

As the project moves along, the initial implementation plan is further refined as more project requirements and risks are uncovered. As the project iterates through the later phases, the plans at each layer (implementation and iteration) will be adjusted based on the results of iteration assessments and as project objectives shift, as is often the case. Furthermore, an iteration plan for the upcoming iteration is created before that iteration begins. Also, the implementation plan must be examined to ensure it is still valid as the iteration plans are created and maintained.

Therefore, at any time on an ERP project, the following plans should be active:

- One implementation plan.
- Two iteration plans: One for the current iteration and a draft for the upcoming iteration.

Planning an ERP Project

Building the Implementation Plan

The implementation plan represents an outline of the project, showing the total number of planned iterations across the project phases, as well as key milestone dates for each of these iterations. Using the estimates for the project and the known priorities, the project manager, along with the team, lays out an implementation plan, mapping requirements (both functional and technical) very roughly to each projected iteration. Each iteration should have an associated objective that contributes toward achieving the overall project goal. The team may find certain requirements pose design or architectural risks, and they should consider assigning them to earlier iterations, in order to address those potential risks as early on in the project as possible.

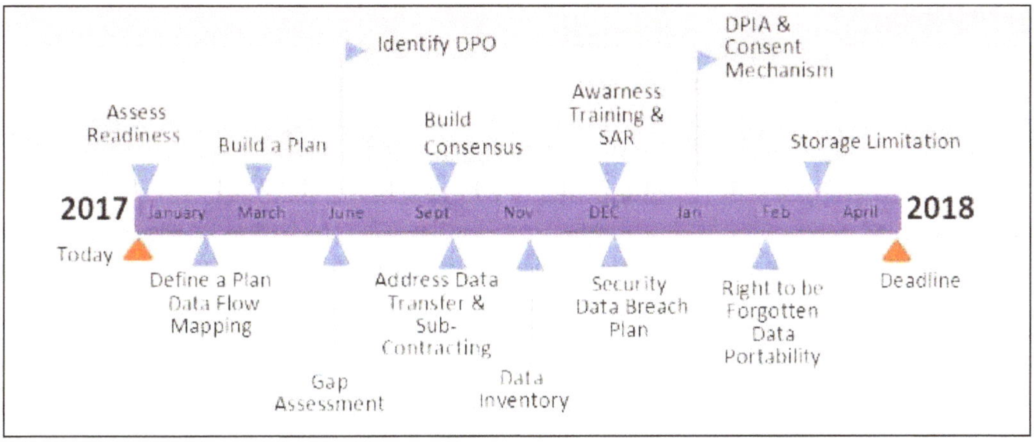

Implementation plan.

The implementation plan above shows a project with one iteration in the Inception phase, two in the Elaboration phase, three in the Construction phase, one in the Transition phase, and one in the Production phase. The triangles at the end of each phase represent the milestones for completion of each project phase.

Iteration Planning

Iteration planning is where the bulk of the planning for a project occurs. In OUM, as with other iterative and incremental methodologies, each phase contains one or more iterations, which should last between two and six weeks, with the duration depending on the type of work being accomplished within the iteration. Each iteration should be planned such that a set of specific objectives are accomplished and a group of project risks are addressed. A project manager will typically analyze and manage the current iteration plan on a daily basis.

The team's capacity is a broad measure of the amount of effort the team will be able to take on in the iteration. The team capacity must be considered when planning the scope of work for the iteration. The capacity is determined by the team's size, availability, and velocity, which refers to the speed at which a team can implement and test user cases and/or user stories and change requests.

The iteration plan information should be compiled into a simple document. The first section of the plan should reflect the scope and objectives of the iteration. The primary goal of the scope is to make clear the iteration's objectives, priorities, and evaluation criteria. This information can be used to track the iteration's progress and drive the iteration assessment. The rest of the plan captures the detailed plan for the execution of the iteration.

Keep in mind that each of the layers – implementation and iteration plans must be kept in synch. The degree to which iteration achieves its objectives will impact future iterations, as well as milestones on the implementation plan. As the phase and iteration assessments are conducted, feedback will be gained, which will lead to the need to adjust the plans.

Partitioning

In a large and/or complex ERP project, the project manager should consider breaking the project into several product partitions — one for each major release of the product to be developed, implemented, or upgraded. Projects which are more than a year in duration, those with high risk factors, projects where there is business value to be gained from delivery of a sub-set of the overall functionality, and/or those where resources are constrained are all candidates for partitioning. This approach allows risk to be spread over a number of releases and permits business value to be delivered sooner.

In the case in which multiple partitions will be used to accomplish the project's objectives, an overall plan should be established to map out the execution of all of the anticipated partitions. Partitions can be executed in parallel, serial or in a staggered fashion, and should be planned, so that the delivery of some subset of the project's benefits is realized through the delivery of working software. This is done by examining the business drivers and schedule goals for the project, laying out the work, and assigning the milestones in the overall plan for one or more partitions.

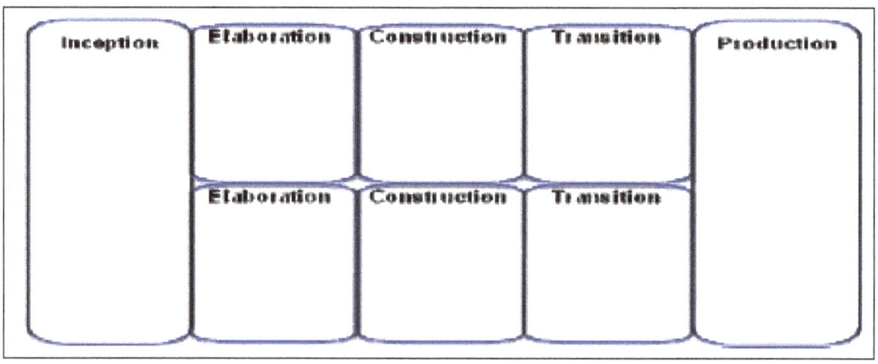

Partitioning the implementation of two business flows.

Considerations for Planning ERP Projects

ERP projects contain many of the same tasks as other IT development projects (business requirements, requirements analysis, analysis, design, implementation, test, etc). As part of requirements analysis, ERP projects must include a mapping be performed of the known requirements onto the products or applications that have been chosen. This is often referred to as "Fit/Gap" or "Map and Gap." Essentially, an analysis of the requirements is done to determine which requirements can be met by configuring the product set and which requirements will drive the development of custom application software. The resulting configurations and custom extensions must be planned such that the resulting custom components are integrated with the configured product software and the resulting integrated system is tested.

Early on, an ERP project's iterations typically emphasize requirements-configuration-analysis-design. These iterations may also include implementation-test activities (of a prototype, for example). Also, in the early phases of a project, iteration is most likely to result in an incremental improvement to models, documentation, and prototypes. Later iterations have a greater emphasis on implementation and test, but will also likely include some refinement of the requirements-configuration-analysis-design work products. Therefore, during the phase in which system construction occurs; an iteration will more likely result in an internal release of software. On projects where heavy custom extensions are built, integration and integration testing tasks should be considered for each iteration to ensure the customizations and configurations work together as a complete system.

Given the fluid nature of ERP project requirements, the iterative and incremental approach will often be managed somewhat differently than in highly agile custom development projects. Project managers should consider planning for "controlled iterations," meaning that the content and objectives of each iteration are planned early in the project and monitored closely throughout the project. The project team determines the content of the iterations by identifying project risks and addressing the highest priority risks in the early iterations. In this more controlled manner, changes in scope can be readily identified and handled through the project's change control process.

Process-based Management

Process-based management is a management approach that views a business as a collection of processes, managed to achieve a desired result. The processes are managed and improved by organisation in purpose of achieving their vision, mission and core value. A clear correlation between processes and the vision supports the company to plan strategies, build a business structure and use sufficient resources that are required to achieve success in the long run.

From a process perspective, an organisation regards its business as a system of vision-achieving vertical processes rather than specific activities and tasks of individual functions. The system is not a method or tool for a particular process, but a holistic approach to manage all the processes in one organisation. Therefore, to manage processes effectively, the organisation must have an effective team network and full knowledge of their vision.

The general management system focuses on specific work-knowledge and direct solutions for cost and budget; on the other hand, process based management applies these financial measurements but in an operational way considering how each performance affects the company as an amalgam of different processes. As a result of recent advances in technology and increased international competition, more companies aim for better methods of grouping and integrating organisational activities.

Vision, Mission and Values

Vision, mission and core value are three crucial factors to manage an organisation from a process perspective. Considering the vision, mission and value as a direction of their business, an organisation can build their corporate strategy and determine the processes they will take into account. As a result, the organisation obtains strengths and competitiveness among other companies.

First, the vision is an aspirational purpose what the organisation would like to achieve in the long run. The vision leads the company to challenge various tasks and develop its own business strategy. In other words, the organisation considers vision as a motivation to build a business structure, determine strategic plans and manage human resources. Therefore, the company carries out the 'vision-achieving operations' as their primary goals.

Mission is a fundamental purpose of a company that remains unchanged over time. The mission provides a guidance for decision making and gives a path to successful results. For instance, mission is different from a vision in that mission is a something to be achieved whereas a vision is something to be aimed for achievement.

Core Values is a principle that helps companies to determine whether the actions and decisions are right or wrong. The value is essential to take decision-making and sustain the company's long-term success.

Advantages of Process-based Management

- Documenting a process provides a clear guideline of how organisation improves their processes and performances over time.
- Process based management measures the full set of activities in one business. For instance, it focuses on internal processes such as customer satisfaction, quality of product and security as well as financial results including revenues, profits, costs, and budget.
- Understanding of the correlations between business processes avoids taking wrong decisions. It reduces costs, time and resources wasting on unnecessary things.
- Analysing the processes, an organisation will be able to predict sources of hazard and choose right decisions.
- The system protects intellectual capital of the organisation. Monitoring the development of processes, the organisation can analyse risks and its weakness.
- Focusing on continuous improvement and customer's requirements, the organisation improves customer services which deliver value to its customers.

- Evaluating the process assures the results a company expecting to obtain.
- Process based management is an integration of both input and output in business process. It controls personnel, technical and financial resources in a holistic viewpoint.
- The organisation can improve IT system that reduces unnecessary complexity and improves the quality of performance measurement.
- Analysing processes and implementing new objects if required, the organisation deal with fast changes in demand.

Three Stages in Process-based Management

Documenting the Process

To manage its business from a process based perspective, an organisation requires to understand what defines the process and which activities they consist of.

A business consists of different departments in charge of specific jobs or functions. Therefore, the processes support these managerial sectors and transform successful outputs. Then a process team performs a set of sequential tasks to analyse whether the organisation delivers useful outputs to the customers.

Basically, processes are built by information that indicates the current state of company and research data such as customer satisfaction. The information includes customer-based agreement, management documentation, purchasing manuals and flow charts. For instance, the flow chart is useful information in order to control the flow of processes and list several steps and activities in detail.

Analysing Process Performance

Analysed and clarified processes are allowed to implement on the actual business. Then, an organisation monitors its business and improves the overall stage of process.

To evaluate the sequence of process, measurement is an essential element that shows results of process performance with numerical and comparative data. In other words, organisations obtain a relevant analysis using the measurements that can be shown as graphical representations such as pie charts, bar charts, cause-and-effect analysis, and gap analysis.

Many organisations highly depend on data and visual analysis processed by information system. For this reason, organisation must obtain accurate analysis based on exact data and must be cautious for mistaken output that impacts whole process of their business.

As a result, the measurements help the company to analyse current state of performance and give guidance for the firm's sustainable improvements.

Implementing the Improvements

Having designed the processes of management system and analysed the performances using useful measurements, the final step is how to improve the system and maintain its effectiveness. Therefore, implementing the improvements is a key activity to examine the processes and improve the flow of the management system.

An organisation determines which part of processes must be improved and modified. It analyses how each process influences a set of activities and applies the improvements to some parts of system. The purpose of implementation is to operate its business strategically and to deliver sufficient resources. In effect, the process based management results in outputs that satisfy their customers and develop the business itself.

Event Chain Methodology

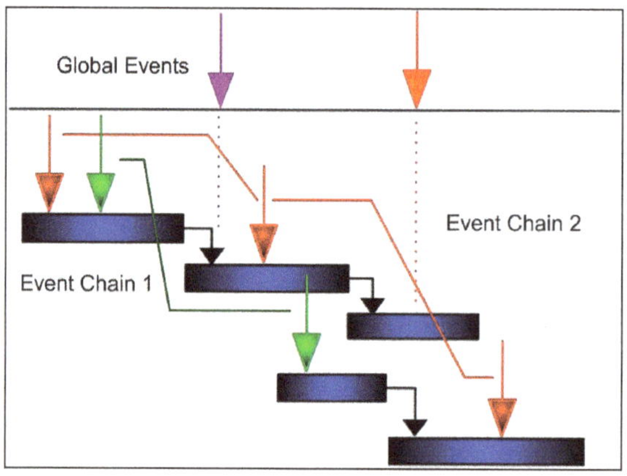

Event chain diagram.

Event chain methodology is a network analysis technique that is focused on identifying and managing events and relationship between them (event chains) that affect project schedules. It is an uncertainty modeling schedule technique. Event chain methodology is an extension of quantitative project risk analysis with Monte Carlo simulations. It is the next advance beyond critical path method and critical chain project management. Event chain methodology helps to mitigate the effect of motivational and cognitive biases in estimating and scheduling. It improves accuracy of risk assessment and helps to generate more realistic risk adjusted project schedules.

Principles

Moment of Risk and State of Activity

Activities (tasks) are not a continuous uniform procedure. Tasks are affected by external events, which transform an activity from one state to another. One of the important properties of an event is the moment when an event occurs during the course of an activity. This moment, when an event occurs, in most cases is probabilistic and can be defined using statistical distribution. The original state is called a ground state, other states are called excited states. For example, if the team completes their job on activity, they can move to other activities. The notion of an activity's state is important because certain events can or cannot occur when activity is in certain state. It means that the state of an activity is subscribed to the events. Events can be local, affecting particular tasks or resources, or global affecting all tasks or resources.

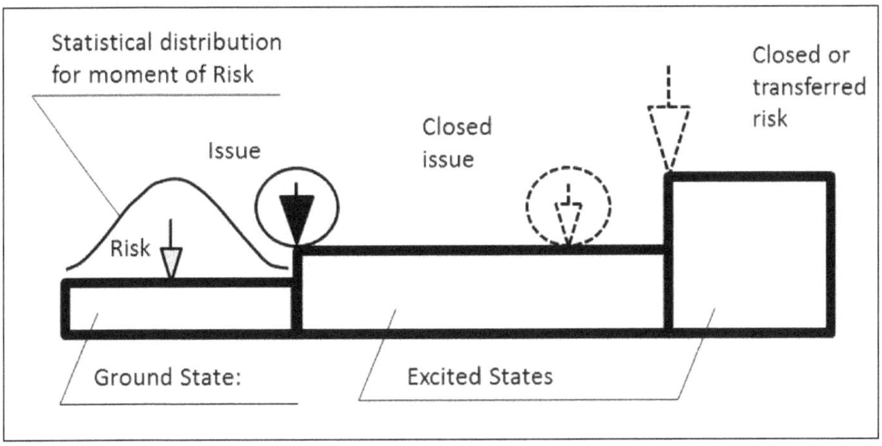

Event chain diagram for one activity.

Event Chains

Events can be related to other events, which will create event chains. These event chains can significantly affect the course of the project. For example, requirement changes can cause an activity to be delayed. To accelerate the activity, the project manager allocates a resource from another activity, which then leads to a missed deadline. Eventually, this can lead to the failure of the project. It could be different relationship between events. One event can trigger one or multiple events.

Events can be correlated with each other without one triggering another one. In this case if one risk has occurred, another one will occur and vice versa. One event assigned in one activity can execute another activity or group of activities. In many cases it the execution of risk response plans. For example, event "structural defect is discovered" can cause one or many activities "Repair". Events can cause other events to occur either immediately or with a delay. The delay is a property of the event subscription. The delay can be deterministic, but in most cases, it is probabilistic. Also risks can be transferred from one activity to another. To define event chains, we need to identify a "sender", the event that initiates the chain of events. The sender event can cause one or more events that effect multiple activities. These are called "receiver" events. In turn, the receiver events can also act as sender events.

Event Chain Diagrams

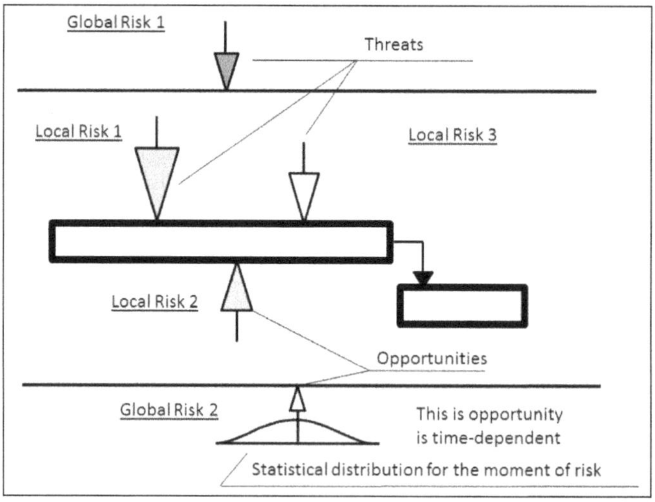

Example of event chain diagram: local and global threats and opportunities with different probabilities and impacts.

Event chain diagram is a visualization that shows the relationships between events and tasks and how the events affect each other. The simplest way to represent these chains is to depict them as arrows associated with certain tasks or time intervals on the Gantt chart. Here are a few important rules:

- Event chains diagrams present events as arrows on the Gantt charts.
- Arrows pointing down are threats. Arrows pointing up are opportunities.
- Issues are shown as an arrow within a circle. Color of the issue arrow is red (dark).
- Closed or transferred risks are shown using dashed lines. Color of arrow is white. Closed issue is shown in the circle with dashed border line.
- Excited states are represented by elevating the associated section of the bar on the Gantt chart.
- Colors represent the calculated impact of the risk. Higher impacts are red or darker shade. Low impacts are green or lighter shade. The size of the arrow represents probability.
- Event chains are shown as lines connecting arrows depicting events.
- Event chains may trigger another activity. In this case event chain line will be connected with the beginning of activity with optional arrow.
- Event chains may trigger a group of activities. In this case this group of activities will be surrounded by the box or frame and event chain line will be connected to the corner of the box or first activity within a frame.

By using event chain diagrams to visualize events and event chains, the modeling and analysis of risks and uncertainties can be significantly simplified.

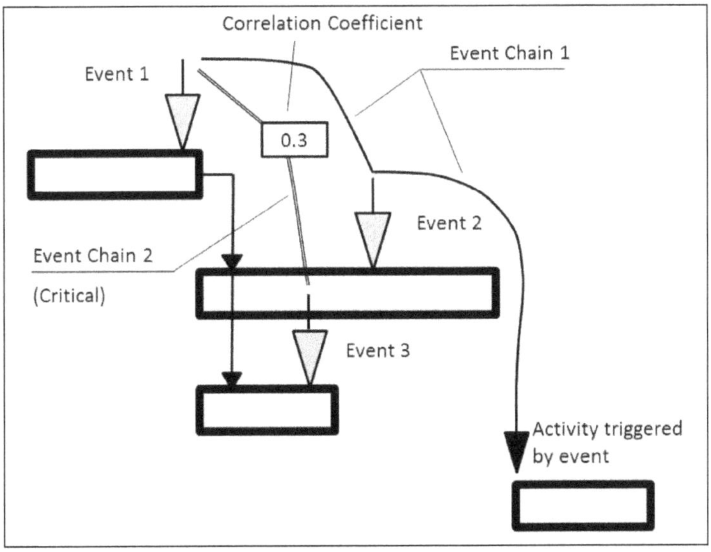

Example of event chain diagram with critical event chain and activity triggered by event.

Another tool that can be used to simplify the definition of events is a state table. Columns in the state table represent events; rows represent the states of an activity. Information for each event in each state includes four properties of event subscription: probability, moment of event, excited state, and impact of the event.

Monte Carlo Simulation

Once events and event chains are defined, quantitative analysis using Monte Carlo simulation can be performed to quantify the cumulative effect of the events. Probabilities and impacts of risks assigned to activities are used as input data for Monte Carlo simulation of the project schedule. In most projects it is necessary to supplement the event based variance with uncertainties as distributions related to duration, start time, cost, and other parameters.

In Event chain methodology, risk can not only affect schedule and cost, but also other parameters such as safety, security, performance, technology, quality, and other objectives. In other words, one event can belong to different categories. The result of the analysis would show risk exposure for different categories as well as integrated project risk score for all categories. This integrated project risk score is calculated based on relative weights for each risk category.

Critical Event Chains

Monte Carlo simulation provides the capability, through sensitivity analysis, to identify single or chains of events. These chains of events can be identified by analyzing the correlations between the main project parameters, such as project duration or cost, and the event chains. These are called "critical events" or "critical chains of events". By identifying critical events or critical chains of events, we can identify strategies to minimize their negative effects: Avoid, Transfer, Mitigate, or Accept. Event and event chain ranking is performed for all risk categories (schedule-related and non-schedule) as part of one process. Integrated risk probability, impact and score can be calculated using weights for each risk category.

Project Control with Event and Event Chains

Monitoring the activity's progress ensures that updated information is used to perform the analysis. During the course of the project, the probability and time of the events can be recalculated based on actual data. The main reason for performance tracking is forecasting an activity's duration and cost if an activity is partially completed and certain events are assigned to the activity. Event chain methodology reduces the risk probability and impact automatically based on the percent of work completed. Advanced analysis can be performed using a Bayesian approach. It is possible to monitor the chance that a project will meet a specific deadline. This chance is constantly updated as a result of the Monte Carlo analysis. Critical events and event chains can be different at the various phases of the project.

Phenomena

Repeated Activities

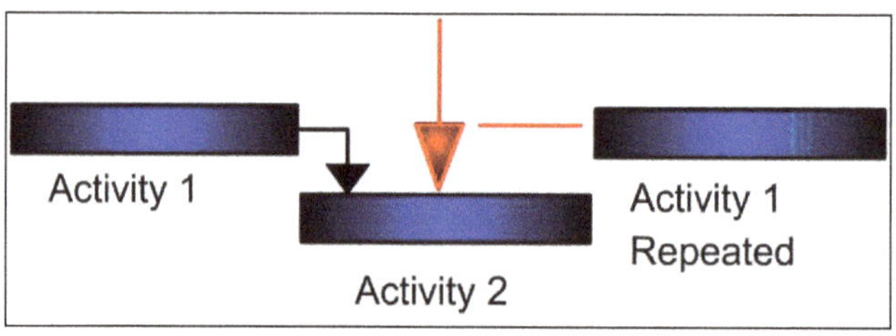

Repeated activity.

Sometimes events can cause the start of an activity that has already been completed. This is a very common scenario for real life projects; sometimes a previous activity must be repeated based on the results of a succeeding activity. Event chain methodology simplifies modeling of these scenarios. The original project schedule does not need to be updated, all that is required is to define the event and assign it to an activity that points to the previous activity. In addition, a limit to the number of times an activity can be repeated must be defined.

Event Chains and Risk Response

If an event or event chain occurs during the course of a project, it may require some risk response effort.

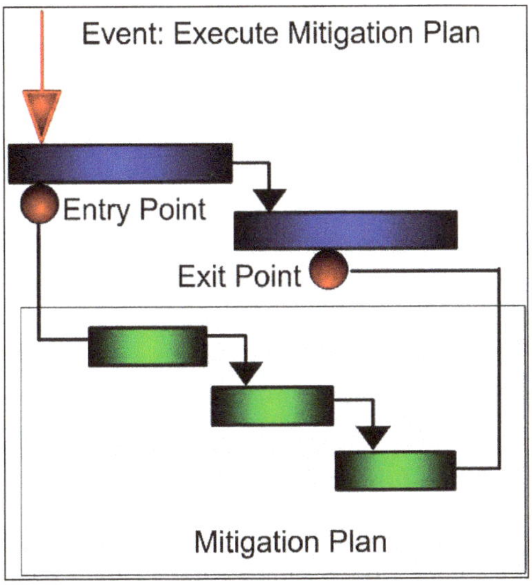

Risk response plans execution are triggered by events, which occur if an activity is in an excited state. Risk response events may attempt to transform the activity from the excited state to the ground state. Response plans are an activity or group of activities (small schedule) that augment the project schedule if a certain event occurs. The solution is to assign the response plan to an event or event chain. The same response plan can be used for one or more events.

Resource Allocation based on Events

One potential event is the reassignment of a resource from one activity to another, which can occur under certain conditions. For example, if an activity requires more resources to complete it within a fixed period, this will trigger an event to reallocate the resource from another activity. Reallocation of resources can also occur when activity duration reaches a certain deadline or the cost exceeds a certain value. Events can be used to model different situations with resources, e.g. temporary leave, illness, vacations, etc.

Waterfall Methodology

Waterfall is a project management approach where a project is completed in distinct stages and moved step by step toward ultimate release to consumers. You make a big plan upfront and then execute in a linear fashion, hoping there won't be any changes in the plan.

When you take traditional project management and apply it to software development, you get Waterfall.

Waterfall was the first software development methodology, inherited from manufacturing and construction industry where you can't afford to iterate (after you've built a tower or a bridge you can't go back to "improve" the foundation). But because the software is prone to frequent change, the waterfall is not the best solution.

Waterfall is often mentioned alongside Agile and stands in contrast to it. The main difference between them is that waterfall doesn't react well to frequent changes, which is why it gets a bad reputation in the software development community, where frequent changes are the norm.

Phases in Waterfall Projects

All tasks on waterfall projects are grouped by type of activity and each project follows the same phases:

- Requirements: Where we analyze business needs and document what software needs to do.
- Design: Where we choose the technology, create diagrams and plan software architecture.
- Coding: Where we figure out how to solve problems and write code.
- Testing: Where we make sure the code does what it supposed to do without breaking anything.
- Operations: Where we deploy the code to a production environment and provide support.

Once you put all the activities on a Gantt chart, you get something that looks like slopes of a waterfall, hence the name.

Usually, 20–40% of the time is spent on requirements and design, 30–40% on coding, and the rest on testing and operations.

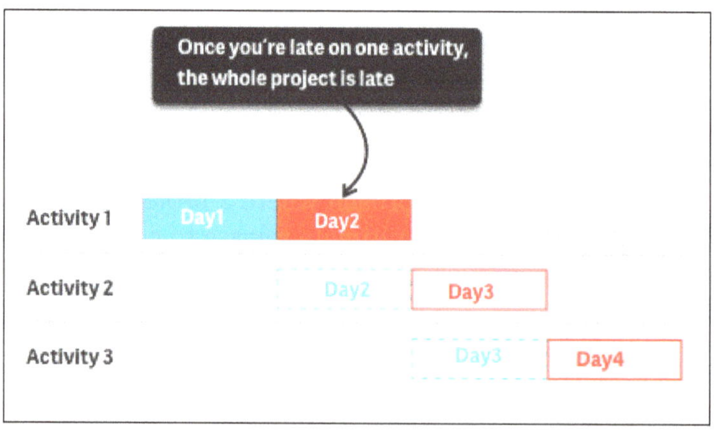

Activities on waterfall projects have to happen in the exact order and one set of activities can't start before the previous one ends. This is why planning is the most important thing on waterfall projects: if you don't plan right, a phase will be late and will push every other subsequent phase, thus putting the whole project over deadline.

The problem with using waterfall method on a software project is that planning is very tricky in software development. You can never be 100% sure how much time you'll need on something or how much time you'll spend debugging. As a result, the waterfall is risky.

Advantages of Waterfall

- Extensive documentation: Because you can't go back to a previous activity, you're forced to create comprehensive documentation from the start, listing all the requirements you can think of.
- Knowledge stays in the organization: When you have extensive documentation, knowledge won't get lost if someone leaves. Also, you don't have to spend time on training new members as they can familiarize with the project by reading the documentation.
- Team members can better plan their time: Because everyone knows in advance on what they'll work, they can be assigned on multiple projects at the same time.
- Easy to understand: Waterfall projects are divided into discrete and easily understandable phases. As a result, project management is straightforward and the process is easily understandable even to non-developers.
- Client knows what to expect: Clients can know in advance the cost and timeline of the project so they can plan their business activities and manage cash flow according to the plan.
- Client input not required: After the requirements phase, client input is minimal (save for occasional reviews, approvals, and status meetings). This means you don't have coordinate with them and wait for when they're available.
- Easier to measure: Because waterfall projects are simple, it's much easier to measure your progress by quickly looking at a Gantt chart.
- Better design: Products have a higher cohesion because during the design phase you know everything that must be taken into account. There is no one-feature-at-a-time problem that leads to usability problems down the road.

Disadvantages of Waterfall

- No going back: Once you're finished with one activity, it's difficult and expensive to go back and make changes. This puts huge pressure on the planning.

- No room for error during the requirements phase: Everything relies heavily on the requirements phase and if you make an error, the project is doomed.
- Deadline creep: Once one activity is late, all the other activities are late too, including the project deadline.
- QA too late to be useful: Testing is done at the end of the project which means that developers can't improve how they write code based on QA feedback.
- Bug ridden software: Because the testing is done at the end, most teams tend to rush the testing in order to deliver the project on time and hit their incentives. These short-term wins lead to sub-par quality and long-term problems.
- Not what the client actually needs: Most of the time, clients can't articulate what they need until they see what they don't need. If the client realizes they need more than they initially thought, the project plan will need a major overhaul (as well as the budget).
- Unexpected problems: Designers can't foresee all the problems that will arise from their design, and once those problems surface, it's very difficult to fix them.

Projects for which Waterfall Methodology is Suitable

Waterfall is suited for projects where:

- Budget, requirements, and scope are fixed (e.g. You're building a one-off project which doesn't need further development).
- You can accurately estimate the work (you're familiar with technology and you've done the same work before).
- You can't afford to iterate (e.g. You're building a heart rate monitoring software).
- Project is innately low-risk (you're building a clone of something that already works).
- Project has a hardship date (e.g. You have to ship a video game by Christmas).
- Your users can't or won't update software (doesn't apply to web applications where updates are seamless).

You shouldn't use a waterfall:

- Where a working prototype is more important than quality (e.g. You first need to test if there's a market demand).
- When you don't know what the final product should look like.
- Where a client doesn't know exactly what they need.

- When the product is made for an industry with rapidly changing standards.
- When you know you won't get the product first the right time and have to incorporate user feedback.
- When your users are happy with v1.0 and you can ship additional features as time goes on.

References

- Critical-chain-project-management-ccpm-28202: techopedia.com, Retrieved 13 May, 2020
- What-is-critical-chain-project-management-rar68-article: simplilearn.com, Retrieved 12 January, 2020
- Goodpasture, John C. (2004). Quantitative Methods in Project Management. J. Ross Publishing. pp. 173–178. ISBN 1-932159-15-0
- Agile-project-management-a-beginners-guide-3156998: cio.com, Retrieved 18 June, 2020
- Erp-oracle-unified-method-approach-5990: pmi.org, Retrieved 02 April, 2020
- Badewi, Amgad (2016). "The impact of project management (PM) and benefits management (BM) practices on project success: Towards developing a project benefits governance framework". International Journal of Project Management. 34 (4): 761–778. doi:10.1016/j.ijproman.2015.05.005
- Waterfall-project-management-methodology, project-management: activecollab.com, Retrieved 16 February, 2020

Processes and Phases 3

- Project Planning
- Dependency
- Aggregate Planning
- Project Charter
- Schedule
- Earned Schedule
- Hammock Activity
- Kickoff Meeting
- Work Breakdown Structure
- Project Workforce Management
- Project Execution
- Project Monitoring
- Project Governance
- Project Communication Management
- Aligning Projects with Business Strategies
- Project Documentation
- Project Networks
- Project Assurance
- Project Quality Management
- Project Accounting

Aggregate planning, work breakdown structure, project monitoring, project communication management, project documentation, project networks, project quality management, project cost management, etc. are some of the processes and phases that are studied under the domain of project management. This chapter discusses the different processes and phases of project management.

Project Planning

Project planning is part of project management, which relates to the use of schedules such as Gantt charts to plan and subsequently report progress within the project environment. Project planning can be done manually or by the use of project management software.

Initially, the project scope is defined and the appropriate methods for completing the project are determined. Following this step, the durations for the various tasks necessary to complete the work are listed and grouped into a work breakdown structure. Project planning is often used to organize different areas of a project, including project plans, work loads and the management of teams and individuals. The logical dependencies between tasks are defined using an activity network diagram that enables identification of the critical path. Project planning is inherently uncertain as it must be done before the project is actually started. Therefore the duration of the tasks is often estimated through a weighted average of optimistic, normal, and pessimistic cases. The critical chain method adds "buffers" in the planning to anticipate potential delays in project execution. Float or slack time in the schedule can be calculated using project management software. Then the necessary resources can be estimated and costs for each activity can be allocated to each resource, giving the total project cost. At this stage, the project schedule may be optimized to achieve the appropriate balance between resource usage and project duration to comply with the project objectives. Once established and agreed, the project schedule becomes what is known as the baseline schedule. Progress will be measured against the baseline schedule throughout the life of the project. Analyzing progress compared to the baseline schedule is known as earned value management.

The inputs of the project planning phase 2 include the project charter and the concept proposal. The outputs of the project planning phase include the project requirements, the project schedule, and the project management plan.

The purpose of the project planning phase is to:

- Establish business requirements.
- Establish cost, schedule, list of deliverables, and delivery dates.
- Establish resources plans.
- Obtain management approval and proceed to the next phase.

The basic processes of project planning are:

- Scope planning: Specifying the in-scope requirements for the project to facilitate creating the work breakdown structure.

- Preparation of the work breakdown structure: Spelling out the breakdown of the project into tasks and sub-tasks.
- Project schedule development: Listing the entire schedule of the activities and detailing their sequence of implementation.
- Resource planning: Indicating who will do what work, at which time, and if any special skills are needed to accomplish the project tasks.
- Budget planning: Specifying the budgeted cost to be incurred at the completion of the project.
- Procurement planning: Focusing on vendors outside your company and sub-contracting
- Risk management: Planning for possible risks and considering optional contingency plans and mitigation strategies.
- Quality planning: Assessing quality criteria to be used for the project.
- Communication planning: Designing the communication strategy with all project stakeholders.

The planning phase refines the project's objectives, which were gathered during the initiation phase. It includes planning the steps necessary to meet those objectives by further identifying the specific activities and resources required to complete the project. Now that these objectives have been recognized, they must be clearly articulated, detailing an in-depth scrutiny of each recognized objective. With such scrutiny, our understanding of the objective may change. Often the very act of trying to describe something precisely gives us a better understanding of what we are looking at. This articulation serves as the basis for the development of requirements. What this means is that after an objective has been clearly articulated, we can describe it in concrete (measurable) terms and identify what we have to do to achieve it. Obviously, if we do a poor job of articulating the objective, our requirements will be misdirected and the resulting project will not represent the true need.

Users will often begin describing their objectives in qualitative language. The project manager must work with the user to provide quantifiable definitions to those qualitative terms. These quantifiable criteria include schedule, cost, and quality measures. In the case of project objectives, these elements are used as measurements to determine project satisfaction and successful completion. Subjective evaluations are replaced by actual numeric attributes.

Examples:

- A web user may ask for a fast system. The quantitative requirement should be all screens must load in under three seconds. Describing the time limit during which the screen must load is specific and tangible. For that reason, you'll know that the requirement has been successfully completed when the objective has been met.

- Let's say that your company is going to produce a holiday batch of eggnog. Your objective statement might be stated this way: Christmas Cheer, Inc. will produce two million cases of holiday eggnog, to be shipped to our distributors by October 30, at a total cost of $1.5 million or less. The objective criteria in this statement are clearly stated and successful fulfillment can easily be measured. Stakeholders will know that the objectives are met when the two million cases are produced and shipped by the due date within the budget stated.

When articulating the project objectives you should follow the SMART rule:

- Specific: Get into the details. Objectives should be specific and written in clear, concise, and understandable terms.
- Measurable: Use quantitative language. You need to know when you have successfully completed the task.
- Acceptable: Agreed with the stakeholders.
- Realistic: In terms of achievement. Objectives that are impossible to accomplish are not realistic and not attainable. Objectives must be centred in reality.
- Time based: Deadlines not durations. Objectives should have a time frame with an end date assigned to them.

Project Life Cycle

The project manager and project team have one shared goal: to carry out the work of the project for the purpose of meeting the project's objectives. Every project has a beginning, a middle period during which activities move the project toward completion, and an ending (either successful or unsuccessful). A standard project typically has the following four major phases (each with its own agenda of tasks and issues): initiation, planning, implementation, and closure. Taken together, these phases represent the path a project takes from the beginning to its end and are generally referred to as the project "life cycle."

Initiation Phase

During the first of these phases, the initiation phase, the project objective or need is identified; this can be a business problem or opportunity. An appropriate response to the need is documented in a business case with recommended solution options. A feasibility study is conducted to investigate whether each option addresses the project objective and a final recommended solution is determined. Issues of feasibility ("can we do the project?") and justification ("should we do the project?") are addressed.

Once the recommended solution is approved, a project is initiated to deliver the approved solution and a project manager is appointed. The major deliverables and the participating work groups are identified, and the project team begins to take shape. Approval is then sought by the project manager to move onto the detailed planning phase.

Planning Phase

The next phase, the planning phase, is where the project solution is further developed in as much detail as possible and the steps necessary to meet the project's objective are planned. In this step, the team identifies all of the work to be done. The project's tasks and resource requirements are identified, along with the strategy for producing them. This is also referred to as "scope management." A project plan is created outlining the activities, tasks, dependencies, and timeframes. The project manager coordinates the preparation of a project budget by providing cost estimates for the labour, equipment, and materials costs. The budget is used to monitor and control cost expenditures during project implementation.

Once the project team has identified the work, prepared the schedule, and estimated the costs, the three fundamental components of the planning process are complete. This is an excellent time to identify and try to deal with anything that might pose a threat to the successful completion of the project. This is called risk management. In risk management, "high-threat" potential problems are identified along with the action that is to be taken on each high-threat potential problem, either to reduce the probability that the problem will occur or to reduce the impact on the project if it does occur. This is also a good time to identify all project stakeholders and establish a communication plan describing the information needed and the delivery method to be used to keep the stakeholders informed.

Finally, you will want to document a quality plan, providing quality targets, assurance, and control measures, along with an acceptance plan, listing the criteria to be met to gain customer acceptance. At this point, the project would have been planned in detail and is ready to be executed.

Implementation (Execution) Phase

During the third phase, the implementation phase, the project plan is put into motion and the work of the project is performed. It is important to maintain control and communicate as needed during implementation. Progress is continuously monitored and appropriate adjustments are made and recorded as variances from the original plan. In any project, a project manager spends most of the time in this step. During project implementation, people are carrying out the tasks, and progress information is being reported through regular team meetings. The project manager uses this information to maintain control over the direction of the project by comparing the progress reports with the project plan to measure the performance of the project activities and take corrective action as needed. The first course of action should always be to bring the project back on course (i.e., to return it to the original plan). If that cannot happen, the team should record variations from the original plan and record and publish modifications to the plan. Throughout this step, project sponsors and other key stakeholders should be kept informed of the project's status according to the agreed-on frequency and format of communication. The plan should be updated and published on a regular basis.

Status reports should always emphasize the anticipated end point in terms of cost, schedule, and quality of deliverables. Each project deliverable produced should be reviewed for quality and measured against the acceptance criteria. Once all of the deliverables have been produced and the customer has accepted the final solution, the project is ready for closure.

Closing Phase

During the final closure, or completion phase, the emphasis is on releasing the final deliverables to the customer, handing over project documentation to the business, terminating supplier contracts, releasing project resources, and communicating the closure of the project to all stakeholders. The last remaining step is to conduct lessons-learned studies to examine what went well and what didn't. Through this type of analysis, the wisdom of experience is transferred back to the project organization, which will help future project teams.

Dependency

In a project network, a dependency is a link amongst a project's terminal elements.

The A Guide to the Project Management Body of Knowledge (PMBOK Guide) does not define the term dependency, but refers for this term to a logical relationship, which in turn is defined as *dependency between two activities, or between an activity and a milestone.*

Standard Types of Dependencies

There are four standard types of dependencies:

- Finish to start (FS):
    - *A* FS *B* means "activity A must finish before activity B can begin" (or "B can't start until A has finished").

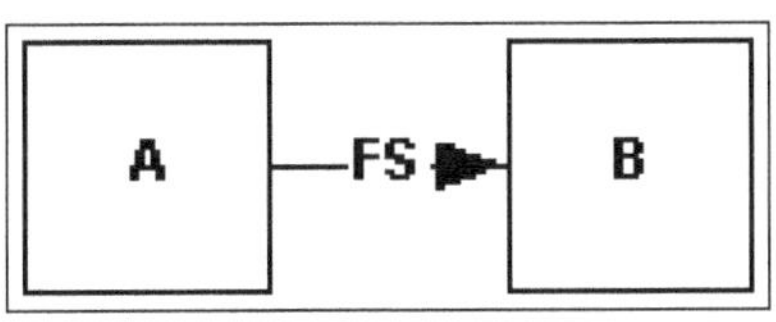

    - (Foundations dug) FS (Concrete poured).

- Finish to finish (FF):
    - A FF B means "activity A must finish before activity B can finish" (or "B can't finish before A is finished").

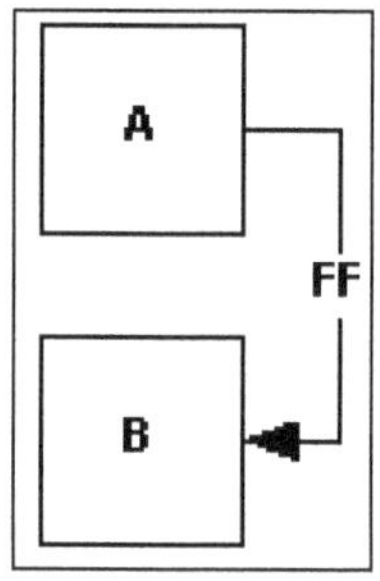

    - (Last chapter written) FF (Entire book written).
- Start to start (SS):
    - A SS B means "activity A must start before activity B can start" (or "B can't start until A has started").

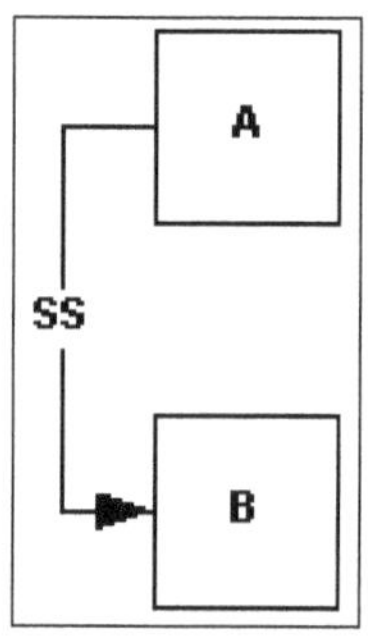

    - (Project work started) SS (Project management activities started.)
- Start to finish (SF):
    - A SF B means "activity A must start before activity B finishes" (or "B can't finish until A has started").

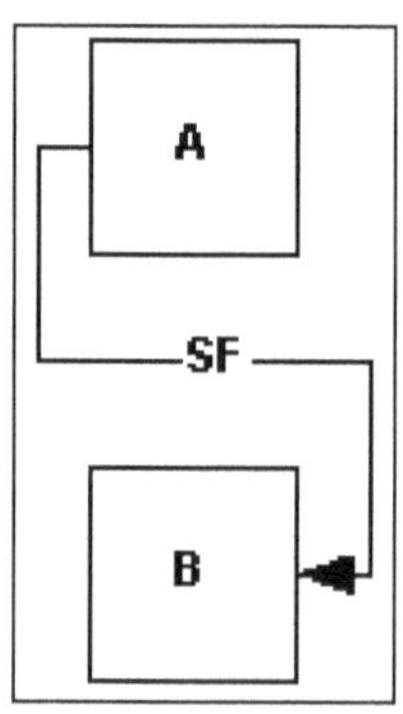

- *(New shift started) SF (Previous shift finished).*

Finish-to-start is considered a "natural dependency". The Practice Standard for Scheduling recommends, that "typically, each predecessor activity would finish prior to the start of its successor activity (or activities)(known as finish-to-start (FS) relationship). Sometimes it is necessarily to overlap activities; an option may be selected to use start-to-start (SS), finish-to-finish (FF) or start-to-finish (SF) relationships. Whenever possible, the FS logical relationship should be used. If other types of relationships are used, they shall be used sparingly and with full understanding of how the relationships have been implemented in the scheduling software being used. Ideally, the sequence of all activities will be defined in such a way that the start of every activity has a logical relationship from a predecessor and the finish of every activity has a logical relationship to a successor".

SF is rarely used, and should generally be avoided. Microsoft recommends to use SF dependency for just-in-time scheduling. It can be easily shown however, that this would only work if resource levelling is not used, because resource levelling can delay a successor activity (an activity, which shall be finished just-in-time) in such a way, that it will finish later than the start of its logical predecessor activity, thus not fulfilling the just-in-time requirement.

There are three kinds of dependencies with respect to the reason for the existence of dependency:

- Causal (logical):
    - It is impossible to edit a text before it is written.
    - It is illogical to pour concrete before you dig the foundations of a building.
- Resource constraints:
    - It is logically possible to paint four walls in a room simultaneously but there is only one painter.
- Discretionary (preferential):
    - I want to paint the living room before painting the dining room, although I could do it the other way round, too.

Early critical path-derived schedules often reflected only on causal (logical) or discretionary (preferential) dependencies because the assumption was that resources would be available or could be made available. Since at least the mid-1980s, competent project managers and schedulers have recognized that schedules must be based on resource availability. The critical chain method necessitates taking into account resource constraint-derived dependencies as well.

Leads and Lags

Dependencies can be modified by leads, and lags. Both leads and lags can be applied to all 4 types of dependencies.

PMBOK defines lag as “the amount of time whereby a successor activity will be delayed with respect to a predecessor activity”.

For example: When building two walls from a novel design, one might start the second wall 2 days after the first so that the second team can learn from the first. This is an example of a *lag* in a Start-Start relationship.

In accordance to PMBOK a lead is “the amount of time whereby a successor activity can be advanced with respect to a predecessor activity. For example, on a project to construct a new office building, the landscaping could be scheduled to start prior to the scheduled punch list completion. This would be shown as a finish-to-start with two-week lead”.

Example:

If you are building a building, you can’t paint the walls before installing the water pipes into the walls.

It would be much faster and less expensive, to install the pipes first, place the concrete to actually build the wall around the pipes, and finally paint the walls.

Advanced Cases of Activities Dependencies

Maximal-Type Relationships

Activity A and Activity B are said to have a Maximal-Type Relationship, if Activity B can start after Activity A, but with the delay of no more than X. Real life examples, which are simulated by Maximal-Type Relation:

- Shoring of the trench has to be done not necessarily immediately after excavation, but within certain time, otherwise the trench will collapse.
- Vaccination of baby has to be done not immediately after birth, but within certain time.
- Renewal of the passport has to be done some time after the current one has been issued, but before it expires.
- Invoice payment does not have to be done immediately, but within certain time after it has been issued.

Maximal-Type relationships are rarely implemented in the project management software, most probably because with this feature it is too easy to create contradictory dependencies.

Aggregate Planning

Aggregate planning is the process of developing, analysing, and maintaining a preliminary, approximate schedule of the overall operations of an organization. The aggregate plan generally contains targeted sales forecasts, production levels, inventory levels, and customer backlogs. This schedule is intended to satisfy the demand forecast at a minimum cost. Properly done, aggregate planning should minimize the effects of short sighted, day-to-day scheduling, in which small amounts of material may be ordered one week, with an accompanying layoff of workers, followed by ordering larger amounts and rehiring workers the next week. This longer-term perspective on resource use can help minimize short-term requirements changes with a resulting cost savings.

In simple terms, aggregate planning is an attempt to balance capacity and demand in such a way that costs are minimized. The term "aggregate" is used because planning at this level includes all resources "in the aggregate;" for example, as a product line or family. Aggregate resources could be total number of workers, hours of machine time, or tons of raw materials. Aggregate units of output could include gallons, feet, pounds of output, as well as aggregate units appearing in service industries such as hours of service delivered, number of patients seen, etc.

Aggregate planning does not distinguish among sizes, colors, features, and so forth. For example, with automobile manufacturing, aggregate planning would consider the total number of cars planned for not the individual models, colors, or options. When units of aggregation are difficult to determine (for example, when the variation in output is extreme) equivalent units are usually determined. These equivalent units could be based on value, cost, worker hours, or some similar measure.

Aggregate planning is considered to be intermediate-term (as opposed to long- or short-term) in nature. Hence, most aggregate plans cover a period of three to 18 months. Aggregate plans serve as a foundation for future short-range type planning, such as production scheduling, sequencing, and loading. The master production schedule (MPS) used in material requirements planning (MRP) has been described as the aggregate plan "disaggregated."

Steps taken to produce an aggregate plan begin with the determination of demand and the determination of current capacity. Capacity is expressed as total number of units per time period that can be produced (this requires that an average number of units be computed since the total may include a product mix utilizing distinctly different production times). Demand is expressed as total number of units needed. If the two are not in balance (equal), the firm must decide whether to increase or decrease capacity to meet demand or increase or decrease demand to meet capacity. In order to accomplish this, a number of options are available.

Options for situations in which demand needs to be increased in order to match capacity include:

- Pricing: Varying pricing to increase demand in periods when demand is less than peak. For example, matinee prices for movie theaters, off-season rates for hotels, weekend rates for telephone service, and pricing for items that experience seasonal demand.
- Promotion: Advertising, direct marketing, and other forms of promotion are used to shift demand.
- Back ordering: By postponing delivery on current orders demand is shifted to period when capacity is not fully utilized. This is really just a form of smoothing demand. Service industries are able to smooth demand by taking reservations or by making appointments in an attempt to avoid walk-in customers. Some refer to this as "partitioning" demand.
- New demand creation: A new, but complementary demand is created for a product or service. When restaurant customers have to wait, they are frequently diverted into a complementary (but not complimentary) service, the bar. Other examples include the addition of video arcades within movie theaters, and the expansion of services at convenience stores.

Options which can be used to increase or decrease capacity to match current demand include:

- Hire/lay off: By hiring additional workers as needed or by laying off workers not currently required to meet demand, firms can maintain a balance between capacity and demand.
- Overtime: By asking or requiring workers to work extra hours a day or an extra day per week, firms can create a temporary increase in capacity without the added expense of hiring additional workers.
- Part-time or casual labor: By utilizing temporary workers or casual labor (workers who are considered permanent but only work when needed, on an on-call basis, and typically without the benefits given to full-time workers).
- Inventory: Finished-goods inventory can be built up in periods of slack demand and then used to fill demand during periods of high demand. In this way no new workers have to be hired, no temporary or casual labor is needed, and no overtime is incurred.
- Subcontracting: Frequently firms choose to allow another manufacturer or service provider to provide the product or service to the subcontracting firm's customers. By subcontracting work to an alternative source, additional capacity is temporarily obtained.

- Cross-training: Cross-trained employees may be able to perform tasks in several operations, creating some flexibility when scheduling capacity.
- Other methods: While varying workforce size and utilization, inventory buildup/backlogging, and subcontracting are well-known alternatives, there are other, more novel ways that find use in industry. Among these options are sharing employees with counter-cyclical companies and attempting to find interesting and meaningful projects for employees to do during slack times.

Aggregate Planning Strategies

There are two pure planning strategies available to the aggregate planner: a level strategy and a chase strategy. Firms may choose to utilize one of the pure strategies in isolation, or they may opt for a strategy that combines the two.

Level Strategy

A level strategy seeks to produce an aggregate plan that maintains a steady production rate and/or a steady employment level. In order to satisfy changes in customer demand, the firm must raise or lower inventory levels in anticipation of increased or decreased levels of forecast demand. The firm maintains a level workforce and a steady rate of output when demand is somewhat low. This allows the firm to establish higher inventory levels than are currently needed. As demand increases, the firm is able to continue a steady production rate/steady employment level, while allowing the inventory surplus to absorb the increased demand.

A second alternative would be to use a backlog or backorder. A backorder is simply a promise to deliver the product at a later date when it is more readily available, usually when capacity begins to catch up with diminishing demand. In essence, the backorder is a device for moving demand from one period to another, preferably one in which demand is lower, thereby smoothing demand requirements over time.

A level strategy allows a firm to maintain a constant level of output and still meet demand. This is desirable from an employee relations standpoint. Negative results of the level strategy would include the cost of excess inventory, subcontracting or overtime costs, and backorder costs, which typically are the cost of expediting orders and the loss of customer goodwill.

Chase Strategy

A chase strategy implies matching demand and capacity period by period. This could result in a considerable amount of hiring, firing or laying off of employees; insecure and unhappy employees; increased inventory carrying costs; problems with labor unions; and erratic utilization of plant and equipment. It also implies a great deal of flexibility on the firm's part. The major advantage of a chase strategy is that it allows inventory to be held to the lowest level possible, and for some firms this is a considerable savings.

Most firms embracing the just-in-time production concept utilize a chase strategy approach to aggregate planning.

Most firms find it advantageous to utilize a combination of the level and chase strategy. A combination strategy (sometimes called a hybrid or mixed strategy) can be found to better meet organizational goals and policies and achieve lower costs than either of the pure strategies used independently.

Techniques for Aggregate Planning

Techniques for aggregate planning range from informal trial-and-error approaches, which usually utilize simple tables or graphs, to more formalized and advanced mathematical techniques. This general procedure consists of the following steps:

- Determine demand for each period.
- Determine capacity for each period. This capacity should match demand, which means it may require the inclusion of overtime or subcontracting.
- Identify company, departmental, or union policies that are pertinent. For example, maintaining a certain safety stock level, maintaining a reasonably stable workforce, backorder policies, overtime policies, inventory level policies, and other less explicit rules such as the nature of employment with the individual industry, the possibility of a bad image, and the loss of goodwill.
- Determine unit costs for units produced. These costs typically include the basic production costs (fixed and variable costs as well as direct and indirect labor costs). Also included are the costs associated with making changes in capacity. Inventory holding costs must also be considered, as should storage, insurance, taxes, spoilage, and obsolescence costs. Finally, backorder costs must be computed. While difficult to measure, this generally includes expediting costs, loss of customer goodwill, and revenue loss from cancelled orders.
- Develop alternative plans and compute the cost for each.
- If satisfactory plans emerge, select the one that best satisfies objectives. Frequently, this is the plan with the least cost. Otherwise, return to step 5.

An example of a completed informal aggregate plan can be seen in figure. This plan is an example of a plan determined utilizing a level strategy. Notice that employment levels and output levels remain constant while inventory is allowed to build up in earlier periods only to be drawn back down in later periods as demand increases. Also, note that backorders are utilized in order to avoid overtime or subcontracting. The computed costs for the individual variables of the plan are as follows:

Output costs:

- Regular time = $5 per unit.

- Overtime = $8 per unit.
- Subcontracted = $12 per unit.

Other costs:

- Inventory carrying cost = $3 per unit per period applied to average inventory.
- Backorders = $10 per unit per period.

Cost of aggregate plan utilizing a level strategy:

Output costs:

- Regular time = $5 × 1,500 = $7,500.
- Overtime = $8 × 0 = 0.
- Subcontracted = $10 × 0 = 0.

Other costs:

- Inventory carrying cost = $3 × 850 = $2,400.
- Backorders = $10 × 100 = $1,000.
- Total cost = $10,900.

A second example, presents the same scenario but demonstrates the use of a combination strategy (i.e., a combination of level and chase) to meet demand and seek to minimize costs. For this example, let's assume that company policy prevents us from utilizing backorders and limits our plan to no more than 50 units of overtime per period. Notice that the regular output level is constant, implying a level workforce, while overtime and subcontracting are used to meet demand on a period by period basis (chase strategy). One will notice that the cost of the combination plan is slightly lower than the cost of the level plan.

Output costs:

- Regular time = $5 × 1,200 = $6,000.
- Overtime = $8 × 100 = 800.
- Subcontracted = $12 × 250 = 2,500.

Other costs:

- Inventory carrying cost = $3 × 325 = 975.
- Backorders = $10 × 0 = 0.

- Total cost = \$10,275

Period		1	2	3	4	5	6
Fore Cast		100	150	300	300	500	150
Output							
	Regular	250	250	250	250	250	250
	Overline						
	Sub Contract						
Output-forecast		150	100	-50	-50	-250	100
Inventory							
	Beginning	0	150	250	200	150	0
	Ending	150	250	200	150	0	100
	Average	75	200	225	175	75	50
Back Log	0	0	0	0	0	100	0
Cost of aggregate plan utilizing a level strategy: Output: Regular time =\$ 5 X 1500 = \$ 7500 Overtime = \$ 8 X 0 = 0 Subcontracted = \$ 10 X 0 0 = 0 Inventory Carrying Cost = \$ 3 X 850 = 2550 Back Orders =\$ 10 X 100 = 1000 Total Cost \$ 11050							

Mathematical Approaches to Aggregate Planning

The following are some of the better known mathematical techniques that can be used in more complex aggregate planning applications.

Linear Programming

Linear programming is an optimization technique that allows the user to find a maximum profit or revenue or a minimum cost based on the availability of limited resources and certain limitations known as constraints. A special type of linear programming known as the Transportation Model can be used to obtain aggregate plans that would allow balanced capacity and demand and the minimization of costs. However, few real-world aggregate planning decisions are compatible with the linear assumptions of linear programming.

Mixed-integer Programming

For aggregate plans that are prepared on a product family basis, where the plan is essentially the summation of the plans for individual product lines, mixed-integer programming may prove to be useful. Mixed-integer programming can provide a method for determining the number of units to be produced in each product family.

Linear Decision Rule

Linear decision rule is another optimizing technique. It seeks to minimize total production costs (labor, overtime, hiring/lay off, inventory carrying cost) using a set of cost-approximating functions (three of which are quadratic) to obtain a single quadratic equation. Then, by using calculus, two linear equations can be derived from the quadratic equation, one to be used to plan the output for each period and the other for planning the workforce for each period.

Management Coefficients Model

The management coefficients model, formulated by E.H. Bowman, is based on the suggestion that the production rate for any period would be set by this general decision rule: $P_t = aW_{t-1} - bI_{t-1} + cF_{t+1} + K$, where

- P_t = the production rate set for period t
- W_{t-1} = the workforce in the previous period
- I_{t-1} = the ending inventory for the previous period
- F_{t+1} = the forecast of demand for the next period
- a, b, c, and K are constants

Period		1	2	3	4	5	6
Fore Cast		100	150	300	300	500	150
Output							
	Regular	200	200	200	200	200	200
	Overline				50	50	
	Sub Contract					250	
Output-forecast		100	50	-100	-50	0	50
Inventory							
	Beginning	0	100	150	50	0	0

	Ending	100	150	50	0	0	50
	Average	50	125	100	25	0	25
Back Log	0	0	0	0	0	0	0

Cost of aggregate plan utilizing a level strategy:

Output

Regular time =$ 5 X 1200 = $ 6000

Overtime = $ 8 X 100 = 800

Subcontracted = $ 12 X 250 = 3000

Inventory Carrying Cost = $ 3 X 325 = 975

Back Orders =$ 10 X 0 = 0

Total Cost $ $ 10775

It then uses regression analysis to estimate the values of a, b, c, and K. The end result is a decision rule based on past managerial behavior without any explicit cost functions, the assumption being that managers know what is important, even if they cannot readily state explicit costs. Essentially, this method supplements the application of experienced judgment.

Search Decision Rule

The search decision rule methodology overcomes some of the limitations of the linear cost assumptions of linear programming. The search decision rule allows the user to state cost data inputs in very general terms. It requires that a computer program be constructed that will unambiguously evaluate any production plan's cost. It then searches among alternative plans for the one with the minimum cost. However, unlike linear programming, there is no assurance of optimality.

Simulation

A number of simulation models can be used for aggregate planning. By developing an aggregate plan within the environment of a simulation model, it can be tested under a variety of conditions to find acceptable plans for consideration. These models can also be incorporated into a decision support system, which can aid in planning and evaluating alternative control policies. These models can integrate the multiple conflicting objectives inherent in manufacturing strategy by using different quantitative measures of productivity, customer service, and flexibility.

Functional Objective Search Approach

The functional objective search (FOS) system is a computerized aggregate planning system that incorporates a broad range of actual planning conditions. It is capable of realistic, low-cost operating schedules that provide options for attaining different planning goals. The system works by comparing the planning load with available capacity. After management has chosen its desired actions and associated planning objectives for specific load conditions, the system weights each planning goal to reflect the functional emphasis behind its achievement at a certain load condition. The computer then uses a computer search to output a plan that minimizes costs and meets delivery deadlines.

Aggregate Planning in Services

For manufacturing firms the luxury of building up inventories during periods of slack demand allows coverage of an anticipated time when demand will exceed capacity. Services cannot be stockpiled or inventoried so they do not have this option. Also, since services are considered "perishable," any capacity that goes unused is essentially wasted. An empty hotel room or an empty seat on a flight cannot be held and sold later, as can a manufactured item held in inventory.

Service capacity can also be very difficult to measure. When capacity is dictated somewhat by machine capability, reasonably accurate measures of capacity are not extremely difficult to develop. However, services generally have variable processing requirements that make it difficult to establish a suitable measure of capacity.

Historically, services are much more labor intensive than manufacturing, where labor averages 10 percent (or less) of total cost. This labor intensity can actually be an advantage because of the variety of service requirements an individual can handle. This can provide quite a degree of flexibility that can make aggregate planning easier for services than manufacturing.

Project Charter

Project Charter refers to a statement of objectives in a project. This statement also sets out detailed project goals, roles and responsibilities, identifies the main stakeholders, and the level of authority of a project manager.

It acts as a guideline for future projects as well as an important material in the organization's knowledge management system.

The project charter is a short document that would consist of new offering request or a request for proposal. This document is a part of the project management process, which is required by Initiative for Policy Dialogue (IPD) and Customer Relationship Management (CRM).

The Role of Project Charter

Following are the roles of a Project Charter:

- It documents the reasons for undertaking the project.
- Outlines the objectives and the constraints faced by the project.
- Provides solutions to the problem in hand.
- Identifies the main stakeholders of the project.

Benefits of Project Charter

Following are the prominent benefits of Project Charter for a project:

- It improves and paves way for good customer relationships.
- Project Charter also works as a tool that improves project management processes.
- Regional and headquarter communications can also be improved to a greater extent.
- By having a project charter, project sponsorship can also be gained.
- Project Charter recognizes senior management roles.
- Allows progression, which is aimed at attaining industry best practices.

Elements in Project Charter

Since project charter is a project planning tool, which is aimed at resolving an issue or an opportunity, the below elements are essential for a good charter project.

For an effective charter project, it needs to address these key elements:

- Identity of the project.
- Time: The start date and the deadline for the project.
- People involved in the project.
- Outlined objectives and set targets.
- The reason for a project charter to be carried out often referred to as 'business case'.
- Detailed description of a problem or an opportunity.
- The return expected from the project.

- Results that could be expected in terms of performance.
- The expected date that the objectives are to be achieved.
- Clearly defined roles and responsibilities of the participants involved.
- Requirement of resources that will be needed for the objectives to be achieved.
- Barriers and the risks involved with the project.
- Informed and effective communication plan.

Out of all above elements, there are three most important and essential elements that need further elaboration.

Business Case

This outlines the need for a project charter to take place. A business case should set out the benefits gained from carrying out a project charter. Benefits need not only be in terms of finance such as revenue, cost reduction, etc., but also the benefit that the customer receives.

Following are the characteristics of a good business case:

- The reasons of undertaking the project.
- The benefits gained from undertaking the project now.
- The consequences of not doing the project.
- The factors that would conclude that it fits the business goals.

Project Scope

As the name denotes, it refers to the scope that the project will give the business if they undertake the project.

Before doing a project, the following concerns need to be addressed:

- The within scope and out of scope needs to be considered.
- The process that each team will focus upon.
- The start and end points for a process.
- Availability of resources.
- Constraints under which the team will work.
- Time limitations.
- The impact on the normal workload if the project is to be undertaken.

The need for a Good Communication Plan

The need for a good communication plan is at its utmost necessity when it comes to planning a project. Project managers need to work on building a good communication plan which will help in meeting the overall objectives of a Project Charter.

When creating a communication plan, the project manager needs to take the following into consideration:

- Who: Responsibility of each individuals participating in the project.
- What: The motive and the reason for communication plan.
- Where: Location where the receiver could find information.
- When: The duration and the frequency of the communication plan.
- How: The mechanism which is used to facilitate the communication.
- Whom: The receivers of the communication.

Schedule

In project management, a schedule is a listing of a project's milestones, activities, and deliverables, usually with intended start and finish dates. Those items are often estimated by other information included in the project schedule of resource allocation, budget, task duration, and linkages of dependencies and scheduled events. A schedule is commonly used in the project planning and project portfolio management parts of project management. Elements on a schedule may be closely related to the work breakdown structure (WBS) terminal elements, the Statement of work, or a Contract Data Requirements List.

In many industries, such as engineering and construction, the development and maintenance of the project schedule is the responsibility of a full-time scheduler or team of schedulers, depending on the size and the scope of the project. The techniques of scheduling are well developed but inconsistently applied throughout industry. Standardization and promotion of scheduling best practices are being pursued by the Association for the Advancement of Cost Engineering (AACE), the Project Management Institute (PMI), and the US Government for acquisition and accounting purposes.

Project management is not limited to industry; the average person can use it to organize their own life. Some examples are:

- Homeowner renovation project.
- Keeping track of all the family activities.

- Coaching a team.
- Planning a vacation.
- Planning a wedding.

Some project management software programs provide templates, lists, and example schedules to help their users with creating their schedule.

Methods

Before a project schedule can be created, the schedule maker should have a work breakdown structure (WBS), an effort estimate for each task, and a resource list with availability for each resource. If these components for the schedule are not available, they can be created with a consensus-driven estimation method like Wideband Delphi. The reason for this is that a schedule itself is an estimate: each date in the schedule is estimated, and if those dates do not have the buy-in of the people who are going to do the work, the schedule will be inaccurate.

To develop a project schedule, the following needs to be completed:

- Project scope.
- Sequence of activities.
- Tasks grouped into 5 project phases (conception, definition & planning, launch, performance, close).
- Task dependencies map.
- Critical path analysis.
- Project milestones.

In order for a project schedule to be healthy, the following criteria must be met:

- The schedule must be constantly (weekly works best) updated.
- The EAC (Estimation at Completion) value must be equal to the baseline value.
- The remaining effort must be appropriately distributed among team members (taking vacations into consideration).

The schedule structure may closely follow and include citations to the index of work breakdown structure or deliverables, using decomposition or templates to describe the activities needed to produce the deliverables defined in the WBS.

A schedule may be assessed for the quality of the schedule development and the quality of the schedule management.

Earned Schedule

Earned schedule (ES) is an extension to the theory and practice of earned value management (EVM).

It has been stated that Earned Schedule provides a useful link between traditional Earned Value Analysis and traditional project schedule analysis - a link that some say has been missing in traditional EVM theory.

Earned Schedule Measures

Traditionally, EVM tracks schedule variances *not* in units of time, but in units of currency (e.g. dollars) or quantity (e.g. labor hours). Of course, it is more natural to speak of schedule performance in units of time, but the problems with traditional schedule performance metrics are even deeper. Near the end of a project - when schedule performance is often a primary concern - the usefulness of traditional schedule metrics is demonstrably poor. When a project is completed, its SV is always 0 and SPI is always 1, even if the project was delivered unacceptably late. Similarly, a project can languish near completion (e.g. SPI = 0.95) and never be flagged as outside acceptable numerical tolerance. (Using traditional SV as an exception threshold, it is not uncommon that an SPI > 0.9 is considered acceptable.)

To correct these problems, Earned Schedule theory represents the two measures SV and SPI in 2 separate domains: currency and time. They are named as SV($) and SPI($), to indicate they relate to currency; and SV(t) and SPI(t), to indicate they relate to time.

A stated advantage of Earned Schedule methods is that no new data collection processes are required to implement and test Earned Schedule; it only requires updated formulas. Earned Schedule theory also provides updated formulas for predicting project completion date, using the time-based measures.

Limitation

In spite of more than a decade using Earned Schedule, the general appreciation to that was less than it was expected. One of the most significant reasons of this occurrence is the great difference of forecasting one period from the other periods. The following information was gained from the documents of final processes of a completed project which depicts the results of applying the new index in various time periods.

1226	1136	1046	956	866	776	686	596	AT
1283	1283	1283	1283	1283	1283	1283	1283	AD
1236	1564	2884	2233	2799	3574	3465	3665	IEAC(t)

AT in which is a day the report is prepared and AD is the actual time been spent on the completion of operating the project. As it is noticed, the more we get close to the actual completion of the project (AD=1283), the presented results get more realistic. However the variance in different time estimate in is notable. For instance the estimate at the end of the sixth period has the discrepancy of more than 1000 days with the estimate at the end of the seventh day however there is a gap of only 90 days between these two periods. The most important feedback of such a problem may vary from the distrust of stakeholders of management reports to their changing their turnabout to proceed with the project (considering the estimate of the sixth period). Concerning this issue, while investigating the way to calculate the mentioned index, we decided to evaluate its conformity to the gained actuality. In order to do so, the planned and actual graph of progress of the project has been considered.

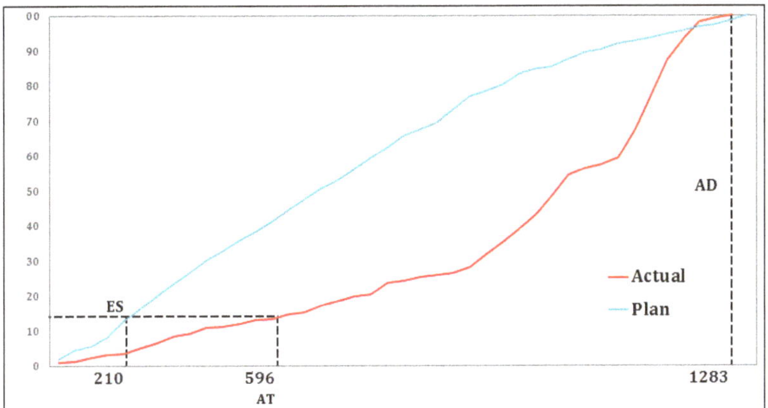

Figure 1- The planned and actual graph of progress of the project No. 1

ES = 210

AD = 1283

AT = 596

IEAC(t) = 3665

Since the amount of AD in all the reported forecasts is similar, it can be concluded that the estimates are relevant to the reverse of schedule performance index of time (SPI ((T)). In better words, independent estimation at completion (IEAC (T)) is calculated based on schedule performance index at the moment of "t". Unaware of the fact that the actual progress at the moment "t" can have an illogical ascending performance, affected by the sharp decline of budget, the unusual descending performance or increase of human resource at a certain time.

In addition, given that in order to calculate ES, the actual progress curve is depicted on planned progress curve. Forecasting the future condition of the project is based on the assumption that all the next periods will encounter the deviation from the schedule based on the current amount SPI (T). While with the assumption of making special conditions, the mentioned index may be reported more or less because of the illogical reasons. For instance if at the point AT= 626 we forecasted the future of the project, the following information would be gained:

ES = 243

AD = 1283

AT = 626

IEAC(t) = 3376

However the study on the condition of progress around this point shows that this condition had a sudden growth at the end of 2013 only due to the injection of budget. Thus, the first problem of the method ES can be known as the ignoring the actual progress of curve performance in predicting the future condition. Because of that problem, the new method which is named "Forecasting at completion" had presented in Industrial Engineering and Operation Management conference. This method is base on linear regression and polynomial regression.

Hammock Activity

A summary or hammock activity is used to represent groups of activities in a project schedule. It is used to summarize the schedule information for a group of activities and to allow the entire project to be summarized as a relatively few summary activities. The summary activity shows the start and finish for a group of activities as one Gantt bar. If the early starts and early finishes are being used for the schedule, the bar will show the earliest early start and the latest early finish for any of the activities in the group.

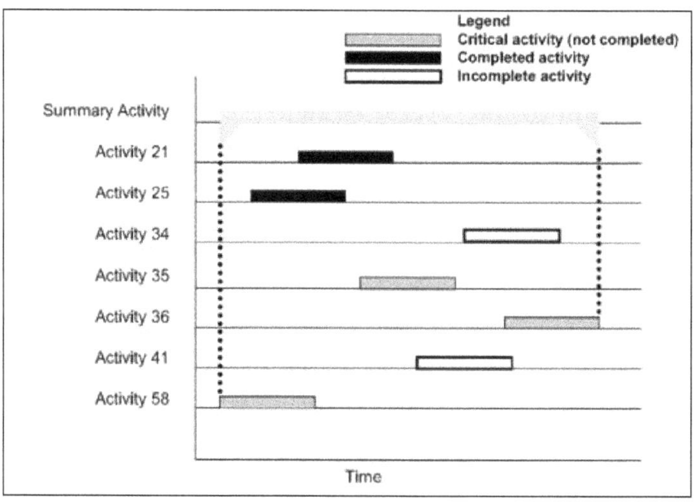

Activity chart.

The summary activity has come into use since the development of project management software. The advantage of summary activities over milestones is that it is not necessary to set up elaborate logical relationships to make sure that the milestone is rescheduled when activities in the group represented by the milestone are moved.

The milestone shows only a single date. This can be the start or finish of a group of activities, or it can be some major event or commitment date. The summary activity shows the start and finish for a group of activities. The computer will search through the group of activities and find the earliest early start date and the latest early finish date if the project is being scheduled according to the early schedule. If the project is being scheduled by the late schedule or a combination of the two, the computer will search for the earliest and the latest scheduled dates in the group of activities.

On the Gantt chart the milestones will have duration of zero and are generally shown as triangles. Summary activities are shown on the Gantt chart as schedule activity bars and usually have a graphic to distinguish them from the normal scheduled activities. In Microsoft Project the summary bars have small triangles below the bar at each end of the bar. The summary activities are created by selecting the activities to be summarized and clicking on the right arrow on the tool bar above them.

The work breakdown structure is entered the same way. The WBS will make a convenient set of summary activities and may be sufficient for your reporting system. If not, other summary activities may be entered as needed.

Kickoff Meeting

A kickoff meeting is the first meeting with the project team and the client of the project. This meeting would follow definition of the base elements for the project and other project planning activities. This meeting introduces the members of the project team and the client and provides the opportunity to discuss the role of team members. Other base elements in the project that involve the client may also be discussed at this meeting (schedule, status reporting, etc).

If there are any new team members, the process to be followed is explained so as to maintain quality standards of the organization. Clarity is given by the project lead if there exists any ambiguity in the process implementations.

There is a special discussion on the legalities involved in the project. For example, the design team interacting with the testing team may want a car to be tested on city roads. If the legal permissions are not mentioned by the concerned stakeholder during kickoff, the test may get modified later to comply with local traffic laws (this causes unplanned delay in project implementation). So, it would be best to have a discussion about this during the kickoff meeting and to follow it up separately, rather than to proceed on assumptions and later be forced to replan test procedures.

The kickoff meeting is an enthusiasm-generator for the customer and displays a full summary of the project so far. By displaying a thorough knowledge of the goal and steps on how to reach it, the customer gains confidence in the team's ability to deliver the work. Kickoff means that the work starts.

Work Breakdown Structure

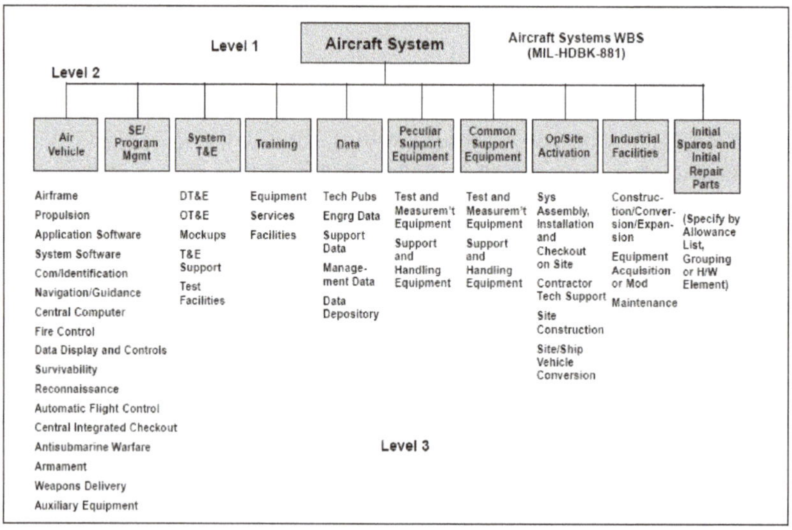

Example from MIL-HDBK-881, which illustrates the first three levels of a typical aircraft system.

A work-breakdown structure (WBS) in project management and systems engineering, is a deliverable-oriented breakdown of a project into smaller components. A work breakdown structure is a key project deliverable that organizes the team's work into manageable sections. The Project Management Body of Knowledge (PMBOK 5) defines the work-breakdown structure "A hierarchical decomposition of the total scope of work to be carried out by the project team to accomplish the project objectives and create the required deliverables."

Working on a project WBS.

A work-breakdown structure element may be a product, data, service, or any combination thereof. A WBS also provides the necessary framework for detailed cost estimating and control along with providing guidance for schedule development and control.

WBS is a hierarchical and incremental decomposition of the project into phases, deliverables and work packages. It is a tree structure, which shows a subdivision of effort required to achieve an objective; for example a program, project, and contract. In a project or contract, the WBS is developed by starting with the end objective and successively subdividing it into manageable components in terms of size, duration, and responsibility (e.g., systems, subsystems, components, tasks, subtasks, and work packages) which include all steps necessary to achieve the objective.

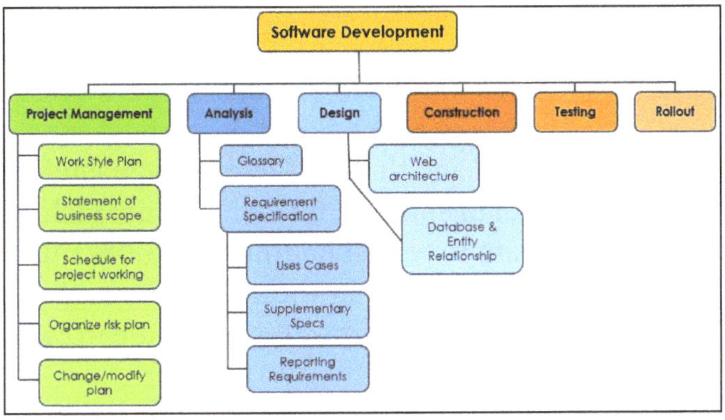

Example of work breakdown structure.

The work breakdown structure provides a common framework for the natural development of the overall planning and control of a contract and is the basis for dividing work into definable increments from which the statement of work can be developed and technical, schedule, cost, and labor hour reporting can be established.

A work breakdown structure permits summing of subordinate costs for tasks, materials, etc., into their successively higher level "parent" tasks, materials, etc. For each element of the work breakdown structure, a description of the task to be performed is generated. This technique (sometimes called a *system breakdown structure*) is used to define and organize the total scope of a project.

The WBS is organized around the primary products of the project (or planned outcomes) instead of the work needed to produce the products (planned actions). Since the planned outcomes are the desired ends of the project, they form a relatively stable set of categories in which the costs of the planned actions needed to achieve them can be collected. A well-designed WBS makes it easy to assign each project activity to one and only one terminal element of the WBS. In addition to its function in cost accounting, the WBS also helps map requirements from one level of system specification to another, for example, a cross reference matrix mapping functional requirements to high level or low level design documents. The WBS may be displayed horizontally in outline form, or vertically as a tree structure (like an organization chart).

The development of the WBS normally occurs at the start of a project and precedes detailed project and task planning.

Design Principles

100% Rule

An important design principle for work breakdown structures is called the 100% rule. It has been defined as follows:

> The 100% rule states that the WBS includes 100% of the work defined by the project scope and captures all deliverables – internal, external, interim – in terms of the work to be completed, including project management. The 100% rule is one of the most important principles guiding the development, decomposition and evaluation of the WBS. The rule applies at all levels within the hierarchy: the sum of the work at the "child" level must equal 100% of the work represented by the "parent" and the WBS should not include any work that falls outside the actual scope of the project, that is, it cannot include more than 100% of the work. It is important to remember that the 100% rule also applies to the activity level. The work represented by the activities in each work package must add up to 100% of the work necessary to complete the work package.

Mutually Exclusive Elements

Mutually exclusive: In addition to the 100% rule, it is important that there is no overlap in scope definition between different elements of a work breakdown structure. This ambiguity could result in duplicated work or miscommunications about responsibility and authority. Such overlap could also cause confusion regarding project cost accounting. If the WBS element names are ambiguous, a WBS dictionary can help clarify the distinctions between WBS elements. The WBS Dictionary describes each component of the WBS with milestones, deliverables, activities, scope, and sometimes dates, resources, costs, quality.

Plan Outcomes and not Actions

If the work breakdown structure designer attempts to capture any action-oriented details in the WBS, the designer will likely include either too many actions or too few actions. Too many actions will exceed 100% of the parent's scope and too few will fall short of 100% of the parent's scope. The best way to adhere to the 100% rule is to define WBS elements in terms of outcomes or results, not actions. This also ensures that the WBS is not overly prescriptive of methods, allowing for greater ingenuity and creative thinking on the part of the project participants. For new product development projects, the most common technique to ensure an outcome-oriented WBS is to use a product breakdown structure. Feature-driven software projects may use a similar technique which is to employ a feature breakdown structure. When a project provides professional services, a common technique is to capture all planned deliverables to create a deliverable-oriented WBS. Work breakdown structures that subdivide work by project phases (e.g. preliminary design phase, critical design phase) must ensure that phases are clearly separated by a deliverable also used in defining entry and exit criteria (e.g. an approved preliminary or critical design review).

Level of Detail

One must decide when to stop dividing work into smaller elements. For most projects a hierarchy of two to four levels will suffice. This will assist in determining the duration of activities necessary to produce a deliverable defined by the WBS. There are several heuristics or "rules of thumb" used when determining the appropriate duration of an activity or group of activities necessary to produce a specific deliverable defined by the WBS.

- The first is the "80 hour rule" which means that no single activity or group of activities at the lowest level of detail of the WBS to produce a single deliverable should be more than 80 hours of effort.
- The second rule of thumb is that no activity or group of activities at the lowest level of detail of the WBS should be longer than a single reporting period. Thus if the project team is reporting progress monthly, then no single activity or series of activities should be longer than one month long.
- The last heuristic is the "if it makes sense" rule. Applying this rule of thumb, one can apply "common sense" when creating the duration of a single activity or group of activities necessary to produce a deliverable defined by the WBS.

A work package at the activity level is a task that:

- Can be realistically and confidently estimated.
- Makes no sense practically to break down any further.
- Can be completed in accordance with one of the heuristics defined above.
- Produces a deliverable which is measurable.
- Forms a unique package of work which can be outsourced or contracted out.

Coding Scheme

It is common for work breakdown structure elements to be numbered sequentially to reveal the hierarchical structure. The purpose for the numbering is to provide a consistent approach to identifying and managing the WBS across like systems regardless of vendor or service. For example, 1.1.2 Propulsion (in the example below) identifies this item as a Level 3 WBS element, since there are three numbers separated by a decimal point. A coding scheme also helps WBS elements to be recognized in any written context and allows for mapping to the WBS Dictionary.

A practical example of the WBS coding scheme is:

1.0 Aircraft System

1.1 Air Vehicle

1.1.1 Airframe

1.1.1.1 Airframe Integration, Assembly, Test and Checkout

1.1.1.2 Fuselage

1.1.1.3 Wing

1.1.1.4 Empennage

1.1.1.5 Nacelle

1.1.1.6 Other Airframe Components 1..n (Specify)

1.1.2 Propulsion

1.1.3 Vehicle Subsystems

1.1.4 Avionics

1.2 System Engineering

1.3 Program Management

1.4 System Test and Evaluation

1.5 Training

1.6 Data

1.7 Peculiar Support Equipment

1.8 Common Support Equipment

1.9 Operational/Site Activation

1.10 Industrial Facilities

1.11 Initial Spares and Repair Parts

Terminal Element

The lowest element in a tree structure, a terminal element is one that is not further subdivided. In a Work Breakdown Structure such elements (activity or deliverable), also known as work packages, are the items that are estimated in terms of resource requirements, budget and duration; linked by dependencies; and scheduled. At the juncture of the WBS element and organization unit, control accounts and work packages are established and performance is planned, measured, recorded and controlled. A WBS can be expressed down to any level of interest. Three levels are the minimum recommended, with additional levels for and only for items of high cost or high risk, and two levels of detail at cases such as systems engineering or program management, with the standard showing examples of WBS with varying depth such as software development at points going to 5 levels or fire-control system to 7 levels.

Consistent to Norms

The higher WBS structure should be consistent to whatever norms or template mandates exist within the organization or domain. For example, shipbuilding for the U.S. Navy must respect that the nautical terms and their hierarchy structure put into MIL-STD are embedded in Naval Architecture and that matching Navy offices and procedures have been built to match this naval architecture structure, so any significant change of WBS element numbering or naming in the hierarchy would be unacceptable.

Example of Work breakdown structure:

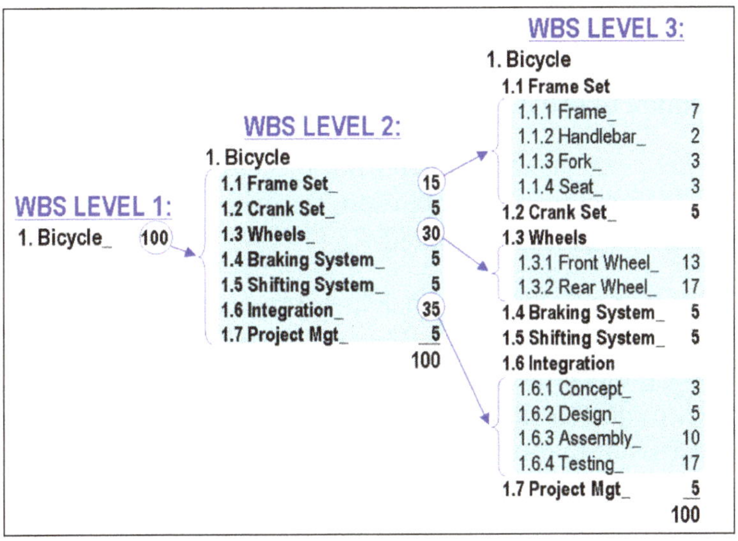

The WBS construction technique employing the 100% rule during WBS construction.

The figure on the left shows a work breakdown structure construction technique that demonstrates the 100% rule and the "progressive elaboration" technique. At WBS Level 1 it shows 100 units of work as the total scope of a project to design and build a custom bicycle. At WBS Level 2, the 100 units are divided into seven elements. The number of units allocated to each element of work can be based on effort or cost; it is not an estimate of task duration.

The three largest elements of WBS Level 2 are further subdivided at Level 3. The two largest elements at Level 3 each represent only 17% of the total scope of the project. These larger elements could be further subdivided using the *progressive elaboration* technique described above.

WBS design can be supported by software (e.g. a spreadsheet) to allow automatic rolling up of point values. Estimates of effort or cost can be developed through discussions among project team members. This collaborative technique builds greater insight into scope definitions, underlying assumptions, and consensus regarding the level of granularity required to manage the projects.

Project Workforce Management

Project workforce management is the practice of combining the coordination of all logistic elements of a project through a single software application (or workflow engine). This includes planning and tracking of schedules and mileposts, cost and revenue, resource allocation, as well as overall management of these project elements. Efficiency is improved by eliminating manual processes, like spreadsheet tracking to monitor project progress. It also allows for at-a-glance status updates and ideally integrates with existing legacy applications in order to unify ongoing projects, enterprise resource planning (ERP) and broader organizational goals. There are a lot of logistic elements in a project. Different team members are responsible for managing each element and often, the organisation may have a mechanism to manage some logistic areas as well.

By coordinating these various components of project management, workforce management and financials through a single solution, the process of configuring and changing project and workforce details is simplified.

A project workforce management system defines project tasks, project positions, and assigns personnel to the project positions. The project tasks and positions are correlated to assign a responsible project position or even multiple positions to complete each project task. Because each project position may be assigned to a specific person, the qualifications and availabilities of that person can be taken into account when determining the assignment. By associating project tasks and project positions, a manager can better control the assignment of the workforce and complete the project more efficiently.

When it comes to project workforce management, it is all about managing all the logistic aspects of a project or an organisation through a software application. Usually, this software has a workflow engine defined. Therefore, all the logistic processes take place in the workflow engine.

Technical Field

This invention relates to project management systems and methods, more particularly to a software-based system and method for project and workforce management.

Software Usage

Due to the software usage, all the project workflow management tasks can be fully automated without leaving many tasks for the project managers. This returns high efficiency to the project management when it comes to project tracking proposes. In addition to different tracking mechanisms, project workforce management software also offer a dashboard for the project team. Through the dashboard, the project team has a glance view of the overall progress of the project elements.

Most of the times, project workforce management software can work with the existing legacy software systems such as ERP (enterprise resource planning) systems. This easy integration allows the organisation to use a combination of software systems for management purposes.

Workflow Engine

When it comes to project workforce management, it is all about managing all the logistic aspects of a project or an organisation through a software application. Usually, this software has a workflow engine defined in them. So, all the logistic processes take place in the workflow engine.

The regular and most common types of tasks handled by project workforce management software or a similar workflow engine are:

Planning and Monitoring Project Schedules and Milestones

Regularly monitoring your project's schedule performance can provide early indications of possible activity-coordination problems, resource conflicts, and possible cost overruns. To monitor schedule performance. Collecting information and evaluating it ensure a project accuracy.

The project schedule outlines the intended result of the project and what's required to bring it to completion. In the schedule, we need to include all the resources involved and cost and time constraints through a work breakdown structure (WBS). The WBS outlines all the tasks and breaks them down into specific deliverables.

Tracking the Cost and Revenue aspects of Projects

The importance of tracking actual costs and resource usage in projects depends upon the project situation.

Tracking actual costs and resource usage is an essential aspect of the project control function.

Resource Utilisation and Monitoring

Organisational profitability is directly connected to project management efficiency and optimal resource utilisation. To sum up, organisations that struggle with either or both of these core competencies typically experience cost overruns, schedule delays and unhappy customers.

The focus for project management is the analysis of project performance to determine whether a change is needed in the plan for the remaining project activities to achieve the project goals.

Other Management aspects of Project Management

Project Risk Management

Risk identification consists of determining which risks are likely to affect the project and documenting the characteristics of each.

Project Communication Management

Project communication management is about how communication is carried out during the course of the project

Project Quality Management

It is of no use completing a project within the set time and budget if the final product is of poor quality. The project manager has to ensure that the final product meets the quality expectations of the stakeholders. This is done by good:

- Quality planning: Identifying what quality standards are relevant to the project and determining how to meet them.
- Quality assurance: Evaluating overall project performance on a regular basis to provide confidence that the project will satisfy the relevant quality standards.
- Quality control: Monitoring specific project results to determine if they comply with relevant quality standards and identifying ways to remove causes of poor performance.

Project Workforce Management vs. Traditional Management

There are three main differences between Project Workforce Management and traditional project management and workforce management disciplines and solutions:

Workflow-driven

All project and workforce processes are designed, controlled and audited using a built-in graphical workflow engine. Users can design, control and audit the different processes involved in the project. The graphical workflow is quite attractive for the users of the system and allows the users to have a clear idea of the workflow engine.

Organisation and Work Breakdown Structures

Project Workforce Management provides organization and work breakdown structures to create, manage and report on functional and approval hierarchies, and to track information at any level of detail. Users can create, manage, edit and report work breakdown structures. Work breakdown structures have different abstraction levels, so the information can be tracked at any level. Usually, project workforce management has approval hierarchies. Each workflow created will go through several records before it becomes an organisational or project standard. This helps the organisation to reduce the inefficiencies of the process, as it is audited by many stakeholders.

Connected Project, Workforce and Financial Processes

Unlike traditional disconnected project, workforce and billing management systems that are solely focused on tracking IT projects, internal workforce costs or billable projects. Project Workforce Management is designed to unify the coordination of all project and workforce processes, whether internal, shared (IT) or billable.

Project Execution

The Project Execution Phase of the project management lifecycle is all about deliverables & outputs. It is here that the intended product or service is delivered to the customer for approval.

In official terms – The Project Management Body of Knowledge (PMBOK) states – "The Executing Process Group consists of those processes performed to complete the work defined in the project management plan to satisfy the project specifications."

The Project Execution Phase is usually the longest phase in the project management life cycle and consumes the most energy and resources. It is pretty evident by now as to how crucial it is to ensure your plans are realized with clinical precision and none to minimal deviation.

To enable you to monitor and control the project during this phase, you will need to implement a range of project management processes. These processes help you to manage time, cost, quality, change, risks and issues. They also help you to manage procurement, customer acceptance and communications.

The primary objective of Execution and Control is to construct deliverables as per the master project plan and consistently evaluate the processes and plans involved to deliver the output as per the agreed specifications.

It is all about action and direction. The Execution Phase will broadly involve the following actions. The priority or sequence is entirely dependent on the nature of the project and organizational practices and preferences. But nevertheless, they are performed to enable successful project execution.

- Acquire Develop & Manage the Team who will work on the project.
- Execute Project Scope.
- Recommend changes, bug fixes, preventive and corrective actions coming from Planning, Executing and Monitoring and Controlling process groups.
- Timely Communication with all stakeholders.
- Implemented approved changes to the processes, documentation and plans.
- Team Building exercises.
- Give recognition and rewards to team members and keep them motivated.
- Hold Status Review meetings to ensure project is on track and any deviations are attended to at the earliest.
- Use Work Authorization systems to allocate work.
- Request Seller responses to your tender and outsourcing needs.
- Select Seller for your procurement needs.

What does Execution Phase Produce?

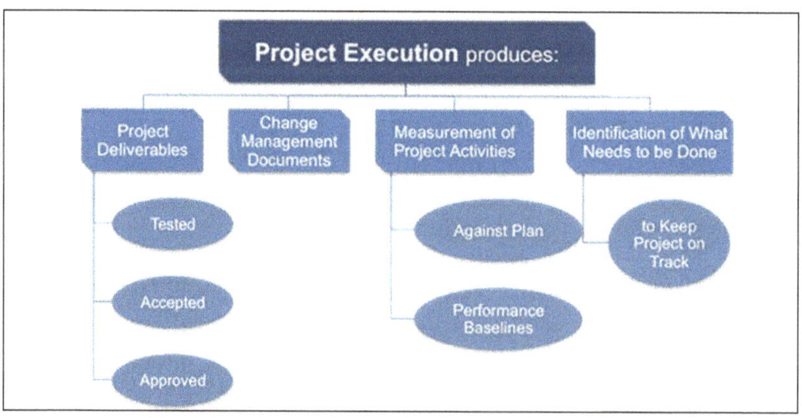

Project Deliverables

Project deliverables are the primary reason why projects are run. They are the tangible expectations and results produced from our projects. As part of the execution process we ensure, that the deliverables are well tested, meet the acceptance criteria and are approved by the customer and/or business sponsor.

It is of utmost importance that the project deliverables are of the agreed quality and meet the defined objectives and specifications.

Change Management Documents

Change is unavoidable in project management too. And in its true sense it is more of an asset. When handled properly, the change management process goes a long way in minimizing loss of precious project resources and reducing scope creep.

This is where the project management change plan comes in. The plan, as detailed in the project management change document, sets out the process by which any changes to the project's goals, schedule, and/or resource usage are to be managed. In short, the change document is a vital component in managing projects of any size and complexity, and it heavily influences project success.

Change Management Document includes 3 items:

- Change Management Goals: Spell out the goals of the project's change management plan. For example, changes are clearly determined, evaluated, approved, and tracked effectively and efficiently. It also details how the overall project change plan is designed to benefit the project.

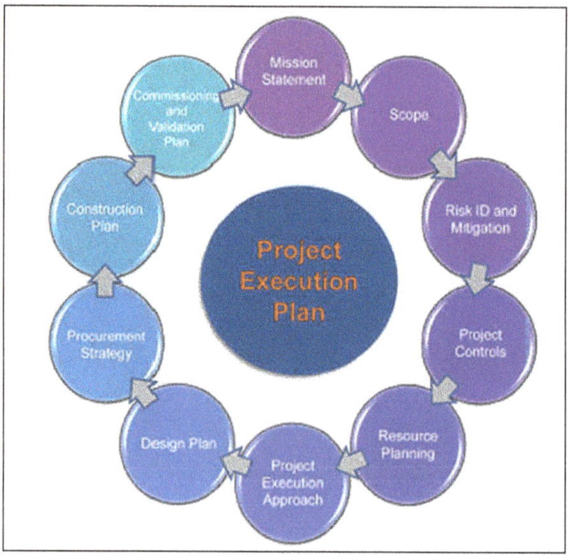

- Change Management Responsibilities: In this area of the change document you need to define the responsibilities of all the parties involved in the project that may be affected by a project change. So, for example, you should define who will receive project change requests, who will evaluate them, and how will project changes be communicated to project personnel, upper management, and project clients or stakeholders.
- Change Management Model: Clearly lay out the details of the change management process. You should describe how project change requests are made and evaluated, who is authorized to approve them, and how they will be recorded.
- Measuring Project Activities: Measuring performance is a critical factor in optimizing performance. Consistent Monitoring and Control measures are required to stay on track.

Project performance, on the surface, seems easy to measure; just track time, cost and scope and it's done.

As part of optimizing your execution, you must perform certain key activities:

- Time Management.
- Cost Management.
- Quality Management.
- Change Management.
- Risk Management.

- Procurement Management.
- Acceptance Management.
- Stakeholder Engagement.
- Communication Management.

Processes Included in Project Execution

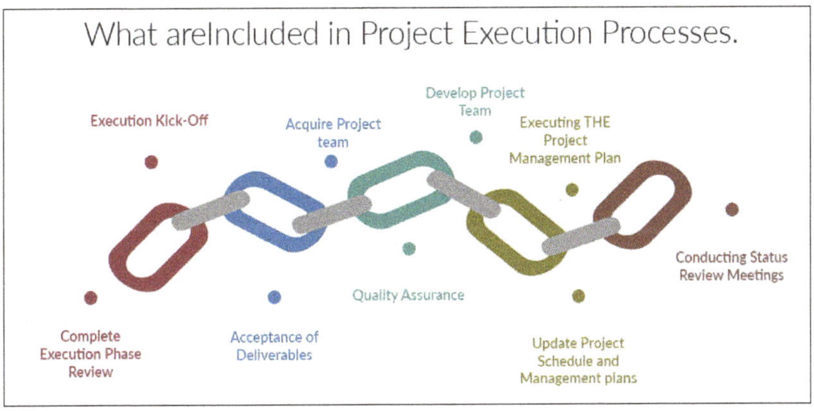

Execution Kick-off

The Project Manager can begin the phase activities following the completion of all planning activities including approval of the PMP, functional specifications & project funding.

Acquire Project Team

The project manager follows necessary steps to obtain the human resources needed to complete the project. Resource calendars are built and resource allocation for the project is done based on the negotiations and acquisitions with the involved business units and resource pool managers.

Develop Project Team

The project manager evaluates each individual skill sets to ensure that the each team member has the proper skill sets for each upcoming project phase. Your training plan, schedule and costs come in handy.

Project leaders that can align their vision and work with their teams will successfully deliver key programs and projects. The alignment of vision and strategy to implementation will help you close those gaps.

Executing the Project Management Plan

The project manager executes the project management plan activities by performing the activities contained within each of the plans such as Communication Plan, Risk management plan, etc.

The project manager will direct the various technical and organizational resources that exist in the project to execute the work defined in the project management plans.

Conducting Status Review Meetings (PSR)

Project status meetings help project managers in reviewing the status collected from the team members. They help the project managers in assessing what has been accomplished till date and compare them with the planned activities.

They allow project managers in the assessment of current problem areas and project risk areas; as well as communicating critical project information with quick feedback. Having these project status meetings also eliminates the communication problem that arises out of an assumption or belief that "everyone knows what's going on in this project". Often team members do not know, because they are busy with their own tasks.

The project execution phase will reveal unanticipated problems or issues, so project leaders must be prepared to pivot and make tactical changes.

Update Project Schedule and Management Plans

In most organizations, the project management team is the group of people responsible for updating the project plan. The project plan is many things to the project manager. It is a record of what has occurred on the project. It illustrates what is happening on the project right now. And, it prepares the project team by showing what will be coming up.

Keeping the plan current is an important role of the project manager (or project administrator). Project updates focus on the three project management constraints, cost, time and scope. An effective project manager knows that a change in one of these areas results in changes in the other two. A current project plan will show the effect of these changes on the overall project.

Therefore, any changes and updates from the previously defined plan must be duly recorded and approved by the relevant parties along with revision history info for audit trail. Any lapse in maintaining an accurate plan or one that is outdated has significant impact to the overall project success.

Quality Assurance

In the Project Management Body of Knowledge (PMBOK), Quality Assurance is part of the Executing process group and is performed throughout the duration of the project. Quality Assurance is the process of auditing the quality requirements and the results from quality control measurements to ensure that appropriate quality standards and operational definitions are used. The key benefit of this process is that it facilitates the improvement of quality processes.

Acceptance of Deliverables

Acceptance criteria for project deliverables establishes in advance an agreed upon standard of performance or capability that the user will accept in a specific deliverable The Performance Plan developed in the Project Planning Phase articulates the project deliverables and acceptance criteria.

Acceptance criteria then become the fundamental guideline for the design team to build a solution that the user will find acceptable.

The execution phase ends when the user has agreed to accept the deliverables in the state that they exist. The acceptance criterion is the standard that the user uses to judge if each deliverable is satisfactory.

In some cases, the deliverable may not meet all acceptance criteria but, from an overall view, the deliverable will meet the requirements of the user. The user must authenticate acceptance of each deliverable. The user will also identify any issues that remain outstanding and the agreed to plan for resolution of any outstanding issues.

Complete Execution Phase Review

The project manager contacts all participating stakeholders to review and document lessons learned in the execution phase. A formal Phase Review form is duly filled and sent to the Project Sponsor for approval.

It is basically to seek permission to proceed to the next phase and closure of the existing phase. All deliverables are reviewed, accepted & approved, any pending issues are documented along with their resolution plan and all relevant plans and documents are updated accordingly.

Project Monitoring

Project Monitoring plays a vital part in project management as well as the project manager's decision making processes.

However, it is a method often overlooked and only done for the sake of fulfilling the requirements of a project management plan. But if put into practice, project monitoring can help project managers and their teams foresee potential risks and obstacles that if left unaddressed, could derail the project. It clarifies the objectives of the project, links the activities to the objectives, sets the target, reports the progress to the management and keeps the management aware of the problems which crop up during the implementation of the project. It supports and motivates the management to complete the project within the budget and on time.

Project Monitoring refers to the process of keeping track of all project-related metrics including team performance and task duration, identifying potential problems and taking corrective actions necessary to ensure that the project is within scope, on budget and meets the specified deadlines. To simply put, project monitoring is overseeing all tasks and keeping an eye on project activities to make sure you're implementing the project as planned.

The process of project monitoring begins during the planning phase of the project. During this phase, it is important to define how the project success will look like and how the goals can be measured using KPIs (Key performance indicators).

Why is Project Monitoring Important?

When project managers make important decisions without verified data, it is like taking a stab in the dark. Your decisions will be based on very little to no evidence, so the action may not be very efficient and could only be a waste of time and resources. Getting a PMP certification will help you grow and become a successful, object-oriented Project Manager.

That's why it is important to monitor projects diligently and use the data you gathered to come up with intelligent decisions. Here are some questions answered through project monitoring:

- Are tasks being carried out as planned?
- Are there any unforeseen consequences that arise as a result of these tasks?
- How is your team performing at a given period of time?
- What are the elements of the project that needs changing?
- What is the impact of these changes?

- Will these actions lead you to your expected results?

Automated tools and technologies can simplify the tedious process of project monitoring. Most project managers have already adopted project management tools to delegate tasks and monitor their projects. However, project monitoring is a complex process and there are only a few project management apps out there that can support the project manager's requirement to have laser-focus on individual tasks and team efficiency.

Types of Project Monitoring

Project Monitoring can be attained via:

- Staff Meetings, which can be conducted on a Weekly, Monthly or an Annual basis.
- Partners meeting, Learning forums (FGD, Surveys) or Retreats.
- Participatory reviews by the stakeholders.
- Monitoring and Supervision Missions that can be Self, Donor or Joint.
- Statistics or Progress reports.

How to Implement Project Monitoring and Control in Projects?

The following are the steps to implement Project Monitoring and Control (PMC) in projects:

- Monitor the parameter of project planning: It requires the monitoring of project parameters like effort, costing, schedule, timeline, etc. It is the responsibility of a Project Manager to track such metrics while working on a project.
- Monitor Commitments: Being a Project Manager, you will have to keep track of the commitments of different stakeholders in the project. The stakeholders can include anyone: the team members, management, peers, vendors as well as clients.
- Monitor the Project Risks: It is important to keep a track of all the risks that might be involved with the project. There are various types of risks that can be involved in a project, including process, people, technology, tools, etc.
- Data Management monitoring: Keeping track of all of the configuration items, which includes software, hardware as well as documentation of the project.
- Monitoring the Stakeholder involvement: As a Project Manager, it is important that you keep track of how all the stakeholders are involved in the project. This can be done through different types of meetings, status reports, etc.

- Manage Progress Reviews: Conduct and manage the project progress reviews with the help of different techniques which includes the work progress of team members, client meetings, milestones reviews, etc. Based on these activities, various status reports are created, which are shared with the stakeholders as well.
- Manage actions to closure: Based on the progress of the project, it is important to take corrective actions to get control over the progress of the project plan. These corrective actions are then tracked by the Project Managers till the project closure or until the progress is under control.

Why Project Monitoring?

Project monitoring aids various purposes. It brings out the problems which occur or which might occur during the implementation of the project and which demands solutions for smoother progress in the project. Effective monitoring helps in knowing if the intended results are being achieved as planned, what actions are needed to achieve the intended results during the project execution, and whether these initiatives are creating a positive impact towards the project execution.

- To assess the project results: To know how the objectives are being met and the desired changes are being met.
- To improve process planning: It helps in adapting to better contextual and risk factors which affect the research process, like social and power dynamics.
- To promote learning: It will help you learn how various approaches to participation influences the outcomes.
- To understand stakeholder's perspectives: Through direct participation in the process of monitoring and evaluation, learn about the people who are involved in the research project. Understand their values and views, as well as design methods to resolve conflicting views and interests.
- To ensure accountability: To assess if the project has been effectively, appropriately and efficiently executed, so that they can be held accountable.

Ways to Track and Re-Plan a Project

It is said that projects never go according to what we have planned. Hence, one must be ready to make any amendments as needed. You can also opt for the following three-step approach:

- Check and understand the progress of the project: Before starting to re-plan your project, you should be sure of the current state and status of the work. Setting up a meeting for the whole team together to get to know about the updates of the current work, upcoming tasks and issues will be beneficial. Also, recognize the important milestones in this meeting.

- Search for and Manage Exceptions: Stay on a look-out for exceptions like risks, issues and change requests. Open issues will have to be resolved so that road-blocks can be removed, and a risk mitigation plan will have to be developed.
- Re-plan the project: You have an idea of how to re-plan the project. The following steps will help you do so:
- Keep the important project documents updated, which includes the project charter.
- Share the new plan with the shareholders.
- As per the demand, re-assign the work. Communicate with the team members regarding the new assignments and send automated reminders to them.
- As required, make changes on the project site with the updates reports and dashboards.

Project Governance

Project governance is the management framework within which project decisions are made. Project governance is a critical element of any project, since the accountabilities and responsibilities associated with an organization's business as usual activities are laid down in their organizational governance arrangements; seldom does an equivalent framework exist to govern the development of its capital investments (projects). For instance, the organization chart provides a good indication of who in the organization is responsible for any particular operational activity the organization conducts. But unless an organization has specifically developed a project governance policy, no such chart is likely to exist for project development activity.

Therefore, the role of project governance is to provide a decision making framework that is logical, robust and repeatable to govern an organization's capital investments. In this way, an organization will have a structured approach to conducting both its business as usual activities and its business change, or project, activities.

Three Pillars of Project Governance

The decision making framework is supported by three pillars:

Structure

This refers to the governance committee structure. In the first instance the Capital Expenditure Board that sanctions resources (capital, human and other) to projects. Secondly the portfolio committee who ensures that the right project are selected. As well as there being a Project Board or Project Steering Committee, the broader governance environment may include various stakeholder groups and perhaps user groups. Additionally, there may be a Programme, governing a group of related projects of which this is one, and possibly some form of portfolio decision making group. The decision rights of all these committees and how they relate must be laid down in policy and procedural documentation. In this way, the project's governance can be integrated within the wider governance arena.

The other governing bodies include the following:

- Functional Management responsible for the tactical governance of project team members and their work and deliverables.
- Project team for operational governance of project resources and activities.
- Review and auditing functions as independent process governance and deliverable and information quality.
- Financial auditing for independent financial compliance auditing.

People

The effectiveness of the committee structure is dependent upon the people that populate the various governance committees. Committee membership is determined by the nature of the project - other factors come into play when determining membership of programme and a portfolio board - which in turn determines which organisational roles should be represented on the committee.

Information

This concerns the information that informs decision makers and consists of regular reports on the project, issues and risks that have been escalated by the Project Manager and certain key documents that describe the project, foremost of which is the business case.

Core Project Governance Principles

Project governance frameworks should be based around a number of core principles in order to ensure their effectiveness.

1. Ensure a single point of accountability for the success of the project.

The most fundamental project accountability is accountability for the success of the project. A project without a clear understanding of who assumes accountability for its success has no clear leadership. With no clear accountability for project success, there is no one person driving the solution of the difficult issues that beset all projects at some point in their life. It also slows the project during the crucial project initiation phase since there is no one person to take the important decisions necessary to place the project on a firm footing. The concept of a single point of accountability is the first principle of effective project governance.

However, it is not enough to nominate someone to be accountable – the right person must be made accountable. There are two aspects to this. The accountable person must hold sufficient authority within the organisation to ensure they are empowered to make the decisions necessary for the project's success. Beyond this however is the fact that the right person from the correct area within the organisation be held accountable. If the wrong person is selected, the project is no better placed than if no one was accountable for its success. The single person who will assume accountability for the success of the project is the subject of Principle 2.

2. Project ownership independent of Asset ownership, Service ownership or other stakeholder group.

Often organisations promote the allocation of the Project Owner role to the service owner or asset owner with the goal of providing more certainty that the project will meet these owner's fundamental needs, which is also a critical project success measure. However, the result of this approach can involve wasteful scope inclusions and failure to achieve alternative stakeholder and customer requirements:

- The benefit of the doubt goes to the stakeholder allocated with the Project Owner responsibility, skewing the project outcome.
- Project owner requirements receive less scrutiny, reducing innovation and reducing outcome efficiency.
- Different skill sets surround Project ownership, Asset ownership and Service ownership placing sound project decision making and procedure at risk.
- Operational needs always prevail, placing the project at risk of being neglected during such times.
- Project contingencies are at risk of being allocated to additional scope for the stakeholder allocated project ownership.

The only proven mechanism for ensuring projects meet customer and stakeholder needs, while optimising value for money, is to allocate Project ownership to specialist party, that otherwise would not be a stakeholder to the project. This is principle No. 2 of project governance.

The Project Owner is engaged under clear terms which outline the organisations key result areas and the organisation's view of the key project stakeholders. Often, organisations establish a Governance of Projects Committee, which identifies the existence of projects and appoints project owners as early as possible in a project's life, establishes

Project Councils which form the basis of customer and stakeholder engagement, establishes the key result areas for a project consistent with the organisations values, and, oversees the performance of projects. These parameters are commonly detailed in a Project Governance Plan which remains in place for the life of the project (and is distinct from a Project Management Plan which is more detailed and only comes into existence during the development of the project).

Projects have many stakeholders and an effective project governance framework must address their needs. The next principle deals with the manner in which this should occur.

3. Ensure separation of stakeholder management and project decision making activities.

The decision making effectiveness of a committee can be thought of as being inversely proportional to its size. Not only can large committees fail to make timely decisions, those it does make are often ill-considered because of the particular group dynamics at play.

As project decision making forums grow in size, they tend to morph into stakeholder management groups. When numbers increase, the detailed understanding of each attendee of the critical project issues reduces. Many of those present attend not to make decisions but as a way of finding out what is happening on the project. Not only is there insufficient time for each person to make their point, but those with the most valid input must compete for time and influence with those with only a peripheral involvement in the project. Further not all present will have the same level of understanding of the issues and so time is wasted bringing everyone up to speed on the particular issues being discussed. Hence, to all intents and purposes, large project committees are constituted more as a stakeholder management forum than a project decision making forum. This is a major issue when the project is depending upon the committee to make timely decisions.

There is no question that activities, project decision making and stakeholder management, are essential to the success of the project. The issue is that they are two separate activities and need to be treated as such. This is the third principle of effective project governance. If this separation can be achieved, it will avoid clogging the decision making forum with numerous stakeholders by constraining its membership to only those select stakeholders absolutely central to its success.

There is always the concern that this solution will lead to a further problem if disgruntled stakeholders do not consider their needs are being met. Whatever stakeholder management mechanism that is put in place must adequately address the needs of all project stakeholders. It will need to capture their input and views and address their concerns to their satisfaction. This can be achieved in part by chairing of any key stakeholder groups by the chair of the Project Board. This ensures that stakeholders have the project owner (or SRO) to champion their issues and concerns within the Project Board.

4. Ensure separation of project governance and organisational governance structures.

Project governance structures are established precisely because it is recognised that organisation structures do not provide the necessary framework to deliver a project. Projects require flexibility and speed of decision making and the hierarchical mechanisms associated with organisation charts do not enable this. Project governance structures overcome this by drawing the key decision makers out of the organisation structure and placing them in a forum thereby avoiding the serial decision making process associated with hierarchies.

Consequently, the project governance framework established for a project should remain separate from the organisation structure. It is recognised that the organisation has valid requirements in terms of reporting and stakeholder involvement. However dedicated reporting mechanisms established by the project can address the former and the project governance framework must itself address the latter. What should be avoided is the situation where the decisions of the steering committee or project board are required to be ratified by one or more persons in the organisation outside of that project decision making forum; either include these individuals as members of the project decision making body or fully empower the current steering committee/project board. The steering committee/project board is responsible for approving, reviewing progress, and delivering the project outcomes, and its intended benefits, therefore, they must have capacity to make decisions, which may commit resources and funding outside the original plan. This is the final principle of effective project governance.

Adoption of this principle will minimise multi layered decision making and the time delays and inefficiencies associated with it. It will ensure a project decision making body empowered to make decisions in a timely manner.

Additional and Complementary Principles of Governance

The board has overall responsibility for governance of project management. The roles, responsibilities and performance criteria for the governance of project management are clearly defined. Disciplined governance arrangements, supported by appropriate methods and controls are applied throughout the project life cycle. A coherent and supportive relationship is demonstrated between the overall business strategy and the project portfolio.

All projects have an approved plan containing authorisation points, at which the business case is reviewed and approved. Decisions made at authorisation points are recorded and communicated. Members of delegated authorisation bodies have sufficient representation, competence, authority and resources to enable them to make appropriate decisions. The project business case is supported by relevant and realistic information that provides a reliable basis for making authorisation decisions. The board or its delegated agents decide when independent scrutiny of projects and project management systems is required, and implement such scrutiny accordingly.

There are clearly defined criteria for reporting project status and for the escalation of risks and issues to the levels required by the organisation. The organisation fosters a culture of improvement and of frank internal disclosure of project information. Project stakeholders are engaged at a level that is commensurate with their importance to the organisation and in a manner that fosters trust.

Principles for Multi-owned Projects

Multi-owned is defined as being a project where the board shares ultimate control with other parties. The principles are:

- There should be formally agreed governance arrangements.
- There should be a single point of decision making for the project.
- There should be a clear and unambiguous allocation of authority for representing the project in contacts with owners, stakeholders and third parties.
- The project business case should include agreed, and current, definitions of project objectives, the role of each owner, their incentives, inputs, authority and responsibility.
- Each owner should assure itself that the legal competence and obligations and internal governance arrangements of co-owners, are compatible with its acceptable standards of governance for the project.
- There should be project authorisation points and limiting constraints to give owners the necessary degree of control over the project.
- There should be agreed recognition and allocation or sharing of rewards and risks taking into account ability to influence the outcome and creating incentives to foster co-operative behaviour.
- Project leadership should exploit synergies arising from multi-ownership and should actively manage potential sources of conflict or inefficiency.
- There should be a formal agreement that defines the process to be invoked and the consequences for assets and owners when a material change of ownership is considered.
- Reporting during both the project and the realisation of benefits should provide honest, timely, realistic and relevant data on progress, achievements, forecasts and risks to the extent required for good *governance by owners.
- There should be a mechanism in place to invoke independent review or scrutiny when it is in the legitimate interests of one or more of the project owners.
- There should be a dispute resolution process agreed between an owners that does not endanger the achievement of project objectives.

Roles

A key role in project governance is that of the project sponsor. The project sponsor has three main areas of responsibility which are to the board, the project manager and the project stakeholders.

The Board

For the board, the sponsor provides leadership on culture and values, owns the business case, keeps the project aligned with the organisation's strategy and portfolio direction, governs project risk, works with other sponsors, focuses on realisation of benefits, recommends opportunities to optimise cost/benefits, ensures continuity of sponsorship, provides assurance and provides feedback and lessons learnt.

The Project Manager

For the project manager, the sponsor provides timely decisions, clarifies decision making framework, clarifies business priorities and strategy, communicates business issues, provides resources, engenders trust, manages relationships, and promotes ethical working.

Project Stakeholders

For other project stakeholders, the project sponsor engages stakeholders, governs stakeholder communications, directs client relationship, directs governance of users, directs governance of suppliers and arbitrates between stakeholders.

Elements

Project governance will:

- Outline the relationships between all internal and external groups involved in the project.
- Describe the proper flow of information regarding the project to all stakeholders.
- Ensure the appropriate review of issues encountered within each project.
- Ensure that required approvals and direction for the project is obtained at each appropriate stage of the project.

Important specific elements of good project governance include:

- A compelling business case, stating the objects of the project and specifying the in-scope and out-of-scope aspects.
- A mechanism to assess the compliance of the completed project to its original objectives.

- Identifying all stakeholders with an interest in the project.
- A defined method of communication to each stakeholder.
- A set of business-level requirements as agreed by all stakeholders.
- An agreed specification for the project deliverables.
- The appointment of a project manager.
- Clear assignment of project roles and responsibilities.
- A current, published project plan that spans all project stages from project initiation through development to the transition to operations.
- A system of accurate upward status- and progress-reporting including time records.
- A central document repository for the project.
- A centrally-held glossary of project terms.
- A process for the management and resolution of issues that arise during the project.
- A process for the recording and communication of risks identified during the project.
- A standard for quality review of the key governance documents and of the project deliverables.

Project Communication Management

Project Communications Management includes the processes necessary to ensure that the information needs of the project and its stakeholders are met through development of artifacts and implementation of activities designed to achieve effective information exchange.

It is one of the ten key knowledge areas that lays the foundation of Project Management framework and plays a major role in keeping the entire project team on the same page. Without proper communication management, the entire project management framework can crumble down as a lack of communication may result in the breakdown in various processes. This can further put a negative effect on the final deliverable and thus resulting in an unsuccessful project.

Project Communications Management covers various processes which ensure that the correct project information is delivered to the correct teams and at the correct time.

Effective communication helps in establishing a healthy relationship between diverse stakeholders with varying cultural and organizational backgrounds, expertise levels, interests, and perspectives. All together they can influence the project execution and the final product. The complete process of project communications management is an aggregation of two parts:

- The first part deals with the development of a strategy that ensures an effective communication system for stakeholders.
- The second part aims to perform the activities which are required for implementing the communication strategies.

On average, a project manager spends approx 85-90% of his total project time in communicating. Thus for a project manager, maintaining an effective communication flow becomes very important. In order to do so, he must decide on a project strategy at the very beginning of the project and follow it throughout the project lifecycle. Some of the highly recommended skills for a project manager that help in establishing effective communication are listed below:

- Strong active listening.
- Proficient writing.
- Fluent speaking ability.
- Questioning and exploring ideas.
- Establishing and managing expectations.
- Motivating team to become and stay engaged.
- Guide team to enhance performance.
- Conflict resolution.
- Ability to Summarize and reiterate.
- Identify the next most efficient step.

Along with the above-listed skills, a project manager must also follow the 5 C's of communication that will help in creating an uninterrupted and systematic communication throughout the project. These five C's are:

Correct Concise Clear Coherent Controlled

In terms of project management, communication can be of various types:

- Written Communication: It is one of the most precise forms of communication that is transmitted via a correspondence medium. It can be further segregated into two forms:
  - Written Formal: Project charter, scope statement, project plan, WBS, project status, complex issues, contract related communications, Memos etc.
  - Written Informal: Email, notes, letters, regular communication with team members etc.
- Oral Communication: This type of communication has a high degree of flexibility is done through the medium of personal contact, the team meets, telephonic etc. It can be further categorized into two forms:
  - Oral Formal: Presentations, speeches, negotiations etc.
  - Oral Informal: Conversation with team members, project meetings, break-room or war-room conversations etc.
- Non-Verbal Communication: It is the most basic form of communication and approx 55% of communication is done in this form. General examples of this type of communication are facial expressions, hand movements, the tone of voice while speaking, etc.

Communication Management Benefits

- Expectations: Project communication plan helps in setting standards for how and when communication should take place. This aids a manager in maintaining the project control and ensuring that all the stakeholders receive the required information.
- Consistency: With a proper communication plan, a project manager becomes more consistent in handling project activities. Also, it gives the team members a direction following which they can communicate with the rest of the team and stakeholders consistently.
- Productivity: Efficient project management plan keeps all the team members well informed about the project happenings. This way they are always equipped with the information that they need instead of halting the work and look for missing information.

- Outcome: It establishes a proper and clear communication channel between the team and the stakeholders which ensures that the team knows exactly what the stakeholders want, need and expect from the project output.
- Controlled Communication: Communication management also ensures that the right information is delivered to the right people and at the right time. This leaves no space for ambiguity or confusion and provides a smooth flow of communication.
- Project Team Collaboration: Good communication often results in better collaboration among the team members and enhances focus on the whole.
- Effective Kickoff Session: A well-organized communication management plan gives a good kick off to the projects as it ensures that the project and methodologies are discussed and reviewed at a high-level. Once this is ensured further communication processes are expressed and agreed upon by the team members which gives them a clear picture of what will happen next and what their role in the project.

Project Communication Management Processes

The project communication management Knowledge Area is made up of the following three processes:

Plan Communications Management

Plan communication management involves various inputs, tools & techniques and outputs.

Inputs	Tools & Techniques	Outputs

• Project Charter
• Project Management Plan:
  ◦ Resource Management Plan
  ◦ Stakeholder Engagement Plan
• Project Documents:
  ◦ Requirements Documentation
	• Expert Judgment
	• Communication Requirements Analysis
	• Communication Technology
	• Communication Models
	• Communication Methods
	• Interpersonal and Team Skills:
	  ◦ Communication Styles Assessment
		• Communications Management Plan
		• Project Management Plan Updates:
		  ◦ Stakeholder Engagement Plan
		• Project Documents Updates:
		  ◦ Project Schedule

◦ Stakeholder Register • Enterprise Environmental Factors • Organizational Process Assets	◦ Political Awareness ◦ Cultural Awareness • Data Representation: ◦ Stakeholder Engagement Assessment Matrix • Meetings	◦ Stakeholder Register

Plan Communication Mangement is the initial process of project communication management knowledge area. In this process, a systematic and effective plan is developed for the activities involved in project communication. It majorly makes use of the information like the requirement of each and every stakeholder and teams, organizational assets available and the project needs. Plan communication management process is performed in periodic intervals throughout the project life cycle. It primarily helps in the timely presentation of the relevant data through a documented approach that keeps the stakeholders engaged in an efficient manner.

Manage Communications

The second process of project communication management is Manage Communications which mainly aims to collect, create, distribute, store, retrieve, manage, monitor and finally dispose of the project information in an appropriate and timely manner. It is performed throughout the project lifecycle in order to provide an effortless and efficient flow of information from the project team to stakeholders and vice-versa. This process also helps in identifying different aspects of effective communication along with the most suitable methodologies, technologies, and techniques. Furthermore, it allows the entire communication system to be more flexible by providing space for any adjustments in methods and techniques. It helps in accommodating the changing demands and needs of the stakeholders without disrupting the communication flow.

Inputs	Tools & Techniques	Outputs
• Project Management Plan: ◦ Resource Management Plan ◦ Communications Management Plan ◦ Stakeholder Engagement Plan • Project Documents: ◦ Change Log ◦ Issue Log ◦ Lessons Learned Register	• Communication Technology • Communication Methods • Communication Skills: ◦ Communication Competence ◦ Feedback ◦ Nonverbal ◦ Presentations • Project Management Information System	• Project Communications • Project Management Plan Updates: ◦ Communication Management Plans ◦ Stakeholder Engagement Plan • Project Document Updates: ◦ Issue Log

◦ Quality Report ◦ Risk Report ◦ Stakeholder Register • Work Performance Reports Enterprise Environmental Factors • Organizational Process Assets	• Project Reporting • Interpersonal and Team Skills: ◦ Active Listening ◦ Conflict Management ◦ Cultural Awareness Meeting Management ◦ Networking ◦ Political Awareness • Meetings	◦ Lessons Learned Register ◦ Project Schedule ◦ Risk Register • Stakeholder Register Organizational Process Assets Updates

Monitor Communications

Monitor Communications is the final process of the communication management knowledge area. This process ensures that all the information needs and requirements of the project and the involved stakeholders are met by its completion. It is performed throughout the project lifecycle and helps in optimizing the flow of the information as per the communication management and stakeholder engagement plan.

Below table contains the list of various inputs, tools & techniques and outputs involved in the final process of project communication management:

Inputs	Tools & Techniques	Outputs
• Project Management Plan: ◦ Resource Management Plan ◦ Communications Management Plan ◦ Stakeholder Engagement Plan • Project Documents: ◦ Issue Log ◦ Lessons Learned Register ◦ Project Communications • Work Performance Reports • Enterprise Environmental Factors • Organizational Process Assets	• Expert Judgement • Project Management Information System • Data Analysis: ◦ Stakeholder Engagement Assessment Matrix • Interpersonal & Team Skills: ◦ Observation/Conversation • Meetings	• Work Performance Information • Change Requests • Project Management Plan Updates: ◦ Communication Management Plans ◦ Stakeholder Engagement Plan • Project Document Updates: ◦ Issue Log ◦ Lessons Learned Register ◦ Stakeholder Register

Aligning Projects with Business Strategies

A project doesn't end with delivery but with the realization of its benefits to the business.

Without a clear understanding of corporate strategy, there is a real danger that projects will be delivered which are of no real value to the business – or even detrimental to the organization's end goals. Not only is this a huge waste of resources which could have been better placed elsewhere, it may also have a damaging knock on effect at programme and portfolio level.

The reason for this mismatch often comes down to project managers being tasked with delivering a project without knowledge of the wider, long term corporate goals – and therefore have no context to review progress. They are, in effect, running projects blindfolded. In other cases, the company may not actually have a defined strategy, meaning there is no baseline against which to monitor any gains.

Avoiding these outcomes demands a corporate commitment to the cause. Developing a robust strategy in the first instance and then cascading it down through the organization so that it is embedded in all programme activity.

In practical terms this means:

- Building the strategy into the project management policy. It should almost become mandatory; where critical thinking becomes second nature and no project is allowed to continue without questioning if it is still right for the company.
- Linking the project benefits to the strategy. This means recognizing that even if a project is profitable, this short-term gain can't be justified if it doesn't support overall business objectives.
- Using best practice frameworks. Much needed governance can be provided by project management tools, such as PRINCE2, which validate the business case. Adopting this method will prompt evaluation at important stages in a project's lifecycle and ensure it remains a worthwhile investment.
- Setting reviews: Having regular checkpoints will establish whether the project is still fit for purpose. Updates, steering meetings, risk assessments are all forums that can be used as an opportunity to challenge output and decide if a project still has a viable business case.
- Establishing open lines of communication: Regular contact between portfolio manager and project manager is essential. If anything changes at organizational level that could impact the project – or vice versa – then this development can be handled collaboratively.

Project Documentation

Project documentation is a vital part of Project management. The essential two functions of documentation substantiate it: To make sure that project requirements are fulfilled and to establish traceability concerning what has been done, who has done it, and when it has been done.

Documentation must lay the foundation for quality, traceability, and history for both the individual document and for the complete project documentation. It is also essential that the documentation is well arranged, easy to read, and adequate.

Project Documentation Uses

Experienced project managers excel at making and following standard templates for their project documents. They reuse successful project plans, business cases, requirement sheets, and project status reports to help them focus on their core competency of managing the project rather than balancing the unmanageable paperwork.

Project management usually follows major phases: Initiation, Planning, Control, and Closure.

Initiation	Planning	Executive	Control	Closure
Feasibility Report	Requirement Specification	Trace ability Matrix	Change Management	Technical Document
Project Charter	Design Document	Issue Tracker	Test Document	Functional Document
	Work Plan/Estimate			User Manual
				Transition/Rollout Plan
				Handover Document
				Contract Closure
				Lessons Learnt

Details of Project Documentation Phases

Feasibility Report

The purpose of a feasibility report is to investigate and showcase task requirements and to determine whether the project is worthwhile and feasible. Feasibility is verified by five primary factors – technology and system, economic, legal, operational, and schedule. Secondary feasibility factors include market, resource, culture, and financial factors.

Project Charter

Project charter is sometimes also known as the project overview statement. A project charter includes high-level planning components of a project, laying the foundation for the project. It acts as an anchor, holding you to the project's objectives and guiding you as a navigator through the milestones. It is formal approval of the project.

Requirement Specification

A requirement specification document is a complete description of the system to be developed. It contains all interactions users will have with the system as well as non-functional requirements.

Design Document

The design document showcases the high- or low-level design components of the system. The design document used for high-level design gradually evolves to include low-level design details. This document describes the architectural strategies of the system.

Work Plan/Estimate

A work plan sets out the phases, activities, and tasks needed to deliver a project. The timeframes required to deliver a project, as well as resources and milestones, are also shown in a work plan. The work plan is referred to continually throughout the project. Actual progress is reviewed daily against the stated plan and is, therefore, the most critical document to deliver projects successfully.

Traceability Matrix

A traceability matrix is a table that traces a requirement to the tests that are needed to verify that the requirement is fulfilled. A useful traceability matrix will provide backward and forward traceability: A requirement can be traced to a test and a test to a requirement.

Issue Tracker

An issue tracker manages and maintains a list of issues. It helps add issues, assign them to people, and track the status and current responsibilities. It also helps develop a knowledge base that contains information on resolutions to common problems.

Change Management Document

A change management document is used to capture progress and to record all changes made to a system. This helps in linking unanticipated adverse effects of a change.

Test Document

A test document includes a test plan and test cases. A test case is a detailed procedure that thoroughly tests a feature or an aspect of a feature. While a test plan describes what to test, a test case describes how to perform a particular test.

Technical Document

The technical document includes product definition and specification, design, manufacturing/development, quality assurance, product/system liability, product presentation, description of features, functions, and interfaces, safe and correct use, service and repair of a technical product as well as its safe disposal.

Functional Document

Functional specifications define the inner workings of the proposed system. They do not include the specification of how the system function will be implemented. Instead, this project documentation focuses on what various other agents (such as people or a computer) might observe when interacting with the system.

User Manual

User Manual is the standard operating procedure for the system.

Transition/Rollout Plan

The rollout plan includes detailed instructions on how to implement the system in an organization. It consists of the schematic planning of the rollout steps and phases. It also describes the training plan for the system.

Handover Document

The handover document is a synopsis of the system with a listing of all the deliverables of the system.

Contract Closure

Contract closure refers to the process of completing all tasks and terms that are mentioned as deliverable and outstanding upon the initial drafting of the contract. This is only applicable in cases of outsourced projects.

Project Networks

Project network is the technological framework, an online service or the web site intended for provision of a possibility of self-organization to the participants possessing key competences in project team for execution of actions with initially set purposes, achievement of which defines project completion.

Theoretical Aspects

Studying specialized networks to which the offered design networks belong in theoretical aspect is far from end - it is connected with an advancing of practical application of network structures over their theoretical research. At the same time use of modern opportunities of information technologies allows to take a new look at the processes of formation of the scientific, technical and technological design groups and all aspects connected with the process of initiation and performance of work on the projects. Many, at first sight, diverse, researches in technology, sociology, telecommunication and other sciences are based on a postulate of not reducibility of structural descriptions to uniform models of specialized networks. However any researches and developments which are carried out with use of information technologies in many areas, it is possible to consider through a prism of classical project management. In this regard the theory developed is applicable for the social networks, but obviously needs a certain modification.

Approaches in Research of Project Networks

At the moment, theories of social networks research, generally the following questions:

- Statistical properties of networks.
- Models of networks.
- Forecasting of the processes happening in networks.

In applied researches are used typical characteristics, such as: Network size, network density, degree and density of centrality and equivalence.

The general approaches applied to the analysis of social networks can be applied also to the analysis of project networks, it is natural taking into account certain specifics of initiation and maintaining projects. First of all, these specifics are reflected in elements which form a project network.

For further research of project networks it is reasonable to enter some concepts. At the initial stage the project network is in the "sleep mode", so there is a regular, for a social network, information exchange between potential participants of project teams and, therefore, in a network "traditional agents" or other actors. After that, within processes of initiation of projects, there are project teams that are expressed in the emergence of nodes with the increased concentration of connections, the project network leaves "sleep mode" and begins to carry out the functions on ensuring implementation of the initiated projects. For designation of the working teams that the nodes made in a project network with the increased concentration of connections between actors the concept of the actor of 1 level is entered. This basic concept for a project network as it designates availability in a project network of the operating command executing the project. If actors of 1 level establish connection among themselves, for example, within a matrix organizational structure, the concept of the actor 2 levels is entered. The graphical representation of actors of 1 and 2 levels is given in figure.

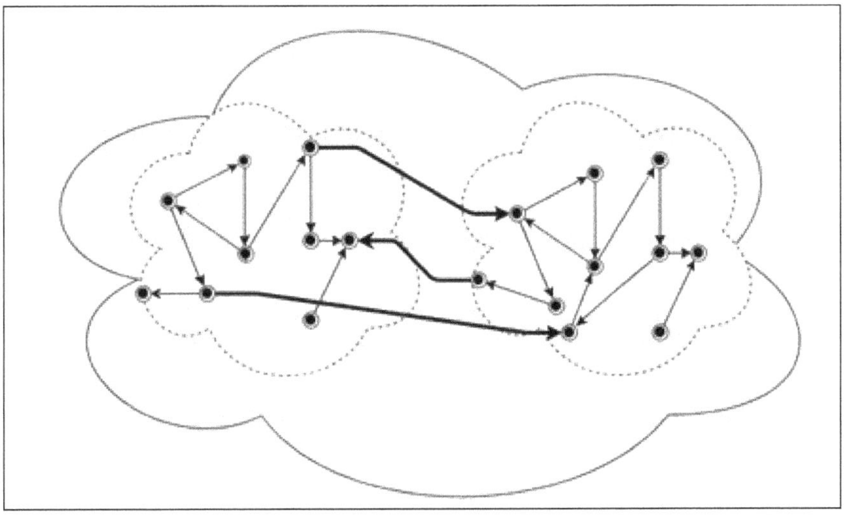

The graphical representation of actors of 1 and 2 levels.

One of important elements of the research of project networks is creation of models which reflect specifics of their functioning. Applying the classification given in for the creation of one of the models of project networks, it is possible to suggest to use statistical models of social networks and, in particular, model of weak connections.

In the modern society these specialized networks of the informal relations allow to find a job, through "on-line exchange", to carry out information exchange, to resolve problems, passing the government and other traditional institutions, in some cases, they allow to receive orders on accomplishment small on amount of works (freelancers). There are bases to believe that increase of the status of a professional group (including project), leads to increase in a flow of information in networks of informal social and professional contacts. And, so-called weak information connections, i.e. connections with a little famous colleagues or project teams, can be more effective, than "strong connections" — with permanent employees, at the same time manifestation of effect of a synergy is not excluded.

In case of the creation of models of project networks, by analogy with social networks, it is necessary to enter the concept of clusterization. For example, if in the network count are available connection between tops 1 and 2, and between 2 and 3 it inevitably leads to connection between 1 and 3. In such models concepts of elasticity and coefficient of correlation of a network have an important role.

If to apply concept of an accidental network to the description of a specific social or project network, then from mathematics line items it will not be correct. In work it is specified that it is possible to pass to the concept of an accidental network through creation of statistical ensemble of networks (a set of networks) in which everyone the specific network has the probability of implementation, that is each network of ensemble has own statistical weight. After creation of such ensemble it is possible to calculate average value for some size in an accidental network, by averaging of this size on all implementations, accepting in attention their statistical weight. This, to a certain extent simplified approach is realized in accidental networks which are usually represented by accidental columns (Erdos-Renyi model). At this model in which statistical ensemble counts with a quantity of nodes X and a quantity of connections Y are provided all columns (networks) have the identical statistical weight of implementation. From this a conclusion follows that the probability of existence of connection between any two nodes is identical to such networks.

One of key characteristics of accidental networks, which is important for understanding of properties and processes which in them happen is such statistical characteristic of an accidental network as distribution of nodes on number of connections (DD, degree distribution).

The characteristic of DD, distribution of knots on number of connections of P(q) is probability that incidentally chosen knot in a casual network has the power of q:

$$P(q) = \{N(q)\} / N$$

Here {N(q)} — average of knots of degree of q in networks, at the same time averaging undertakes on the whole ensemble. The total number of knots at all members of this ensemble is identical and can be expressed as:

$$N = \sum_{i=1}^{n} q\{N(q)\}$$

Researches have shown that distribution of nodes, in the considered accidental networks, on number suitable connections can be described according to the distribution law of Poisson. From this it is possible to draw a conclusion that in classical accidental networks approximately identical number of connections approaches nodes and there are no dominating nodes with a large number of connections (hubs). From the point of view of such approach the processes happening on small social networks and some types of specialized networks can be studied.

On number of connections on large social networks it is reasonable to apply sedate or exponential distribution to the description of probability of distribution of nodes. The conducted pilot studies have shown that real large networks have slowly falling down distribution of nodes on number of connections, and nodes, with the dominating number of connections, constitute noticeable part from connections of all network structure. Sedate distribution $p(q) = e^{-\lambda^* q}$ in case of great values of q - a regular example of slowly falling down distribution of nodes on number of connections. In figure (a) distribution of accidental process under Poisson's law and an approximate graphic representation of a network for q = 4, and is given in figure (b) for normal, exponential and sedate laws for which the approximate graphic representation of a network is given.

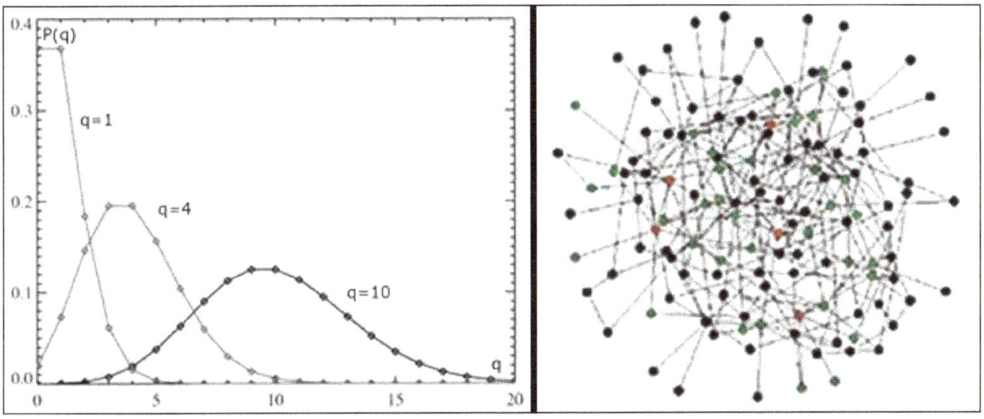

(a) Distribution of accidental process under Poisson's law and an approximate graphic representation of a network for q=4.

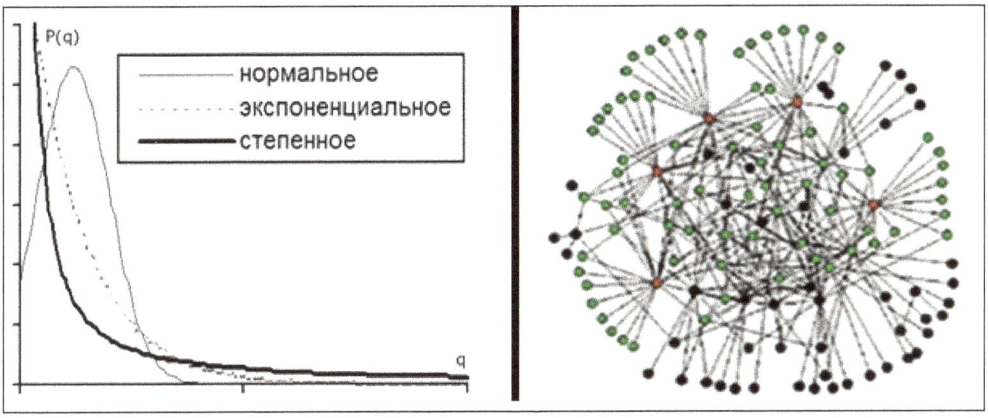

(b) Distribution of accidental process for normal, exponential and sedate laws and an approximate graphic representation of a network (Sedate distribution of connections in nodes).

The important work allowing to understand one of approaches to creation of project networks is research P. Albert and L. Barabasha, on topology of computer networks which within pilot studies has found and actors concentrators (hubs) in different types of networks having the dominating number of communications in comparison with "regular" actors have theoretically proved. They have entered concept of the scale free networks and have revealed two conditions in case of accomplishment of which this type of networks arises:

- Growth condition: After formation of a network with some small number of actors of n1, on each discrete temporary step the new actor with n (n ≤ n1) communications is added, and n condition ≤ is satisfied by n1 which connect the educated actor to n various already existing actors.
- Condition of preference of accession: In case of the choice of actors with whom the new actor establishes connection, it is considered that the probability of joining of the new actor to existing depends on former number of communications of the last.

The term "free scale network" means that in a network there are no nodes with some typical number of communications. The free scale network is a characteristic distinctive feature their increased resistance to damages. The model authentically interprets project networks as actors of 1 level poorly interact with each other and the project, being the one-time entity possesses final time of existence, but in case of offices of projects in a network actors concentrators (hubs) begin to be formed. According to the theory R. Albert and L. Barabasha concentrators are often surrounded with smaller concentrators, and those, in turn smaller, etc. It also provides the increased stability of this kind of network structures. Loss of one of concentrators not crucially for a network as general communications will remain due to existence of other concentrators. Availability in the free scale networks Albert-Barabasha of concentrators of different "amount" does not contradict the fact that in project networks, by determination, teams of various number will be present and function. The larger the project is – the bigger number of actors unites in the actor of 1 level that is in project team. However questions of interaction between actors of various levels need additional research. The internal infrastructure of project networks will be determined their properties and to develop by the principles or self-organization, or under external impact (influence) on a network.

Based on the given material it is possible to make the assumption that according to the characteristic of the DD network can be revolutionizing. At the formation stage, for example, of some social or project network, distribution of nodes on number of communications will submit to Poisson's law, and with growth of its popularity users will have expressed nodes concentrators and the characteristic of DD shall be described by the sedate law. It is not excluded that in case of recession of popularity users on a social network will have the return process that is the network will "breathe". Thus, a network, social or project, it is possible to research as the dynamic system possessing a certain initial condition. This approach allows studying dynamics of the processes happening in network structures in case of process of transition of system of one condition in another. Set of all admissible conditions of dynamic system usually is represented through its phase space. Questions on the modeling of project networks through their representation as dynamic systems with specific initial conditions and research of their phase spaces are of a certain scientific and practical interest, but do not enter a task of this work.

Universality the scale free networks specifies a way of further development of idea of creation and enhancement of project networks. So availability of larger, than from formation of numerous project teams, or even offices of the projects, actors concentrators in a network having a large number of communications can be treated as emergence in project networks of virtual associations on an industry sign, for example on nanotechnology, biology, the software, etc. Integration of such project network into the Unified information system of the Russian Academy of Sciences or into a scientific and innovative network of Russia can be the following level (emergence of super concentrators). Within international cooperation the Canadian "Network of the centers of perfection (NCE)", the German program "Network Management of the East (NEMO)", the French network of the scientific researches CNRS or such programs of the EU as "Eureka" and the European Technological Platforms can act as super concentrators of a project network, for example.

The analysis of the main approaches to the research and the modeling of project networks is at the initial stage. It is required to execute a large volume of work for creation of mathematical models of project networks of various degree of complexity and to determine a technique for studying of the processes happening in these structures. In case of the description of some properties of project networks (correlation, transitivity, structure of consolidation), at the moment, we have to rely on the factors possessing high degree of uncertainty.

The creation of theoretical bases of the analysis and synthesis of project networks will be important for practical implementation of this perspective view of the network structure.

Project Assurance

Project or Programme Assurance is a discipline that seeks to provide an independent and objective oversight of the likely future performance of major projects for those responsible for sanctioning, financing or insuring such undertakings. The discipline has emerged as a response to consistent problems in major projects and the need to provide confidence for project or programme stakeholders of technologically advanced, high capital or high risk projects.

Project/Programme Assurance use technical, strategic and contractual expertise to audit project plans and personnel and develop a forecast of likely technical, economic, and safety performance and critical success factors. Project assurance professionals typically serve and report to the Board of Directors of private companies and publicly held companies, governmental bodies, banking concerns (development, investment and commercial banks), insurance, surety companies, and any other entity that is responsible for project investments that often exceed $1 billion. Project assurance is in contrast with related disciplines of project management, project benchmarking, value assurance or phase–gate model and project risk assessment. It is particularly well suited for projects with a major financial decision point beyond which revisions become exceptionally expensive.

An eight-step assurance procedure was outlined in a 2013 paper produced by the BT Centre for Major Programme Management at the University of Oxford. The key features of this approach to project assurance are a critical review of the project plan and personnel by an expert independent organisation with expertise in benchmarking and project execution. Project assurance is also recognised by PRojects IN Controlled Environments (PRINCE2) – a project management methodology, in an attempt to address the need in project organisation for monitoring all aspects of the project's performance and products independently of the project manager.

According to the Office of Government Commerce, Project Assurance helped manage risk and improved delivery confidence. Project Assurance supported SROs (Senior Responsible Owner) and others responsible for successful delivery whilst providing funders and other stakeholders with the confidence that the project could deliver to time, budget and quality. This they called the Project Assurance Function. The UK Government has also set up a project assurance organisation called the Major Projects Authority that works with HM Treasury to grow project assurance capabilities in Government and deliver project assurance services for high risk Government-sponsored projects.

The term has expanded in its use to a more complete solution. It is now recognised that the original approach of audits of hard disciplines (methods, tools, processes) and soft skills (leadership, people management) need to be extended to include elements such as the context, content and complexity of a project and its environment - with appropriate levels of granularity and precision – to identify critical success factors and barriers to success.

In the U.S., Project or Programme (Program) Assurance has been defined as:

> "Project Assurance: An objective examination and independent assessment of a Capital Investment (Portfolio, Program, and/or Project) risks, controls, processes, and governance. Focus areas may include risk, financial, performance, compliance, system security, due diligence and/or dispute resolution engagements. Mega-Project Assurance would be specific to (Portfolios, Program, and/or Projects) that exceed $1 Billion in estimated investment value."

> "The core concepts of Mega Project Assurance: Risk is governable, leadership is accountable, cost must be properly managed and is recoverable, efficiency is attainable, fraud and waste are nearly preventable, and failure is unacceptable."

Project Quality Management

Project quality management is the process through which quality is managed and maintained throughout a project. While the context may imply that "quality" means "perfection," in this case, is usually more about ensuring quality consistency throughout a project. However, what is exactly meant by "quality" is beholden to what the customer or stakeholder needs from the project, and therefore can be different on a per-project basis.

Modern quality management and project management are complementary. They both emphasize customer satisfaction and the underlying belief that quality leads to customer satisfaction. The main objective in project quality management is making sure that the project meets the needs it was originally created to meet—nothing more, nothing less.

In other words, to ensure quality, you must meet the needs of the stakeholder. Meeting or exceeding requirements, however, is not part of project quality management. Quality is "the degree to which a set of inherent characteristics fulfill requirements." The project manager and project management team have a special responsibility to balance quality and grade (a category or rank assigned to products or services having the same functional use but different technical characteristics).

This responsibility ensures quality expectations are met. This means that it might be possible and reasonable to have a quality, low-grade product, but it is never acceptable to have a low-quality product. At the beginning of the project, requirements are determined with the stakeholders. These requirements become the foundation for the work of the project. After that, the project manager's job is to ensure that the work is done with no extras included. Quality is not about giving the customer extras or completing extra work. The notion of extras is often based on possibly erroneous perceptions of what you believe the customer wants. These extras add time, possible costs and other impacts to a project but do not always result in increased customer satisfaction.

Project quality management consists of three major processes:

- Quality management planning: This involves identifying the quality requirements and standards for the project and product. The goal of the project quality management should be clearly shared with all stakeholders, and appropriate tasks should be delegated to those responsible.
- Quality assurance: This involves auditing the quality requirements and quality control results to ensure appropriate quality standards are used. When standards are not met or goals aren't achieved, necessary steps and corrective actions should be employed to fix these issues.
- Quality control: This involves monitoring and recording the results of quality activities to assess performance and recommend necessary changes.

What is the Definition of "Quality" in "Project Quality Management"?

The definition of quality is central to understanding these three processes. To be able to define quality, you need to be clear about the meaning of the following terms:

- Validation: Assurance that the product meets the agreed-upon needs.
- Verification: Compliance with requirements.
- Precision: Repeatable measures in a tight grouping.
- Accuracy: Closeness of a measure to the true value.
- Tolerance: Range of acceptable results.

What should a Good Project Quality Management Plan Entail?

The quality management planning process determines the quality standards that are applicable to the project and devising a way to satisfy them. The goal is to create a quality management plan which documents the following:

- The way the team will implement the quality policy.
- The way the quality of both the project and the product will be assured during the project.
- The resources required to ensure quality.
- The additional activities necessary to carry out the quality plan.

Identifying these items might require updates to the project management plan or schedule, which emphasizes the evolving nature of the plan and project documents. The plan, like other components created during the planning phase, is written by the project manager with input from stakeholders. When planning for quality on a project follow the corporate quality policies that are in place. If a corporate quality policy does not exist, the project team should create one for the project. The project team might even need to adapt an existing policy to better suit the nature of the project.

Project Accounting

Project accounting is a specialised form of accounting that corresponds to the ever-evolving needs of project delivery, which helps adequately track, report and analyse financial results and implications. This includes the practice of creating financial reports specifically designed to track the financial progress of projects, which can then be used by managers to aid project management.

Traditionally, project accounting and its principles were largely used to track and report predominantly large construction, engineering and government projects. Today, project management delivery methodologies have expanded into several other sectors, including financial, technology and legal. Subsequently, project accounting has needed to follow to cover these areas to ensure corresponding financial tracking and financial implications are understood and considered.

The need for project accounting arose as a specialised field from the nature of projects being treated as separate temporary individualised entities set up for the purpose of delivering one or more business products. As the nature of each project may be different from the business-as-usual activities run by the business, existent management accounting and financial accounting skills were recognised as insufficient to accurately advise on the treatment and financial reporting of a project. Hence, a new field emerged within the accounting sphere – project accounting.

Project accounting therefore includes:

- A separate accounting system or cost centre to track and report project specific transactions, with project revenues, costs, assets and liabilities identified and allocated to the project.
- Frequent reporting, with the frequency often increasing as the project approaches completion.
- A layer of simplified reporting, including key performance indicators relevant to whether the project is on or off track. For instance traffic lights on a dashboard.
- A process for identifying project related transactions in the main accounting system and allocating or apportioning these to the project accounting system.
- Forecasting of costs to complete the project. Key stakeholders are often not only focused on the costs incurred to date, but also those committed and the expected final cost.

Projects differ from the day-to-day business-as-usual (BAU) activities in that they frequently cross organisational boundaries, may last for anything from a few days or weeks to a number of years, during which time budgets may also be revised many times. They may also be one of a number of projects that make up a larger overall project or program.

Consequently, in a project management environment costs (both direct and overhead) and revenues are also allocated to projects, which may be subdivided into a work breakdown structure, and grouped together into project hierarchies. Project accounting permits reporting at any such level that has been defined, and often allows comparison with historical as well as current budgets.

Project accounting is commonly used by government contractors, where the ability to account for costs by contract (and sometimes contract line item, or CLIN) is usually a requirement for interim payments.

Percentage-of-completion is frequently independently assessed by a project manager, program management officer (PMO) and project accountant. It includes the continuous recognition of revenues and income related to longer-term projects. By doing this, the seller is able to identify some gain or loss relevant to a project in every accounting period that is ongoing active. Funding advances and actual-to-budget cost variances are calculated using the project budget adjusted to percent-of-completion.

Where labor costs are a significant portion of overall project cost, it is usually necessary for employees to fill out a timesheet in order to generate the data to allocate project costs.

The capital budget processes of corporations and governments are chiefly concerned with major investment projects that typically have upfront costs and longer term benefits. Investment go/no-go decisions are largely based on net present value assessments. Project accounting of the costs and benefits can provide crucially important feedback on the quality of these important decisions.

An interesting specialised form of project accounting is production accounting, which tracks the costs of individual movie and television episode film production costs. A movie studio will employ production accounting to track the costs of its many separate projects.

The project accountant requires the knowledge of management accounting and financial accounting. They combine the complexities of cross-functional involvement, as well as, project delivery frameworks and methodologies used by the business. Within a project delivery framework, the project accountant plays a dual role of:

- Gatekeeper reporting into the business the true and fair view of how the project is tracking financially.
- Advisor advising the project team as to the financial treatment and implications of the various decisions being made, their impact on both the project and the business.

The key benefit of this is the project accountant ultimately plays a Translator role between the project and other finance/accounting functions.

The role of a project accountant depends on the project needs, but as a basic function, the project accountant position is accountable for monitoring the progress of projects, investigating variances, approving expenses, and ensuring that project billings are issued to customers and payments collected.

Percentage of Completion Method

The percentage-of-completion method permits companies to record profits as development is made toward the finishing of the project. This method is not to be used when compelling uncertainty's about the percentage of completion of the remaining costs to be incurred. The method instead works at its finest when it is rationally likely to estimate the stages of the project in process.

The percentage-of-completion may be measured in any of the resulting ways:

- Cost-to-cost method: This is an example of the contract cost acquired to date the total expected cost. The price of the products already bought for a contract however have not yet been installed should not be added in the perseverance of the percentage of completion of a project, not unless they were particularly created for the contract. Also, assign the cost of equipment over the contract course, rather than direct, unless title to the supplies is being transported to the customer.

- Efforts-expended method: This is the share of effort consumed to date in comparison to the total effort expected for the agreement. E.g. the percentage of completion may possibly be established on direct work hours, machine hours, or material size.
- Units-of-delivery-method: This is the portion of units delivered to the buyer to the overall number of units to be brought under the terms of a contract. It should only be in use when the builder produces a number of units to the requirements of a buyer. The recognition is established on:
    - For revenue, the contract price of units delivered.
    - For expenses, the costs reasonably allocable to the units delivered.

However, the necessary steps are the following:

- Subtract the total predicted contract costs from total approximated revenues to appear at the total estimated gross margin.
- Measure the range of process toward completion.
- Increase the total likely contract revenue by the estimated finishing percentage to arrive at the total amount of revenue that can be acknowledged.
- Subtract the contract revenue allowed to date through the foregoing period from the complete amount of revenue that be accepted. Recognise the development in the current accounting period.
- Consider the cost of the received revenue in the same manner. This means raising the same percentage of completion by the total supposed contract cost, and subtracting the amount formerly realised to arrive at the cost of collected revenue to be recognised in the current accounting period.

Calculations

The following calculation is used to determine the completion percentage:

Percent Complete = Cost Incurred to Date/Total Cost Estimate

The current period revenue to be recognised during production would then be:

Current Period Revenue = (Percent Complete x Total Contract Revenue) - Revenue Recognised in Prior Periods

Tools and Techniques 4

- Schedule Compression
- Phase-gate Model
- Constructability
- Value of Work Done
- Value Breakdown Structure
- Responsibility Assignment Matrix
- Program Evaluation and Review Technique
- Graphical Path Method
- Critical Path Method
- SWOT Analysis

There are various tools and techniques that are used for project management such as schedule compression, phase-gate model, value breakdown structure, graphical path method, critical path method, SWOT analysis, integrated master plan, etc. The topics elaborated in this chapter will help in gaining a better perspective of various tools and techniques used in project management.

Schedule Compression

Schedule compression offers two important techniques for scheduling time so projects are executed on schedule. Understanding these techniques and their application in compressing schedules can be very useful, whether in professional or personal spheres.

Schedule compression refers to techniques used when a project manager wants to shorten the duration of the project without changing the scope of the project. It can be used when a project falls behind schedule and needs to catch up or to finish the project sooner than originally scheduled.

The two techniques you can use to shorten the project duration while maintaining the project scope are fast tracking and crashing.

Fast Tracking

Fast tracking is a technique where activities that would have been performed sequentially using the original schedule are performed in parallel. In other words, fast tracking a project means the activities are worked on simultaneously instead of waiting for each piece to be completed separately. But fast tracking can only be applied if the activities in question can actually be overlapped.

When you need to compress a schedule, you should consider this technique first, because fast tracking usually does not involve any costs. This technique simply rearranges the activities in the original schedule.

Although fast tracking may not result in an increase in the cost, it leads to an increase in the risk, because activities now are performed in parallel may lead to needing to rework or rearrange the project. And, reworking the project can cause the project to lose even more time.

As a project manager, you'll have to weigh the pros and cons of fast tracking to understand whether it will be worthwhile to undertake increased risk.

Crashing

Crashing is the technique to use when fast tracking has not saved enough time on the project schedule. With this technique, resources are added to the project for the least cost possible. Cost and schedule tradeoffs are analyzed to determine how to obtain the greatest amount of compression for the least incremental cost. And crashing is expensive because more resources are added to the project.

Crashing analyzes and categorizes activities based on the lowest crash cost per unit time, allowing the team working the project to identify the activities that will be able to deliver the most value at the least incremental cost. The results of a crash analysis are usually presented in a crash graph, where activities with the flattest slope are the ones that will be considered first—they lead to an equal amount of time savings, but have a smaller increase in cost. Crashing only works if the additional resources will actually achieve completing the project sooner.

When the crashing approach is used, any additional costs associated with rushing the project are reviewed against the possible benefits of completing the project within a shorter time span. In addition, you should consider other items when performing a crash analysis, including adding more resources to the project, allowing additional overtime, and paying extra to receive delivery of critical components more quickly, among others.

Phase-gate Model

A phase-gate process (also referred to as a stage-gate process or waterfall process), is a project management technique in which an initiative or project (e.g., new product development, software development, process improvement, business change) is divided into distinct *stages* or *phases*, separated by decision points (known as *gates*).

At each gate, continuation is decided by (typically) a manager, steering committee, or governance board. The decision is made on forecasts and information available at the time, including the business case, risk analysis, and availability of necessary resources (e.g., money, people with correct competencies).

Phases

The traditional phase-gate process has five phases with four gates. The phases are:

- Scoping
- Build business case
- Development
- Testing and validation
- Launch

Ahead of this process there is often a preliminary phase called *ideation* or *discovery*, and after the fifth phase the process typically ends with the post-launch review. Major new products go through the full five-phase process. Moderate risk projects (such as extensions and enhancements) often use a reduced 3-phase version, which combines the scoping with the business case phase, and developing with the testing phase. Very simple changes (such as a marketing request) may be executed using a light two-phase process, where the launch is rolled into development and testing too.

Gates

Gates provide a point during the process where an assessment of the quality of an idea is undertaken. It includes three main issues:

- Quality of execution: Checks whether the previous step is executed in a quality fashion.

- Business rationale: Does the project continue to look like an attractive idea from an economic and business perspective.
- Action plan: The proposed action plan and the requested resources reasonable and sound.

A gate can lead to one of five possible results: Go, kill, hold, recycle, or conditional go. Gates have a common structure and consist of three main elements:

- Inputs: What the project manager and team deliver to the decision point. These deliverables are decided at the output of the previous gate, and are based on a standard menu of deliverables for each gate.
- Criteria: Questions or metrics on which the project is judged in order to determine a result (go/kill/hold/recycle) and make a prioritization decision.
- Outputs: Results of the gate review—a decision (go/kill/hold/recycle), along with an approved action plan for the next gate, and a list of deliverables and date for the next gate.

Discovery or Ideation

Deciding what projects the company desires and is capable to pursue. During this phase it is common for companies to take part in idea generation activities such as brainstorming or other group thinking exercises. Once the idea generation team has selected a project that they would like to go forward with, it must be passed on to the first gate and therefore screened by the organization's decision makers.

When searching for new product ideas it is beneficial for an organization to look to the outside world to suggest business opportunities. Using methods such as those found in empathic design can be quite helpful. Communicating with customers to understand how and why they use products can produce great strides in idea generation. Specifically, communicating with lead users can provide great feedback to the developers, as these customers are most likely to feel most passionately about the product. In addition to communication with lead users, it may be helpful for developers to communicate with suppliers. By understanding all of the types of business that their materials are being used for, developers may be able to act upon previously untapped possibilities.

Scoping

The first phase of the product development process is scoping. During this step the main goal is to evaluate the product and its corresponding market. The researchers must recognize the strengths and weaknesses of the product and what it is going to offer to the potential consumer. The competition must also be evaluated during this phase. It is important for the researchers to understand who and what is already in the market as well as what can potentially be developed. By determining the relative level of threat from competitors, the management team will be able to recognize whether or not they should go forward with the production of the product.

Building the Business Case and Plan

Once the new product passes through the gate at the end of the scoping phase, the next phase in the phase-gate process is building the business case and plan. This is the last phase of concept development where it is crucial for companies to perform a solid analysis before they begin developing the product. This phase is generally difficult, complex, and resource-intensive. However, companies must put forth a strong effort in this phase for it is directly related to the success and development of a new product. There are four main steps that comprise this phase: Product definition and analysis, building the business case, building the project plan, and feasibility review.

Product Definition and Analysis

The first step, product definition and analysis, is composed of a series of activities that will provide the information to define and justify the development of a new product. One of the first of these activities is the user needs and wants study where customer value is determined. This addresses questions about the product such as what benefits does the product provide and what features should the product have. During this time the company should conduct surveys and interviews with existing and potential customers, along with staff members. Next, the company must conduct a market analysis. They must determine the market size and segmentation, rate of growth, customer trends and behavior, and what channels reach these customers. Once the market analysis is complete the company must then conduct a competitive analysis. It is important to know how your competitors operate in addition to their strengths and weaknesses. This will not only help you build a great product, but will also help in determining how and where to launch your new product.

Together these activities will help define the product and provide a foundation for the marketing strategy. Next, the company must build a technically feasible product concept, which includes the substance and methods needed to produce the new product. Once this is completed the company can then produce a production and operations cost analysis along with a market and launch costs analysis. Next, the company can begin to test the concept they have developed. This is when early prototypes are developed and presented to staff and consumers to gain feedback and gauge customer reaction. From this the company can make the necessary changes and see the sales potential of the product. This feedback will also help the company build a solid product definition. Lastly, the company will then conduct the business analysis, risk analysis, and financial analysis of the new product.

Building the Business Case

The business case is a document that defines the product and provides the rationale for developing it. This document will vary in format amongst companies, but the primary components are the following: Results of the activities of product definition and analysis; legal and regulatory requirements; safety, health, and environmental considerations; assumptions needed to draw the conclusions made, and why it is believed they are valid and reasonable; and out-of-bounds criteria that indicate certain changes/events which will mandate an emergency business case review. This document will be referred to throughout the development process and edited when necessary.

Building the Project Plan

The project plan includes: A scheduled list of tasks and events along with timelines for milestones throughout the development process; the personnel, time, and financial resources needed to complete the project; and an expected launch date for the release of the new product.

Feasibility Review

The last step of building the business case and plan is the feasibility review. This is when management, along with other departments of the company, reviews the rationale for pursuing the product. They analyze the information provided by the previous steps in this process to decide whether or not the product should move forward. If it is decided to be pursued then it passes through gate two and moves on to the product development phase.

Development

During the development phase, plans from previous steps are actually executed. The product's design and development is carried out, including some early, simple tests of the product and perhaps some early customer testing. The product's marketing and production plans are also developed. It is important that the company adheres to their overall goal of the project, which is reflected in these production and marketing plans. Doing this will allow them to definitively decide who they will market their product to and how they will get the product to that target audience. The development team maps out a realistic timeline with specific milestones that are described as SMART: *specific, measurable, actionable, realistic,* and *time-bound*. The timeline is frequently reviewed and updated, helping the team stay on task and giving management information about the product's progress. In the development phase, the product builds momentum as the company commits more resources to the project and makes full use of cross-functional teamwork as the marketing, technical, manufacturing, and sales departments all come together to offer their expert opinions. Having a diversified and parallel development phase ensures that the product continues to meet the company's technical and financial goals. A diverse team allows specific roles and leadership positions to develop as team members make contributions using their strongest attributes. With members having clearly defined roles, tasks can be performed concurrently ensuring a much more efficient development process. The ultimate deliverable of the development phase is the prototype, which will undergo extensive testing and evaluation in the next phase of the process.

Testing and Validation

This phase provides validation for the entire project. Areas that will be evaluated include: the product itself, the production/manufacturing process, customer acceptance, and the financial merit of the project. This phase includes three types of testing: *near testing*, *field testing*, and *market testing*.

Near Testing

The main objective of *near testing* is to find any bugs or issues with a product. A key point to remember, is that the product is no longer a prototype and that it has almost all the features of the commercial product. Testing will be done initially by in-house staff, and customers and partners who are close to the firm. It is important to ensure that those testing have an understanding of how the product should perform, so they know what it should or shouldn't be doing. Members of the research and development team are usually present to observe the participants using the product and take any notes or data that may be useful.

Field Testing

Field testing, or beta testing, is done by those who can provide valuable feedback on the product. This usually lasts a long period of time and the participants can include customers, partners, or anyone who is not familiar with the producing company. At this juncture the product fully resembles its planned launch version in all aspects; therefore the participants' interaction rate will be higher because they know all the features and benefits. During this phase there are three primary objectives to be achieved. The first objective is to see how much the participant is interested. It is also worthwhile to note which individual attribute they prefer and if they would buy the product. Next, determine how the customer uses the product and evaluate its durability. Confirm the environment in which the customers will be using the product. Recording and analyzing customer feedback is the final step in the field testing phase. This feedback may be used to help inform any minor design improvements that need to be made. The sales and marketing team will also be a beneficiary of field testing feedback; they can use this information to help focus their sales presentation.

Market Testing

Unlike the other two test activities, market testing is considered optional. A solid marketing and launch plan along with confidence in the product's ability to sell helps to inform the key decision makers at the test and validation gate. If there is any uncertainty in the marketing or launch plans there are two options to consider. First, a simulated market test may be run, in which customers will be exposed to new products in an advertising and purchasing situation. The goal of this test is to obtain an early forecast of sales and make any necessary adjustments to the marketing plan. The second test involves trial sales, and is done through specific channels, regions, or consumer demographics.

Product Launch

The product launch is the culmination of the product having passed all previous gates. The producer must come up with a marketing strategy to generate customer demand for the product. The producer must also decide how large they anticipate the market for a new product to be and thus determine the size of their starting volume production. Part of the launch phase is training sales and support personnel to be familiar with the product so that they can assist in sales of this product. Setting a product price is an aspect of the product launch that the producer must consider. They should avoid either undershooting or overpricing the potential market. Finally, distribution is a major decision making part of the launch process. Selecting a distributor or value-added reseller for a product must be done with careful thought and potential sales in mind.

Having a smooth launch process that includes effective marketing and a knowledgeable and prepared sales force may result in faster time to profit due to early customer acceptance.

Effective Gates

Most firms suffer from having far too many projects in their product development pipelines, for the limited resources available. "Gates with teeth" help to prune the development portfolio of weak projects and deal with a gridlocked pipeline. Also, a robust innovation strategy, coupled with strategic buckets, refocuses resources on high value development initiatives.

Note that gates are not merely project review points, status reports or information updates. Rather, they are tough decision meetings, where the critical go/kill and prioritization decisions are made on projects. Thus the gates become the quality control check points in the process ensuring that you do the right projects and also do the projects right.

Gates must have clear and visible criteria so that senior managers can make go/kill and prioritization decisions objectively. Most importantly, these criteria must be effective—that is, they must be operational (easy to use), realistic (make use of available information) and discriminating (differentiate the good projects from the mediocre ones). These criteria can be:

- Must meet: Knock-out questions in a check list, designed to kill poor projects outright.

- Should meet: Highly desirable characteristics which are rated and added in a point-count scheme.

A sample list of criteria is shown below, from which a scorecard can be developed that can then be used to score projects at a gate meeting.

- Must meet (checklist - yes/no):
  - Strategic alignment (fits business unit strategy).
  - Reasonable likelihood of technical feasibility.
  - Meet EH&S policies.
  - Positive return versus risk.
- Should meet (scored on 0-10 scale):
  - Strategic:
    - Degree to which projects aligns with business unit strategy.
    - Strategic importance.
  - Product advantage:
    - Unique benefits.
    - Meets customer needs better than existing or competing product.
    - Value for money.
  - Market attractiveness:
    - Market size.
    - Market growth.
    - Competitive situation.
  - Synergies (leverages core competencies):
    - Marketing synergies.
    - Technological synergies.
    - Manufacturing/processing synergies.
  - Technical feasibility:
    - Technical gap.

    - Complexity.
    - Technical uncertainty.
  - Operational viability:
    - Go to market.
    - Sales, marketing, and billing.
    - Support and operation.
  - Risk versus return:
    - Expected profitability (e.g., net present value).
    - Return (e.g., internal rate of return).
    - Payback period.
    - Certainty of return.

If the answers are "no" or "low" to many of these questions, the decision should be to send the project back for reconsideration, (such as, to adjust the scope, timelines, funding, or solution) or to kill it off altogether.

Advantages and Disadvantages

There are a number of advantages to using the phase-gate process for product development, which typically result from its ability to identify problems and assess progress before the project's conclusion. Poor projects can be quickly rejected by disciplined use of the process. When using the phase-gate process on a large project, the process can help reduce complexity of what could be a large and limiting innovation process into a straightforward rule-based approach. When a phase-gate process incorporates cost and fiscal analysis tools such as net present value, the organization can potentially be provided with quantitative information regarding the feasibility of developing potential product ideas. Finally, the process is an opportunity to validate the updated business case by a project's executive sponsors.

One problem with the phase-gate process is the potential for structural organization to interfere with creativity and innovation, as overly structured processes may cause creativity to be reduced in importance and to hinder the largely iterative process of innovation.

Opportunity Management

The opportunity management funnel is a visual representation of phase-gate decision making. Opportunity management has been defined as "a process to identify business and community development opportunities that could be implemented to sustain or improve a local economy." The components of opportunity management are:

- Identifying opportunities.
- Evaluating and prioritizing these opportunities: This may involve developing criteria, deliberating, and ranking the alternatives.
- Driving opportunities: Involves assigning leads, accountability, action plans, and project management.
- Constant monitoring: May require one of the following actions:
    - Advance: Commit additional resources to move the idea forward.
    - Rework: More investigation/rethinking.
    - Kill: Stop working on the idea and move on.

The goal of the opportunity management funnel is to eliminate weak or bad ideas before money or resources are contributed to realize these opportunities. The benefit of the opportunity management funnel when utilizing phase-gate decision making is that the funnel generates efficiencies where weak ideas are efficiently eliminated leaving a strong set of viable alternatives. To fulfill its mandate, the opportunity management funnel filters the broadest range of opportunities and ensures that all priority sectors are represented. When selecting which opportunities to filter through the process, economic developers should be aware that initially, there are no bad ideas or limits. The unviable alternatives will be filtered out throughout the process using phase-gate decision making process.

Constructability

Constructability (or buildability) is a project management technique to review construction processes from start to finish during pre-construction phase. It is to identify obstacles before a project is actually built to reduce or prevent errors, delays, and cost overruns.

The term "constructability" defines the ease and efficiency with which structures can be built. The more constructible a structure is, the more economical it will be. Constructability is in part a reflection of the quality of the design documents; that is, if the design documents are difficult to understand and interpret, the project will be difficult to build.

The term refers to:

- The extent to which the design of the building facilitates ease of construction, subject to the overall requirements for the completed building.

- The effective and timely integration of construction knowledge into the conceptual planning, design, construction, and field operations of a project to achieve the overall project objectives in the best possible time and accuracy at the most cost-effective levels.
- The integration of construction knowledge in the project delivery process and balancing the various project and environmental constraints to achieve the project goals and building performance at the optimal level.

Principles

There are 12 principles of construct-ability which are mapped on to the procurement process:

- Integration.
- Construction knowledge.
- Team skills.
- Corporate objectives.
- Available resources.
- External factors.
- Programme.
- Construction methodology.
- Accessibility.
- Specifications.
- Construction innovation.
- Feedback.

Value of Work Done

The value of work done (VOWD) is a project management technique for measuring and estimating the project cost at a point in time. It is mainly used in project environments of the Petroleum industry and is defined as the value of goods and services progressed, regardless of whether or not they have been paid for or received. The primary purpose of determining VOWD is to get an accurate and comprehensive as possible estimate of cost for a project at a point in time. This is used in overall project management including reporting and cost control.

Unlike the earned value, which measures the value of goods and services received as a percentage of the planned value, the VOWD is not measured against the plan, but against the committed cost. Committed costs can be derived from purchase orders, contracts, approved changes, change orders and other forms of commitments. From an earned value management point of view, the VOWD is comparable to the actual cost achieved rather than the earned value. VOWD represents the full value of the work that has been achieved, at a point in time, against the commercial criteria of the commitments for that work, regardless of payment or receipt.

VOWD for Engineering, Procurement and Construction (EPC) Services

VOWD of EPC (contract) services are measured in terms of actual physical progress based on the documentary evidence of the deliverable produced. The VOWD is determined by applying the percentage of physical progress achieved to the current committed value of the cost of that item, which is in general the contract or purchase order value, including any approved changes. For services specifically, incurred hours to a point in time can be used as a basis for progress, including hours recorded and those yet to be recorded for a specific point in time, as long as they were incurred to that point in time.

VOWD for Tagged Equipment

The VOWD for procuring tagged equipment is usually calculated based on a milestone deliverables basis as this type of equipment and its contractual milestones and VOWD are usually closely aligned.

Tagged equipment is any equipment that is one (or a few) of a kind specific to a project and type of equipment required for that project. It is not a commodity and specific for a particular task.

Examples of tagged equipment include; a pump, a motor, a drive, some electrical wire, a control cabinet, some specific instrumentation, a gauge, transformers. It is not bulk in nature.

Milestones examples may include; 10% on order execution, etc.

VOWD for Procured Regular Bulk Materials

The VOWD for procured bulk materials is usually calculated based on the quantities of materials delivered. The percent complete is calculated by dividing the quantity of material received at the site by the total quantity required for the project. The resulting percent is multiplied by the current agreed committed value of the material item to obtain the VOWD for that item.

Examples of regular bulk materials include;

- Standard valves: Such as small valves, with standard and published specifications, easily obtainable from alternative sources, comparable in nature, larger valves with the same characteristics also are regular bulk materials, more than one, a number in quantity, required for a number of applications and locations within/for a project.
- Standard pipe and tubing.
- Steel.

If there are significant quantities with financial and commercial obligations for such items en route, prior to receipt of such goods, these quantities should be included in the VOWD percent complete calculation for regular bulk materials.

VOWD for Procured Non Regular Bulk Materials

The VOWD for procured non regular bulk materials is usually calculated based on estimate of percent complete basis. The percent complete is calculated by dividing the quantity of material progressed at a point in time by the total quantity required for the project. The resulting percent is multiplied by the current agreed committed value of the material item to obtain the VOWD for that item. Adjustments, +/-, to the quantities should be made for other factors that affect the completion of the non-regular bulk material.

Characteristics of non-regular bulk materials are; higher or high quantity of materials, non-routine, unusual, special order, non-regular, special run, non-standard in nature.

Examples of non-regular bulk materials include; -Non regular valves - those that require unique or specialized specification, testing or manufacturing or similar, something that makes them non routine, high or higher volume in total quantity -Non regular pipes, tubes - those that require a special mill run, a large separate order of steel, special testing to meet specification or special manufacturing to meet project requirements, more than one in quantity, usually many -Steel - materials that require unique configuration, design, manufacturing and similar, lots of material, not simply one piece.

Adjustments might include steel mill retooling upfront costs, specialized steps to manufacture, temper, role, test or certify the pipe going through the mill. There is value in these steps that needs to be incorporated into the VOWD determination. To get documentary evidence to support an estimate as to the value of these steps one might use the milestones as inputs, supplier reports, pictures, video, progress reports on KPI's, supplier surveillance, as well as interim costs of shipping, handling and transportation.

VOWD for Procured Major Equipment

A. Weighted value basis One method for determining VOWD for major equipment is based on weighted values of items of equipment. At the outset of the project a list of equipment is prepared, and the weighted (%) value of each piece of equipment, with the sum of the weighted values of all items totaling 100%. When an item of equipment is received on site the percentage contribution of that equipment is added to the previous months weighted value of all other equipment to determine the total cumulative percentage value of equipment received on site. The VOWD of major equipment is calculated by multiplying the weighted percentage value of all equipment received at site by the total current approved contract value of the Major Equipment scope.

B. Percent Complete Basis: When weighted values are not available or appropriate for determining VOWD, an alternative method would be percent complete basis.

The VOWD of major equipment is calculated by multiplying the weighted percentage value of all progress of the major equipment, at a point in time, by the total current approved contract value of the Major Equipment scope.

To get documentary evidence to support an estimate as to the value of these steps one might use the milestones as inputs, as well as supplier reports, pictures, video, progress reports on KPI's, supplier surveillance, as well as interim costs of shipping, handling and transportation. Key inputs into the equipment can also help determining progress, such as key quantities and steps and stages of construction.

Examples of major equipment include; an off shore platform, a vessel, a barge, a steam turbine generator, a large mine hopper, or similar.

VOWD for Construction

For construction the physical percent complete of any element of the work is measured based on a physical measurement system (but not in terms of job-hours expended, as the measurement system needs to be fixed during the project duration).

Apply the same principles as in major equipment to determine the VOWD for construction. Examples of construction include; a building, a manufacturing plant, a complex, multifaceted industrial equipment or facility.

What VOWD is Not

VOWD is not solely based on goods and services receipts. VOWD is not solely based on cash and or invoice payments. VOWD is not simply a milestone based costing valuation. These components are referenced in determining VOWD, however VOWD is a more fulsome valuation determination of the full value of goods and services committed to and obligated to, at a point in time. Regardless of whether they have been paid for or have been completely received.

Value Breakdown Structure

A value breakdown structure (VBS) is a project management technique introduced by Stephen Devaux as part of the total project control (TPC) approach to project and program value analysis.

A work breakdown structure (WBS) in project management and systems engineering is a deliverable-oriented decomposition of a project into smaller components into a tree structure that represents how the work of the project will create the components of the final product. Resources and cost are typically inserted into the activities in a WBS, and summed to create a budget both for summary levels (often called "work packages") and for the whole project or program. Similarly, the expected value-added of each activity and/or component of the project (or projects within a program) are inserted into the VBS.

In most projects (and programs), there are some components and activities (and projects) that are mandatory and others that are optional. Mandatory activities are required, and have the full value of the project investment, as the project cannot be completed without them. In contrast, optional activities have only the value that they are adding to the project, i.e., their value is equal to the delta between the project/program value if they are included and the value if they are omitted.

For example, in creating an automobile, an engine, a driveshaft and wheels may all be considered mandatory, whereas cupholders are optional. If any of the mandatory activities are excluded, the project's value approaches zero. But the value of the cupholders is only the difference between the value of the car with and without cupholders.

The value from the VBS should also be used as the basis for tracking project value through Devaux's Index of Project Performance (DIPP). If scope is changed during execution, that change should be input into the VBS, the numerator in computing the Actual DIPP adjusted, and the DIPP Progress Index thus updated.

Unlike cost, which can be summed up the branches of a WBS to provide an overall budget, value cannot similarly be summed in a VBS. If the value of an automobile is $25,000, there are many components and activities that are mandatory in generating that value – leave any of them out, and the value of the project approaches zero. Therefore, the fact that the engine, driveshaft and wheels are all mandatory, and each therefore has a value-added of $25,000 does NOT make the value of the automobile $75,000.

The main purpose of the VBS is to prioritize components and work by the value they are expected to add, and to ensure that the value of the project investment is not reduced by the inclusion of work which has a value-added that is less than its true cost, which is the sum of its resource costs and its drag cost. This can often happen if the project's critical path changes so that different activities suddenly acquire critical path drag and drag cost: an optional activity that adds $10,000 to the expected value of the project and has a budget of $5,000 may make sense when it can be performed off the critical path but should probably be jettisoned if on the critical path if they now have a negative value-added due to a drag cost of more than $5,000.

Responsibility Assignment Matrix

A responsibility assignment matrix (RAM), also known as RACI matrix or linear responsibility chart (LRC), describes the participation by various roles in completing tasks or deliverables for a project or business process. RACI is an acronym derived from the four key responsibilities most typically used: *Responsible, Accountable, Consulted*, and *Informed*. It is used for clarifying and defining roles and responsibilities in cross-functional or departmental projects and processes. There are a number of alternatives to the RACI model.

Key Responsibility Roles in RACI Model

Role Distinction

There is a distinction between a role and individually identified people: A role is a descriptor of an associated set of tasks; may be performed by many people; and one person can perform many roles. For example, an organization may have ten people who can perform the role of project manager, although traditionally each project only has one project manager at any one time; and a person who is able to perform the role of project manager may also be able to perform the role of business analyst and tester.

- R = Responsible (also Recommender)

Those who do the work to complete the task. There is at least one role with a participation type of *responsible*, although others can be delegated to assist in the work required.

- A = Accountable (also Approver or final approving authority)

The one ultimately answerable for the correct and thorough completion of the deliverable or task, the one who ensures the prerequisites of the task are met and who delegates the work to those *responsible*. In other words, an *accountable* must sign off (approve) work that *responsible* provides. There must be only one *accountable* specified for each task or deliverable.

- C = Consulted (sometimes Consultant or counsel)

Those whose opinions are sought, typically subject matter experts; and with whom there is two-way communication.

- I = Informed (also Informee)

Those who are kept up-to-date on progress, often only on completion of the task or deliverable; and with whom there is just one-way communication.

Very often the role that is *accountable* for a task or deliverable may also be *responsible* for completing it (indicated on the matrix by the task or deliverable having a role *accountable* for it, but no role *responsible* for its completion, i.e. it is implied). Outside of this exception, it is generally recommended that each role in the project or process for each task receive, at most, just one of the participation types. Where more than one participation type is shown, this generally implies that participation has not yet been fully resolved, which can impede the value of this technique in clarifying the participation of each role on each task.

Responsibility Assignment Matrix - RACI Chart

	Jeff	Michael	Reto	YOU	Alex	Anna	Bill	Cindy	Felix	Fred	Hans	John	Livio	Luc	Marco	Paul	Peter	Sue	Ted	Tim
Planning / Schedule	R	A	I	C					C											Q
Risk Management		I	I	Q						A								R		
Quality Management			R	C						R										A
Procurement				R		Q				R								R		A
1. Specifications Listing								A		R								R		R
2. Site Requirements		C	A	R	Q						R									
3. Call for Tenders				Q	A	R	C				R							R		
4. Budget Approval				A	Q					R							R			R
5. Contract Negotiations			A		Q	R	R											R		

* R – Responsible (works on), A – Accountable, C – Consulted, I – Informed, Q – Quality Reviewer

RACI(Q) chart: At least one responsible and exactly one accountable person are designated for each task. Optional consulted and informed roles may also be denoted.

Assigning People to Facilities

The matrix is typically created with a vertical axis (left-hand column) of tasks (from a work breakdown structure) or deliverables (from a product breakdown structure), and a horizontal axis (top row) of roles (from an organizational chart).

Table: Example of a responsibility assignment (or RACI) matrix.

Code	Name	Project sponsor	Business analyst	Project manager	Technical architect	Applications development
Stage A	Manage sales					
Stage B	Assess job					
Stage C	Initiate project					
- C04	Security governance (draft)	C	C	A	I	I
- C10	Functional requirements	A	R	I	C	I

- C11	Business acceptance criteria	A	R	I	C	I
Stage D	Design solution					

Table: Maintenance Crew KPI RACI Chart.

Tasks	Maint Supervisors	Maint Analyst	Maint Planner	Maint Technician	Maint Supert	Rel Specialist	CMMS Proj Engr
Inputting Failure Data	A	C	I	R		C	C
Work Order Completion	R	C	C	C	A	I	I
Work Order Close Out	C	R	C		I	I	A
QA of Failure Data Input	C	R	I	C	I	C	A
Analyze Failure Reports	C	C	I	C	A	R	I
Maintenance Strategy Adjustments	C	I	I	C	A	R	R
Implementing new strategies	R	I	R	C	A	I	I

Alternatives

There are a number of alternatives to the RACI participation types:

PARIS

This is an early version of a Responsibility Assignment Matrix, with the roles defined as:

- Participant
- Accountable
- Review Required
- Input Required
- Sign-off Required

PACSI

This is a version very useful to organizations where the output of activities under the accountability of a single person/function can be reviewed and vetoed by multiple stakeholders, due to the collaborative nature of the culture.

- Perform: The person/function carrying out the activity.

- Accountable: The person/function ultimately answerable for the correct and thorough completion of the deliverable or task, and often the one who delegates the work to the performer.
- Control: The person/function reviewing the result of the activity. He or she has a right of veto; his or her advice is binding.
- Suggest: The person/function consulted to give advice based upon recognized expertise. The advice is non-binding.
- Informed: The person/function who must be informed of the result of the activity.

RASCI

This is an expanded version of the standard RACI, less frequently known as *RASCI*, breaking the *responsible* participation into:

- Responsible: Those responsible for the task, who ensure that it is done as per the approver.
- Support: Resources allocated to responsible. Unlike consulted, who may provide input to the task, support helps complete the task.

RASI

This is an alternative version of the standard RACI, foregoing the *consulted* participation and replacing it with:

- Support: Resources which play a supporting role in implementation.

RACIQ

This is an expanded version of the standard RACI, with an additional participation type:

- Quality Review: Those who check whether the product meets the quality requirements.

RACI-VS

This is an expanded version of the standard RACI, with two additional participation types:

- Verifier: Those who check whether the product meets the acceptance criteria set forth in the product description.
- Signatory: Those who approve the verify decision and authorize the product

hand-off. It seems to make sense that the signatory should be the party being accountable for its success.

CAIRO

This is an expanded version, of the standard RACI, also known as *RACIO* with one additional participation type:

- Out of the loop (or omitted): Designating individuals or groups who are specifically not part of the task. Specifying that a resource does not participate can be as beneficial to a task's completion as specifying those who do participate.

DACI

Another version that has been used to centralize decision making, and clarify who can re-open discussions.

- Driver: A single driver of overall project like the person steering a car.
- Approver: One or more approvers who make most project decisions, and are responsible if it fails.
- Contributors: Are the worker-bees who are responsible for deliverables; and with whom there is two-way communication.
- Informed: Those who are impacted by the project and are provided status and informed of decisions; and with whom there is one-way communication.

RAPID

Another tool used to clarify decision roles and thereby improve decision making, is RAPID, which was created by and is a registered trademark of Bain & Company.

- Recommend: The Recommend role typically involves 80 percent of the work in a decision. The recommender gathers relevant input and proposes a course of action—sometimes alternative courses, complete with pros and cons so that the decision maker's choices are as clear, simple and timely as possible.
- Agree: The Agree role represents a formal approval of a recommendation. The 'A' and the 'R' should work together to come to a mutually satisfactory proposal to bring forward to the Decider. But not all decisions will need an Agree role, as this is typically reserved for those situations where some form of regulatory or compliance sign-off is required.
- Perform: The Perform role defines who is accountable for executing or implementing the decision once it is made. Best-practice companies typically define P's and gather input from them early in the process.

- Input: The Input role provides relevant information and facts so that the Recommender and Decider can assess all the relevant facts to make the right decision. However, the 'I' role is strictly advisory. Recommenders should consider all input, but they don't have to reflect every point of view in the final recommendation.
- Decide: The Decide role is for the single person who ultimately is accountable for making the final decision, committing the group to action and ensuring the decision gets implemented.

RATSI

Another tool used in organization design or roles analysis:

- Responsibility: Identify who is in charge of making sure the work is done.
- Authority: Identify who has final decision power on the work.
- Task: Identify who actually does the work.
- Support: Identify who is involved to provide support to the work.
- Informed: Identify who is informed that the work has been done (or will be started).

DRASCI

A variant of RASCI developed by three Whitehall theorists (Kane, Jackson, Gilbert). This scheme is adapted for use in matrix management environments, and differs only from RASCI in having an additional role of *Driver* and a narrower *definition of Support.*

Driver: An individual or party that assists those who are *Responsible* for delivering a task by both producing supporting collateral and setting timescales for delivery in line with the overarching aim of the individual or party who is *Accountable* for the overall accomplishment of the objective. The distinction between *Driver* and *Support* lies in that the former reinforces and clarifies the parameters of the task on behalf of those who are *Accountable*, while the latter refers to those who help those who are *Responsible* in reaching a given goal.

PDQA

A version developed at U Tokyo and MIT for model-based project management. The PDQA set of roles corresponds to demand for capabilities of teams. Roles include those for work on scope, handling of dependencies as coordination, and exception handling through error detection and decisions across a project organization.

PDQA is used in agent based modeling to simulate the supply of these capabilities by teams in projects.

- Primary: Provides skill-based effort within capacity to complete scope and also manages dependencies through coordination.
- Decision: Handles any decision, including scope acceptable and exception handling decisions leading to rework.(Does not generation nominal scope).
- Quality: Reviews scope as it progresses to detect poor quality and escalates to decision maker as so. (Does not general nominal scope).
- Assist: Provides skill based effort with capacity to complete scope, in assistance to the primary. (Does not manage dependencies through coordination).

DCI

A minimal set of decision making categories used in organisation design or roles analysis:

- Decision Maker: Individual(s) who makes the decision and is accountable for its impact on the business.
- Consulted: Individual(s) accountable for providing guidance based on functional expertise and experience, highlighting issues and raising alternatives to support the Decision Maker.
- Informed: Impacted stakeholder(s) are notified after the decision has been made and who will need to support the execution of the decision.

RASCEIO

To be used when working on governance, risk, compliance (GRC) and outsourcing matters:

- Responsible
- Accountable
- Support
- Consult
- Execute

3rd parties contracted to execute activities in accordance with a service level agreement.

Key GRC roles, such as risk owner, policy owner - where accountability is devolved, but a role is needed to oversee whether accountabilities all fit together.

Variations

There are also a number of variations to the meaning of RACI participation types:

RACI (Alternative Scheme)

There is an alternative *coding*, less widely published but used by some practitioners and process mapping software, which modifies the application of the *R* and *A* codes of the original scheme. The overall methodology remains the same but this alternative avoids potential confusion of the terms *accountable* and *responsible*, which may be understood by management professionals but not always so clearly differentiated by others:

- Responsible: Those responsible for the performance of the task. There should be exactly one person with this assignment for each task.
- Assists: Those who assist completion of the task
- Consulted: Those whose opinions are sought; and with whom there is two-way communication.
- Informed: Those who are kept up-to-date on progress; and with whom there is one-way communication.

ARCi (Decisions)

This alternative is focused only on documenting who has the authority to make which decisions. This can work across all sized work groups.

- Accountable: Authorized to approve an answer to the decision.
- Responsible: Responsible to recommend an answer to the decision.
- Consulted: Those whose opinions are sought; and with whom there is two-way communication.
- Informed: Those who are informed after the decision is made; and with whom there is one-way communication.

Program Evaluation and Review Technique

The program (or project) evaluation and review technique (PERT) is a statistical tool used in project management, which was designed to analyze and represent the tasks involved in completing a given project.

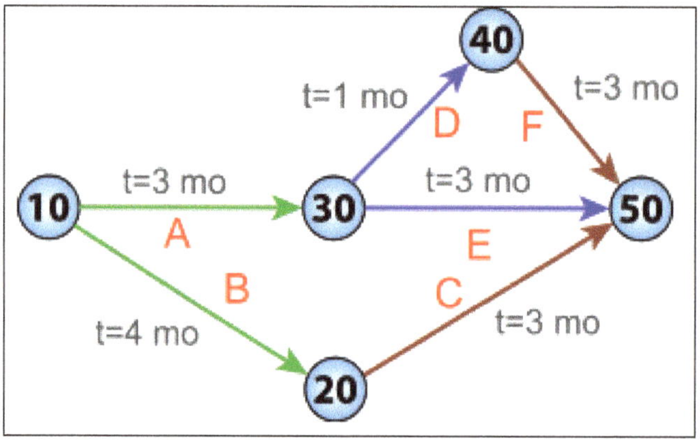

First developed by the United States Navy in the 1958, it is commonly used in conjunction with the critical path method in the year 1957 (CPM).

PERT is a method of analyzing the tasks involved in completing a given project, especially the time needed to complete each task, and to identify the minimum time needed to complete the total project. It incorporates uncertainty by making it possible to schedule a project while not knowing precisely the details and durations of all the activities. It is more of an event-oriented technique rather than start- and completion-oriented, and is used more in these projects where time is the major factor rather than cost. It is applied on very large-scale, one-time, complex, non-routine infrastructure and on Research and Development projects.

PERT offers a management tool, which relies "on arrow and node diagrams of *activities* and *events*: arrows represent the *activities* or work necessary to reach the *events* or nodes that indicate each completed phase of the total project."

PERT and CPM are complementary tools, because "CPM employs one time estimation and one cost estimation for each activity; PERT may utilize three time estimates (optimistic, expected, and pessimistic) and no costs for each activity. Although these are distinct differences, the term PERT is applied increasingly to all critical path scheduling."

Events and Activities

In a PERT diagram, the main building block is the *event*, with connections to its known predecessor events and successor events.

- PERT event: A point that marks the start or completion of one or more activities. It consumes no time and uses no resources. When it marks the completion of one or more activities, it is not "reached" (does not occur) until all of the activities leading to that event have been completed.
- Predecessor event: An event that immediately precedes some other event without any other events intervening. An event can have multiple predecessor events and can be the predecessor of multiple events.

- Successor event: An event that immediately follows some other event without any other intervening events. An event can have multiple successor events and can be the successor of multiple events.

Besides events, PERT also knows activities and sub-activities:

- PERT activity: The actual performance of a task which consumes time and requires resources (such as labor, materials, space, machinery). It can be understood as representing the time, effort, and resources required to move from one event to another. A PERT activity cannot be performed until the predecessor event has occurred.

- PERT sub-activity: A PERT activity can be further decomposed into a set of sub-activities. For example, activity A1 can be decomposed into A1.1, A1.2 and A1.3. Sub-activities have all the properties of activities; in particular, a sub-activity has predecessor or successor events just like an activity. A sub-activity can be decomposed again into finer-grained sub-activities.

Time

PERT has defined four types of time required to accomplish an activity:

- Optimistic time: The minimum possible time required to accomplish an activity (o) or a path (O), assuming everything proceeds better than is normally expected.

- Pessimistic time: The maximum possible time required to accomplish an activity (p) or a path (P), assuming everything goes wrong (but excluding major catastrophes).

- Most likely time: The best estimate of the time required to accomplish an activity (m) or a path (M), assuming everything proceeds as normal.

- Expected time: The best estimate of the time required to accomplish an activity (te) or a path (TE), accounting for the fact that things don't always proceed as normal (the implication being that the expected time is the average time the task would require if the task were repeated on a number of occasions over an extended period of time).

  $$te = (o + 4m + p) \div 6$$

  $$TE = \sum_{i=1}^{n} te_i$$

- Standard deviation of time: The variability of the time for accomplishing an activity (σ_{te}) or a path (σ_{TE}):

$$\sigma_{te} = (p - o) \div 6$$

$$\sigma_{TE} = \sqrt{\sum_{i=1}^{n} \sigma_{tei}^{2}}$$

Management Tools

PERT supplies a number of tools for management with determination of concepts, such as:

- Float or slack is a measure of the excess time and resources available to complete a task. It is the amount of time that a project task can be delayed without causing a delay in any subsequent tasks (free float) or the whole project (total float). Positive slack would indicate ahead of schedule; negative slack would indicate behind schedule; and zero slack would indicate on schedule.
- Critical path: The longest possible continuous pathway taken from the initial event to the terminal event. It determines the total calendar time required for the project; and, therefore, any time delays along the critical path will delay the reaching of the terminal event by at least the same amount.
- Critical activity: An activity that has total float equal to zero. An activity with zero float is not necessarily on the critical path since its path may not be the longest.
- Lead time: The time by which a predecessor event must be completed in order to allow sufficient time for the activities that must elapse before a specific PERT event reaches completion.
- Lag time: The earliest time by which a successor event can follow a specific PERT event.
- Fast tracking: Performing more critical activities in parallel.
- Crashing critical path: Shortening duration of critical activities.

Implementation

The first step for scheduling the project is to determine the tasks that the project requires and the order in which they must be completed. The order may be easy to record for some tasks (e.g. When building a house, the land must be graded before the foundation can be laid) while difficult for others (there are two areas that need to be graded, but there are only enough bulldozers to do one). Additionally, the time estimates usually reflect the normal, non-rushed time. Many times, the time required to execute the task can be reduced for an additional cost or a reduction in the quality.

In the following example there are seven tasks, labeled *A* through *G*. Some tasks can be done concurrently (*A* and *B*) while others cannot be done until their predecessor task is complete (*C* cannot begin until *A* is complete). Additionally, each task has three time estimates: the optimistic time estimate (*o*), the most likely or normal time estimate (*m*), and the pessimistic time estimate (*p*). The expected time (*te*) is computed using the formula $(o + 4m + p) \div 6$.

Activity	Predecessor	Time estimates			Expected time
		Opt. (o)	Normal (m)	Pess. (p)	
A	—	2	4	6	4.00
B	—	3	5	9	5.33
C	A	4	5	7	5.17
D	A	4	6	10	6.33
E	B, C	4	5	7	5.17
F	D	3	4	8	4.50
G	E	3	5	8	5.17

Once this step is complete, one can draw a Gantt chart or a network diagram.

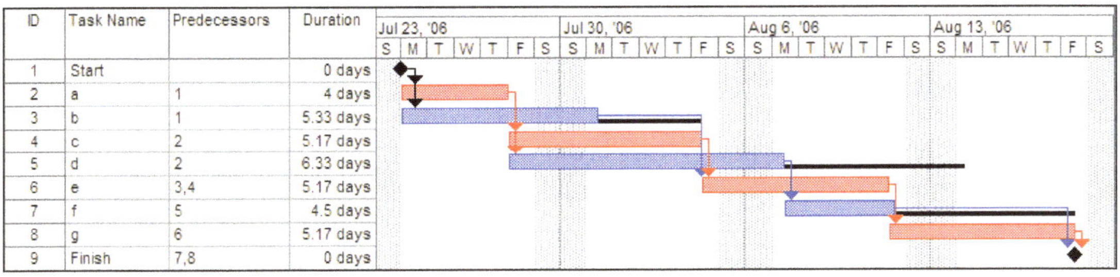

A Gantt chart created using Microsoft Project (MSP). (1) The critical path is in red, (2) the slack is the black lines connected to non-critical activities, (3) since Saturday and Sunday are not work days and are thus excluded from the schedule, some bars on the Gantt chart are longer if they cut through a weekend.

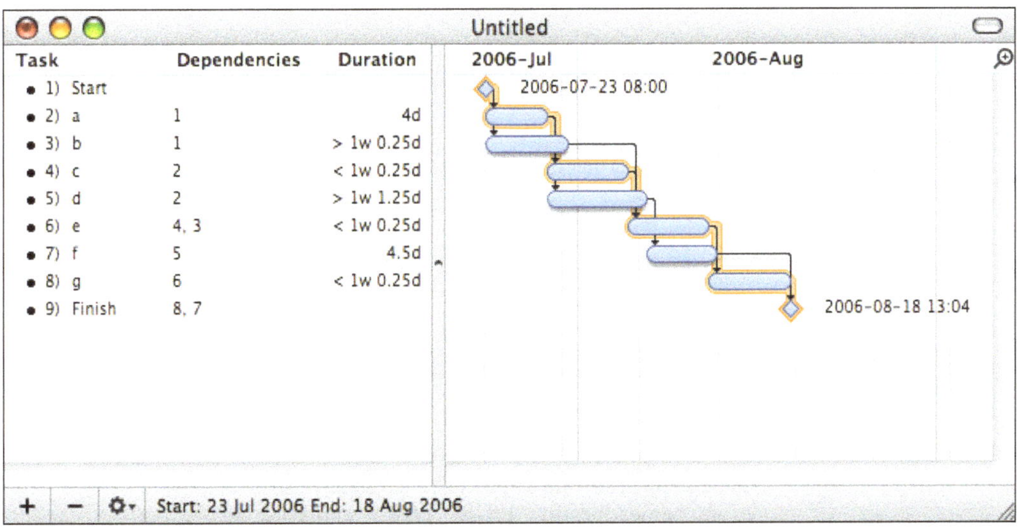

A Gantt chart created using OmniPlan. (1) The critical path is highlighted, (2) the slack is not specifically indicated on task 5 (d), though it can be observed on tasks 3 and 7 (b and f), (3) since weekends are indicated by a thin vertical line, and take up no additional space on the work calendar, bars on the Gantt chart are no longer or shorter when they do or don't carry over a weekend.

creating Network Diagram by Hand or by using Diagram Software

A network diagram can be created by hand or by using diagram software. There are two types of network diagrams, activity on arrow (AOA) and activity on node (AON). Activity on node diagrams is generally easier to create and interpret. To create an AON diagram, it is recommended (but not required) to start with a node named *start*. This "activity" has duration of zero (0). Then you draw each activity that does not have a predecessor activity (*a* and *b* in this example) and connect them with an arrow from start to each node. Next, since both *c* and *d* list *a* as a predecessor activity, their nodes are drawn with arrows coming from *a*. Activity *e* is listed with *b* and *c* as predecessor activities, so node *e* is drawn with arrows coming from both *b* and *c*, signifying that *e* cannot begin until both *b* and *c* have been completed. Activity *f* has *d* as a predecessor activity, so an arrow is drawn connecting the activities. Likewise, an arrow is drawn from *e* to *g*. Since there are no activities that come after *f* or *g*, it is recommended (but again not required) to connect them to a node labeled *finish*.

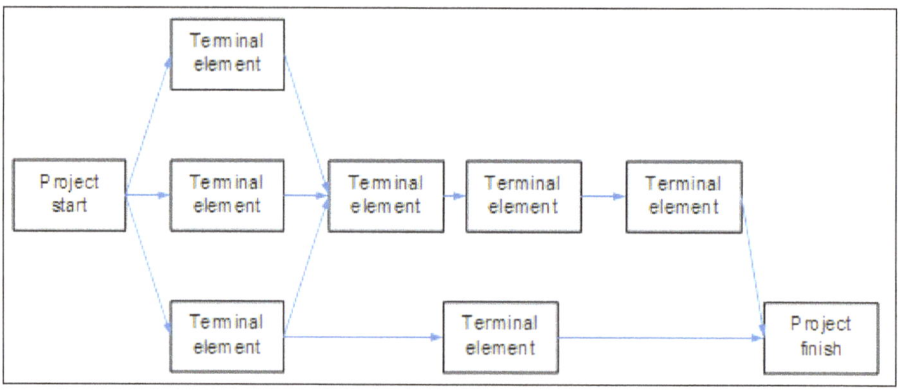

A project network diagram.

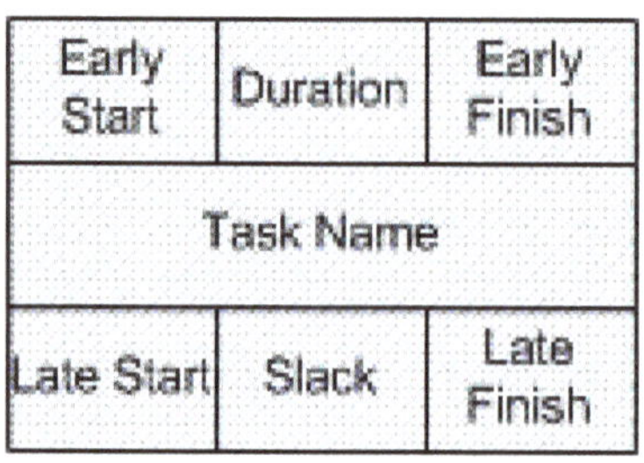

A node like this one can be used to display the activity name, duration, ES, EF, LS, LF, and slack.

By itself, the network diagram does not give much more information than a Gantt chart; however, it can be expanded to display more information. The most common information shown is:

- The activity name.
- The expected duration time.
- The early start time (ES).
- The early finish time (EF).
- The late start time (LS).
- The late finish time (LF).
- The slack.

In order to determine this information it is assumed that the activities and normal duration times are given. The first step is to determine the ES and EF. The ES is defined as the maximum EF of all predecessor activities, unless the activity in question is the first activity, for which the ES is zero (0). The EF is the ES plus the task duration (EF = ES + duration).

- The ES for start is zero since it is the first activity. Since the duration is zero, the EF is also zero. This EF is used as the ES for a and b.
- The ES for a is zero. The duration (4 work days) is added to the ES to get an EF of four. This EF is used as the ES for c and d.
- The ES for b is zero. The duration (5.33 work days) is added to the ES to get an EF of 5.33.
- The ES for c is four. The duration (5.17 work days) is added to the ES to get an EF of 9.17.
- The ES for d is four. The duration (6.33 work days) is added to the ES to get an EF of 10.33. This EF is used as the ES for f.
- The ES for e is the greatest EF of its predecessor activities (b and c). Since b has an EF of 5.33 and c has an EF of 9.17, the ES of e is 9.17. The duration (5.17 work days) is added to the ES to get an EF of 14.34. This EF is used as the ES for g.
- The ES for f is 10.33. The duration (4.5 work days) is added to the ES to get an EF of 14.83.
- The ES for g is 14.34. The duration (5.17 work days) is added to the ES to get an EF of 19.51.

- The ES for finish is the greatest EF of its predecessor activities (f and g). Since f has an EF of 14.83 and g has an EF of 19.51, the ES of finish is 19.51. Finish is a milestone (and therefore has a duration of zero), so the EF is also 19.51.

Barring any unforeseen events, the project should take 19.51 work days to complete. The next step is to determine the late start (LS) and late finish (LF) of each activity. This will eventually show if there are activities that have slack. The LF is defined as the minimum LS of all successor activities, unless the activity is the last activity, for which the LF equals the EF. The LS is the LF minus the task duration (LS = LF – duration).

- The LF for finish is equal to the EF (19.51 work days) since it is the last activity in the project. Since the duration is zero, the LS is also 19.51 work days. This will be used as the LF for f and g.

- The LF for g is 19.51 work days. The duration (5.17 work days) is subtracted from the LF to get an LS of 14.34 work days. This will be used as the LF for e.

- The LF for f is 19.51 work days. The duration (4.5 work days) is subtracted from the LF to get an LS of 15.01 work days. This will be used as the LF for d.

- The LF for e is 14.34 work days. The duration (5.17 work days) is subtracted from the LF to get an LS of 9.17 work days. This will be used as the LF for b and c.

- The LF for d is 15.01 work days. The duration (6.33 work days) is subtracted from the LF to get an LS of 8.68 work days.

- The LF for c is 9.17 work days. The duration (5.17 work days) is subtracted from the LF to get an LS of 4 work days.

- The LF for b is 9.17 work days. The duration (5.33 work days) is subtracted from the LF to get an LS of 3.84 work days.

- The LF for a is the minimum LS of its successor activities. Since c has an LS of 4 work days and d has an LS of 8.68 work days, the LF for a is 4 work days. The duration (4 work days) is subtracted from the LF to get an LS of 0 work days.

- The LF for start is the minimum LS of its successor activities. Since a has an LS of 0 work days and b has an LS of 3.84 work days, the LS is 0 work days.

Determination of Critical Path and Possible Slack

The next step is to determine the critical path and if any activities have slack. The critical path is the path that takes the longest to complete. To determine the path times, add the task durations for all available paths. Activities that have slack can be delayed without changing the overall time of the project. Slack is computed in one of two ways, slack = LF – EF *or* slack = LS – ES. Activities that are on the critical path have a slack of zero (0).

- The duration of path adf is 14.83 work days.
- The duration of path aceg is 19.51 work days.
- The duration of path beg is 15.67 work days.

The critical path is *aceg* and the critical time is 19.51 work days. It is important to note that there can be more than one critical path (in a project more complex than this example) or that the critical path can change. For example, let's say that activities *d* and *f* take their pessimistic (b) times to complete instead of their expected (T_E) times. The critical path is now *adf* and the critical time is 22 work days. On the other hand, if activity *c* can be reduced to one work day, the path time for *aceg* is reduced to 15.34 work days, which is slightly less than the time of the new critical path, *beg* (15.67 work days).

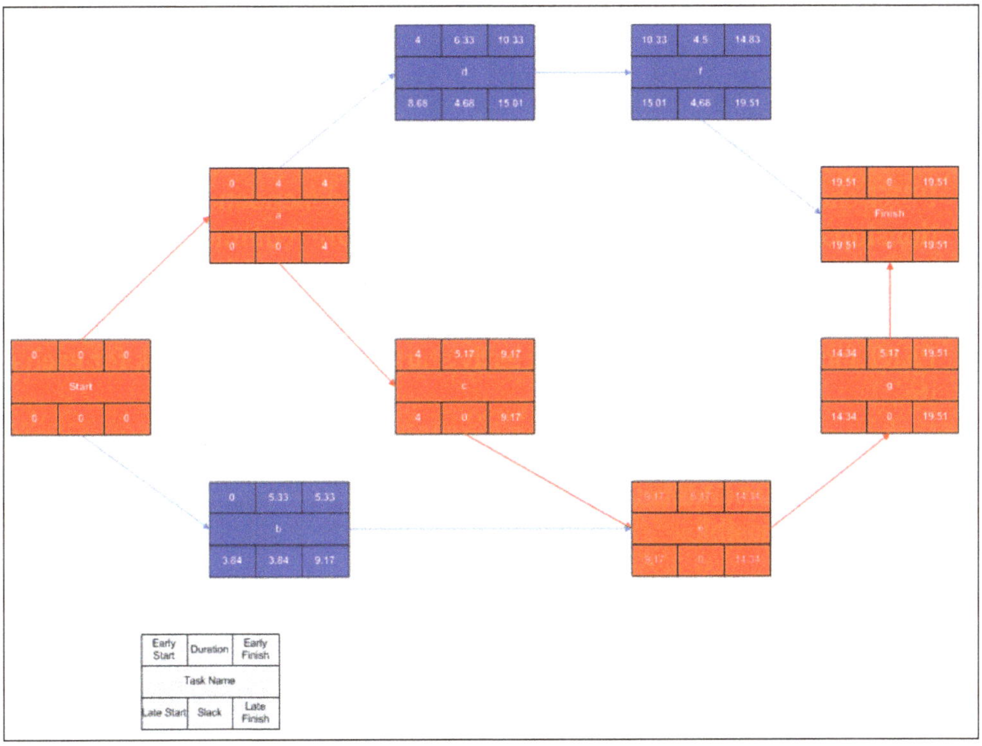

A completed network diagram created using Microsoft Vision. The critical path is in red.

Assuming these scenarios do not happen, the slack for each activity can now be determined.

- Start and finish are milestones and by definition have no duration, therefore they can have no slack (0 work days).
- The activities on the critical path by definition have a slack of zero; however, it is always a good idea to check the math anyway when drawing by hand.
    - $LF_a - EF_a = 4 - 4 = 0$

- $LF_c - EF_c = 9.17 - 9.17 = 0$
- $LF_e - EF_e = 14.34 - 14.34 = 0$
- $LF_g - EF_g = 19.51 - 19.51 = 0$

- Activity b has an LF of 9.17 and an EF of 5.33, so the slack is 3.84 work days.
- Activity d has an LF of 15.01 and an EF of 10.33, so the slack is 4.68 work days.
- Activity f has an LF of 19.51 and an EF of 14.83, so the slack is 4.68 work days.

Therefore, activity *b* can be delayed almost 4 work days without delaying the project. Likewise, activity *d* or activity *f* can be delayed 4.68 work days without delaying the project (alternatively, *d* and *f* can be delayed 2.34 work days each).

Project Scheduling Tool

Advantages

- PERT chart explicitly defines and makes visible dependencies (precedence relationships) between the work breakdown structure (commonly WBS) elements.
- PERT facilitates identification of the critical path and makes this visible.
- PERT facilitates identification of early start, late start, and slack for each activity.
- PERT provides for potentially reduced project duration due to better understanding of dependencies leading to improved overlapping of activities and tasks where feasible.
- The large amount of project data can be organized and presented in diagram for use in decision making.
- PERT can provide a probability of completing before a given time.

Disadvantages

- There can be potentially hundreds or thousands of activities and individual dependency relationships.
- PERT is not easily scalable for smaller projects.
- The network charts tend to be large and unwieldy, requiring several pages to print and requiring specially-sized paper.
- The lack of a timeframe on most PERT/CPM charts makes it harder to show status, although colours can help, e.g., specific colour for completed nodes.

Uncertainty in Project Scheduling

During project execution, however, a real-life project will never execute exactly as it was planned due to uncertainty. This can be due to ambiguity resulting from subjective estimates that are prone to human errors or can be the result of variability arising from unexpected events or risks. The main reason that PERT may provide inaccurate information about the project completion time is due to this schedule uncertainty. This inaccuracy may be large enough to render such estimates as not helpful.

One possible method to maximize solution robustness is to include safety in the baseline schedule in order to absorb the anticipated disruptions. This is called *proactive scheduling*. A pure proactive scheduling is a utopia; incorporating safety in a baseline schedule which allows for every possible disruption would lead to a baseline schedule with a very large make-span. A second approach, termed *reactive scheduling*, consists of defining a procedure to react to disruptions that cannot be absorbed by the baseline schedule.

Graphical Path Method

The Graphical Path Method (GPM) is a mathematically based algorithm used in project management for planning, scheduling and resource control. GPM represents logical relationships of dated objects – such as activities, milestones, and benchmarks – in a time-scaled network diagram.

Technique

To create a GPM schedule, users draw and place objects – such as activities, milestones, and benchmarks – on a time-scaled canvas. Objects are linked together to establish logical, precedence relationships. These relationships are governed by the Logic Diagramming Method (LDM), a blend of the Arrow Diagramming Method (ADM) and the Precedence Diagramming Method (PDM). In total, LDM permits 12 relationship types to account for all possible dependencies between objects. The resulting web of logically related, dated objects and their relationships forms a network diagram.

Object relationships form the backbone of a GPM network. They are used to calculate a number of object attributes, including link gap and object buffer, drift, and float. As objects and their relationships are added to or modified in the schedule, GPM continuously re-calculates and updates gap for all links and float for all dated objects. Link gaps are calculated from the dates of two related activities and floats are algorithmically calculated from gaps.

Differences between GPM and CPM

The Critical Path Method (CPM) is the traditional mathematical algorithm used for schedule logic computation. GPM utilizes a different algorithm than CPM and thus produces its own distinct schedule attributes.

Planned Dates vs. Early Dates

In a GPM network, objects not residing on the critical path, and thus having float, are permitted to be scheduled anywhere within their float range and are not forced to their early or late dates. This action in a GPM network is referred to as scheduling objects on planned dates. This is contrary to CPM logic, where a forward and backward pass algorithm defaults objects to their early dates, unless additional logic is introduced to constrain an object to a later date. GPM logic permits the as-planned scheduling framework because logic links retain their own attributes, namely gap.

Schedule Attributes

Gap

GPM allows users to place an object anywhere in between its early and late dates; consequently, link gap emerges between objects. Link gap permits object scheduling on planned dates while retaining the Total Float value of the network. The link gap values become the basis for calculating floats in a GPM network. The as-planned framework introduces additional schedule values of buffer, drift, and float.

Buffer

CPM calculates available slippage in Free Float and Total Float. CPM measures Free Float by how much a predecessor activity may be delayed without causing a delay to its nearest successor activity. In GPM this is called buffer and it is calculated as the minimum of the link gaps for all logic ties to successor objects.

Drift

Because activities in a CPM network default to their early dates, CPM does not calculate activity movement in the opposite direction – namely, how much an activity may backslide or extend to earlier dates without affecting predecessor activities. GPM permits activity placement between early and late dates and thus introduces this value of "preceding float" as drift. GPM calculates drift as the minimum of the link gaps for all logic ties to predecessor objects.

Float

CPM Total Float is measured by how much an activity may be delayed without delaying the project completion date. In GPM this is called float, with the distinction that it is measured with respect to planned dates rather than early dates. Thus, the GPM value of float plus drift is analogous to Total Float in CPM.

Real-time vs. Sequential Compiling

CPM relies on activity dates as the basis for float calculations, where total float is determined by the difference between late finish dates and early finish dates. This requires a standby calculation engine to perform a forward pass and a backward pass of the entire network when planning ceases or when an interim calculation is necessary for further planning. The result is that planning and scheduling are separate processes performed in sequential order.

In GPM's time-scaled framework, dates are innate, real-time attributes of network objects. This permit GPM to use the link gap between two objects for the float calculation and thus schedule data and object attributes are continuously updated in real-time, as changes to the schedule are committed. This allows for dynamic feedback from the schedule; users are permitted to execute schedule optimization, time and cost trade-offs, resource management and other analysis concurrently as the schedule is being built.

Critical Path Method

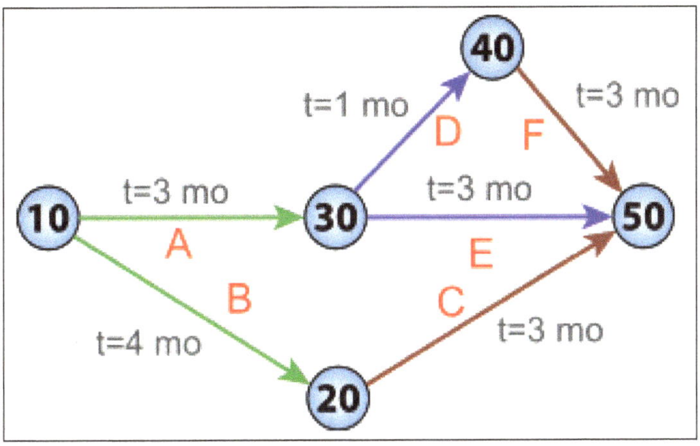

PERT chart for a project with five milestones (10 through 50) and six activities (A through F). The project has two critical paths: activities B and C, or A, D, and F – giving a minimum project time of 7 months with fast tracking. Activity E is sub-critical, and has a float of 1 month.

The critical path method (CPM), or critical path analysis (CPA), is an algorithm for scheduling a set of project activities. It is commonly used in conjunction with the program evaluation and review technique (PERT). A critical path is determined by identifying the longest stretch of dependent activities and measuring the time required to complete them from start to finish.

Basic Technique

The essential technique for using CPM is to construct a model of the project that includes the following:

- A list of all activities required to complete the project (typically categorized within a work breakdown structure).
- The time (duration) that each activity will take to complete.
- The dependencies between the activities.
- Logical end points such as milestones or deliverable items.

Using these values, CPM calculates the longest path of planned activities to logical end points or to the end of the project, and the earliest and latest that each activity can start and finish without making the project longer. This process determines which activities are "critical" (i.e., on the longest path) and which have "total float" (i.e., can be delayed without making the project longer). In project management, a critical path is the sequence of project network activities which add up to the longest overall duration, regardless if that longest duration has float or not. This determines the shortest time possible to complete the project. There can be 'total float' (unused time) within the critical path. For example, if a project is testing a solar panel and task 'B' requires 'sunrise', there could be a scheduling constraint on the testing activity so that it would not start until the scheduled time for sunrise. This might insert dead time (total float) into the schedule on the activities on that path prior to the sunrise due to needing to wait for this event. This path, with the constraint-generated total float would actually make the path longer, with total float being part of the shortest possible duration for the overall project. In other words, individual tasks on the critical path prior to the constraint might be able to be delayed without elongating the critical path; this is the 'total float' of that task. However, the time added to the project duration by the constraint is actually critical path drag, the amount by which the project's duration is extended by each critical path activity and constraint.

A project can have several, parallel, near critical paths; and some or all of the tasks could have 'free float' and/or 'total float'. An additional parallel path through the network with the total durations shorter than the critical path is called a sub-critical or non-critical path. Activities on sub-critical paths have no drag, as they are not extending the project's duration.

CPM analysis tools allow a user to select a logical end point in a project and quickly identify its longest series of dependent activities (its longest path). These tools can display the critical path (and near critical path activities if desired) as a cascading waterfall that flows from the project's start (or current status date) to the selected logical end point.

Visualizing Critical Path Schedule

Although the activity-on-arrow diagram (PERT Chart) is still used in a few places, it has generally been superseded by the activity-on-node diagram, where each activity is shown as a box or node and the arrows represent the logical relationships going from predecessor to successor as shown here in the "Activity-on-node diagram".

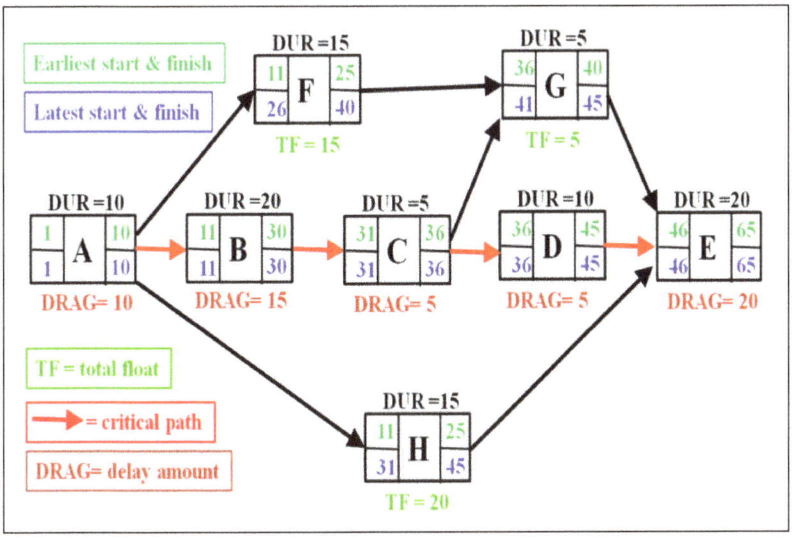

Activity-on-node diagram showing critical path schedule, along with total float and critical path drag computations.

In this diagram, Activities A, B, C, D, and E comprise the critical or longest path, while Activities F, G, and H are off the critical path with floats of 15 days, 5 days, and 20 days respectively. Whereas activities that are off the critical path have float and are therefore not delaying completion of the project, those on the critical path will usually have critical path drag, i.e., they delay project completion. The drag of a critical path activity can be computed using the following formula:

- If a critical path activity has nothing in parallel, its drag is equal to its duration. Thus A and E have drags of 10 days and 20 days respectively.
- If a critical path activity has another activity in parallel, its drag is equal to whichever is less: its duration or the total float of the parallel activity with the least total float. Thus since B and C are both parallel to F (float of 15) and H (float of 20), B has a duration of 20 and drag of 15 (equal to F's float), while C has a duration of only 5 days and thus drag of only 5. Activity D, with a duration of 10 days, is parallel to G (float of 5) and H (float of 20) and therefore its drag is equal to 5, the float of G.

These results, including the drag computations, allow managers to prioritize activities for the effective management of project, and to shorten the planned critical path of a project by pruning critical path activities, by "fast tracking" (i.e., performing more activities in parallel), and/or by "crashing the critical path" (i.e., shortening the durations of critical path activities by adding resources).

Critical path drag analysis has also been used to optimize schedules in processes outside of strict project-oriented contexts, such as to increase manufacturing throughput by using the technique and metrics to identify and alleviate delaying factors and thus reduce assembly lead time.

Crash Duration

Crash duration is a term referring to the shortest possible time for which an activity can be scheduled. It can be achieved by shifting more resources towards the completion of that activity, resulting in decreased time spent and often a reduced quality of work, as the premium is set on speed. Crash duration is typically modeled as a linear relationship between cost and activity duration; however, in many cases a convex function or a step function is more applicable.

Expansion

Originally, the critical path method considered only logical dependencies between terminal elements. Since then, it has been expanded to allow for the inclusion of resources related to each activity, through processes called activity-based resource assignments and resource leveling. A resource-leveled schedule may include delays due to resource bottlenecks (i.e., unavailability of a resource at the required time), and may cause a previously shorter path to become the longest or most "resource critical" path. A related concept is called the critical chain, which attempts to protect activity and project durations from unforeseen delays due to resource constraints.

Since project schedules change on a regular basis, CPM allows continuous monitoring of the schedule, which allows the project manager to track the critical activities, and alerts the project manager to the possibility that non-critical activities may be delayed beyond their total float, thus creating a new critical path and delaying project completion. In addition, the method can easily incorporate the concepts of stochastic predictions, using the program evaluation and review technique (PERT) and event chain methodology.

Currently, there are several software solutions available in industries that use the CPM method of scheduling. The method currently used by most project management software is based on a manual calculation approach developed by Fondahl of Stanford University.

Flexibility

A schedule generated using the critical path techniques often is not realized precisely, as estimations are used to calculate times: If one mistake is made, the results of the analysis may change. This could cause an upset in the implementation of a project if the estimates are blindly believed, and if changes are not addressed promptly. However, the structure of critical path analysis is such that the variance from the original schedule caused by any change can be measured, and its impact either ameliorated or adjusted for. Indeed, an important element of project postmortem analysis is the *as built critical path* (ABCP), which analyzes the specific causes and impacts of changes between the planned schedule and eventual schedule as actually implemented.

SWOT Analysis

SWOT analysis (or SWOT matrix) is a strategic planning technique used to help a person or organization identify strengths, weaknesses, opportunities, and threats related to business competition or project planning. It is designed for use in the preliminary stages of decision-making processes and can be used as a tool for evaluation of the strategic position of a city or organization. It is intended to specify the objectives of the business venture or project and identify the internal and external factors that are favorable and unfavorable to achieving those objectives. Users of a SWOT analysis often ask and answer questions to generate meaningful information for each category to make the tool useful and identify their competitive advantage. SWOT has been described as the tried-and-true tool of strategic analysis, but has also been criticized for its limitations.

Strengths and weakness are frequently internally-related, while opportunities and threats commonly focus on the external environment. The name is an acronym for the four parameters the technique examines:

- Strengths: Characteristics of the business or project that give it an advantage over others.
- Weaknesses: Characteristics of the business that place the business or project at a disadvantage relative to others.
- Opportunities: Elements in the environment that the business or project could exploit to its advantage.
- Threats: Elements in the environment that could cause trouble for the business or project.

The degree to which the internal environment of the firm matches with the external environment is expressed by the concept of strategic fit. Identification of SWOTs is important because they can inform later steps in planning to achieve the objective. First, decision-makers should consider whether the objective is attainable, given the SWOTs. If the objective is *not* attainable, they must select a different objective and repeat the process.

Some authors credit SWOT to Albert Humphrey, who led a convention at the Stanford Research Institute (now SRI International) in the 1960s and 1970s using data from Fortune 500 companies. However, Humphrey himself did not claim the creation of SWOT, and the origins remain obscure.

Internal and External Factors

SWOT analysis aims to identify the key internal and external factors seen as important to achieving an objective. SWOT analysis groups key pieces of information into two main categories:

- Internal factors: The strengths and weaknesses internal to the organization.
- External factors: The opportunities and threats presented by the environment external to the organization.

Analysis may view the internal factors as strengths or as weaknesses depending upon their effect on the organization's objectives. What may represent strengths with respect to one objective may be weaknesses (distractions, competition) for another objective. The factors may include all of the 4Ps as well as personnel, finance, manufacturing capabilities, and so on.

The external factors may include macroeconomic matters, technological change, legislation, and sociocultural changes, as well as changes in the marketplace or in competitive position. The results are often presented in the form of a matrix.

SWOT analysis is just one method of categorization and has its own weaknesses. For example, it may tend to persuade its users to compile lists rather than to think about actual important factors in achieving objectives. It also presents the resulting lists uncritically and without clear prioritization so that, for example, weak opportunities may appear to balance strong threats.

It is prudent not to eliminate any candidate SWOT entry too quickly. The importance of individual SWOTs will be revealed by the value of the strategies they generate. A SWOT item that produces valuable strategies is important. A SWOT item that generates no strategies is not important.

Use

SWOT analysis can be used in any decision-making situation when a desired end-state (objective) is defined, not just profit-seeking organizations. Examples include non-profit organizations, governmental units, and individuals. SWOT analysis may also be used in pre-crisis planning and preventive crisis management. SWOT analysis may also be used in creating a recommendation during a viability study/survey.

Strategy Building

SWOT analysis can be used to build organizational or personal strategy. Steps necessary to execute strategy-oriented analysis involve identification of internal and external factors (using the popular 2x2 matrix), selection and evaluation of the most important factors, and identification of relations existing between internal and external features.

For instance, strong relations between strengths and opportunities can suggest good conditions in the company and allow using an *aggressive* strategy. On the other hand, strong interactions between weaknesses and threats could be analyzed as a potential warning and advice for using a *defensive* strategy.

Matching and Converting

One way of using SWOT is matching and converting. Matching is used to find competitive advantage by matching the strengths to opportunities. Another tactic is to convert weaknesses or threats into strengths or opportunities. An example of a conversion strategy is to find new markets. If the threats or weaknesses cannot be converted, a company should try to minimize or avoid them.

Corporate Planning

As part of the development of strategies and plans to enable the organization to achieve its objectives, that organization will use a systematic/rigorous process known as corporate planning. SWOT alongside PEST/PESTLE can be used as a basis for the analysis of business and environmental factors:

- Set objectives: Defining what the organization is going to do.
- Environmental scanning:
    - Internal appraisals of the organization's SWOT: This needs to include an assessment of the present situation as well as a portfolio of products/services and an analysis of the product/service lifecycle.
- Analysis of existing strategies: This should determine relevance from the results of an internal/external appraisal. This may include gap analysis of environmental factors.
- Strategic issues defined: Key factors in the development of a corporate plan that the organization must address.
- Develop new/revised strategies: Revised analysis of strategic issues may mean the objectives need to change.
- Establish critical success factors: The achievement of objectives and strategy implementation.

- Preparation of operational, resource, projects plans for strategy implementation.
- Monitoring all results: Mapping against plans, taking corrective action, which may mean amending objectives/strategies.

Marketing

In many competitor analyses, marketers build detailed profiles of each competitor in the market, focusing especially on their relative competitive strengths and weaknesses using SWOT analysis. Marketing managers will examine each competitor's cost structure, sources of profits, resources and competencies, competitive positioning and product differentiation, degree of vertical integration, historical responses to industry developments, and other factors.

Marketing management often finds it necessary to invest in research to collect the data required to perform accurate marketing analysis. Accordingly, management often conducts market research (alternately marketing research) to obtain this information. Marketers employ a variety of techniques to conduct market research, but some of the more common include:

- Qualitative marketing research such as focus groups.
- Quantitative marketing research such as statistical surveys.
- Experimental techniques such as test markets.
- Observational techniques such as ethnographic (on-site) observation.
- Marketing managers may also design and oversee various environmental scanning and competitive intelligence processes to help identify trends and inform the company's marketing analysis.

Below is an example SWOT analysis of a market position of a small management consultancy with specialism in HRM.

Strengths	Weaknesses	Opportunities	Threats
Reputation in marketplace	Shortage of consultants at operating level rather than partner level.	Well established position with a well-defined market niche.	Large consultancies operating at a minor level.
Expertise at partner level in HRM consultancy	Unable to deal with multidisciplinary assignments because of size or lack of ability.	Identified market for consultancy in areas other than HRM.	Other small consultancies looking to invade the marketplace.

In Community Organization

The SWOT analysis has been used in community work as a tool to identify positive and negative factors within organizations, communities, and the broader society that promote or inhibit successful implementation of social services and social change efforts. It is used as a preliminary resource, assessing strengths, weaknesses, opportunities, and threats in a community served by a nonprofit or community organization. This organizing tool is best used in collaboration with community workers and/or community members before developing goals and objectives for a program design or implementing an organizing strategy. The SWOT analysis is a part of the planning for social change process and will not provide a strategic plan if used by itself. After a SWOT analysis is completed, a social change organization can turn the SWOT list into a series of recommendations to consider before developing a strategic plan.

SWOT ANALYSIS

	Strengths 1. 2. 3. 4.	Weaknesses 1. 2. 3. 4.
Opportunities 1. 2. 3. 4.	Opportunity-Strength strategies *Use strengths to take advantage of opportunities* 1. 2.	Opportunity-Weakness strategies *Overcome weaknesses by taking advantage of opportunities* 1. 2.
Threats 1. 2. 3. 4.	Threat-Strength strategies *Use strengths to avoid threats* 1. 2.	Threat-Weakness Strategies *Minimize weaknesses and avoid threats* 1. 2.

One example of a SWOT Analysis used in community organizing.

SWOT ANALYSIS

Internal		External	
Strengths	Weaknesses	Opportunities	Threats

A simple SWOT Analysis used in Community Organizing.

Strengths and weaknesses (*internal factors within an organization*):

- Human resources: Staff, volunteers, board members, target population.

- Physical resources: Your location, building, equipment.
- Financial: Grants, funding agencies, other sources of income.
- Activities and processes: Programs you run, systems you employ.
- Past experiences: Building blocks for learning and success, your reputation in the community.

Opportunities and threats (*external factors stemming from community or societal forces*):

- Future trends in your field or the culture.
- The economy: Local, national, or international.
- Funding sources: Foundations, donors, legislatures.
- Demographics: Changes in the age, race, gender, culture of those you serve or in your area.
- The physical environment: Is your building in a growing part of town? Is the bus company cutting routes?
- Legislation: Do new federal requirements make your job harder or easier?
- Local, national, or international events.

Although the SWOT analysis was originally designed as an organizational method for business and industries, it has been replicated in various community work as a tool for identifying external and internal support to combat internal and external opposition. The SWOT analysis is necessary to provide direction to the next stages of the change process. It has been used by community organizers and community members to further social justice in the context of Social Work practice.

Application in Community Organization

SWOT can be crucial to determining the success of a project, while factoring in funding, as well as accessibility and logic. Often, a city will spend a year weighing the Risk-benefits of a project before they even vote on it.

Elements to Consider

Elements to consider in a SWOT analysis include understanding the community that a particular organization is working with. This can be done via public forums, listening campaigns, and informational interviews. Data collection will help inform the community members and workers when developing the SWOT analysis. A needs and assets assessment is tooling that can be used to identify the needs and existing resources of the community. When these assessments are done and data has been collected, an analysis of the community can be made that informs the SWOT analysis.

Steps for Implementation

A SWOT analysis is best developed in a group setting such as a work or community meeting. A facilitator can conduct the meeting by first explaining what a SWOT analysis is as well as identifying the meaning of each term.

One way of facilitating the development of a SWOT analysis includes developing an example SWOT with the larger group then separating each group into smaller teams to present to the larger group after set amount of time. This allows for individuals, who may be silenced in a larger group setting, to contribute. Once the allotted time is up, the facilitator may record all the factors of each group onto a large document such as a poster board, and then the large group, as a collective, can go work through each of the threats and weaknesses to explore options that may be used to combat negative forces with the strengths and opportunities present within the organization and community. A SWOT meeting allows participants to creatively brainstorm, identify obstacles, and possibly strategize solutions/way forward to these limitations.

When to use SWOT Analysis

The uses of a SWOT analysis by a community organization are as follows: to organize information, provide insight into barriers that may be present while engaging in social change processes, and identify strengths available that can be activated to counteract these barriers.

A SWOT analysis can be used to:

- Explore new solutions to problems.
- Identify barriers that will limit goals/objectives.
- Decide on direction that will be most effective.
- Reveal possibilities and limitations for change.
- To revise plans to best navigate systems, communities, and organizations.
- As a brainstorming and recording device as a means of communication.
- To enhance "credibility of interpretation" to be used in presentation to leaders or key supporters.

Benefits and Advantages

The SWOT analysis in social work practice framework is beneficial because it helps organizations decide whether or not an objective is obtainable and therefore enables organizations to set achievable goals, objectives, and steps to further the social change or community development effort. It enables organizers to take visions and produce practical and efficient outcomes that effect long-lasting change, and it helps organizations gather meaningful information to maximize their potential. Completing a SWOT analysis is a useful process regarding the consideration of key organizational priorities, such as gender and cultural diversity and fundraising objectives.

Disadvantages

SWOT is intended as a starting point for discussion and cannot, in itself, show managers how to achieve a competitive advantage. Because the SWOT analysis is a snapshot of the firm at a particular moment in time, the analysis might obscure the fact that both the internal and external environment are rapidly changing.

Some findings from Menon and Hill and Westbrook have suggested that SWOT may harm performance and that "no-one subsequently used the outputs within the later stages of the strategy". Others have critiqued the misuse of the SWOT analysis as a technique that can be quickly designed without critical thought leading to a misrepresentation of strengths, weaknesses, opportunities, and threats within an organization's internal and external surroundings. If a firm becomes preoccupied with a single strength, such as cost control, they can neglect their weaknesses, such as product quality.

Another limitation includes the development of a SWOT analysis simply to defend previously decided goals and objectives. This misuse leads to limitations on brainstorming possibilities and "real" identification of barriers. This misuse also places the organization's interest above the well-being of the community. Further, a SWOT analysis should be developed as a collaborative with a variety of contributions made by participants including community members.

References

- Fast-tracking-vs-crashing-article: simplilearn.com, Retrieved 17 April, 2020
- Dinsmore, Paul C. (2012). Enterprise project governance : a guide to the successful management of projects across the organization. Rocha, Luiz. New York: AMACOM. ISBN 0814417469. OCLC 780445038
- Devaux, Stephen A. (2015). Total Project Control (2nd Edition): A Practitioner's Guide to Managing Projects as Investments. CRC Press. ISBN 978-1498706773
- Harold Kerzner (2003). Project Management: A Systems Approach to Planning, Scheduling, and Controlling (8th ed.). Wiley. ISBN 0-471-22577-0
- Mubarak, Saleh (2010). Construction Project Scheduling and Control, Second Edition. John Wiley and Sons. ISBN 978-0-470-50533-5
- Dess, Gregory (2018). Strategic Management. United States: McGraw-Hill. p. 73. ISBN 9781259927621
- Project-management-tools: projectsmart.co.uk, Retrieved 19 June, 2020

Project Management Software 5

- **Fast Track Schedule**
- **Spider Project**
- **Time-tracking Software**
- **Onepager Pro**
- **Teamwork**
- **Smartsheet**
- **Employee Scheduling Software**
- **Rational Plan**

Project management software helps project managers and teams to manage and meet goals on time while managing resources and cost. Its functions include task distribution, time tracking, budgeting, resource planning, team collaboration, etc. This chapter delves into the subject of project management software for a thorough understanding of it.

Project management software is software used for project planning, scheduling, resource allocation and change management. It allows project managers (PMs), stakeholders and users to control costs and manage budgeting, quality management and documentation and also may be used as an administration system. Project management software is also used for collaboration and communication between project stakeholders.

Although project management software is used is a variety of ways, its main purpose is to facilitate the planning and tracking of project components, stakeholders and resources.

Project management software caters to the following primary functions:

- Project planning: To define a project schedule, a project manager (PM) may use the software to map project tasks and visually describe task interactions.

- Task management: Allows for the creation and assignment of tasks, deadlines and status reports.
- Document sharing and collaboration: Productivity is increased via a central document repository accessed by project stakeholders.
- Calendar and contact sharing: Project timelines include scheduled meetings, activity dates and contacts that should automatically update across all PM and stakeholder calendars.
- Bug and error management: Project management software facilitates bug and error reporting, viewing, notifying and updating for stakeholders.
- Time tracking: Software must have the ability to track time for all tasks maintain records for third-party consultants.

Fast Track Schedule

Fast Track Schedule 10.2 is the leading easy-to-use project management software for planning, tracking, and reporting project goals. Ideal for both new and experienced project managers, Fast Track Schedule 10.2 Concurrent-Users Versions help teams effectively and successfully manage projects.

Fast Track Schedule 10.2 Concurrent-Users Versions are scalable for all networks and project teams of various sizes. Available in 5, 10, and 25-User configurations, Fast Track Schedule 10.2 Concurrent-Users Versions provide all the key features of the popular desktop version plus many other time and cost saving benefits.

- Reduced per user cost for medium to large project teams.
- Lower IT costs with a single installation and single point for updates.
- Scalability with built-in Key Code System for adding additional licenses.
- Global default templates for project teams.
- Locally stored user preferences.
- Concurrent-usage monitoring.
- Make Fast Track Schedule available to a larger volume of occasional users without the expense and administration of single-user licenses.
- Increased accuracy of license records for planning, purchasing, evaluation, and potential software audits.

Network administrators can also establish a global default schedule and templates by capturing preferred settings for dates, data columns, layouts, filters, and sorts—even bar styles and milestones.

Spider Project

Spider Project is a project management software, developed by a Russian company, Spider Project Team.

Spider Project is primarily a tool for project and portfolio scheduling and associated resource, materials, cost and risk management. It does not have features like project-related communication management, issue tracking, and document management.

According to Spider Project's publisher, the product provides CPM functions and metrics, and can calculate critical path drag, which tells the user how much each critical path activity delays project completion. Spider provides automatic scheduling, driven by resource allocation and resource leveling, and does not stress manual scheduling features.

Spider Project's publisher says it is closely linked with "Success Driven Project Management (SDPM)"—a methodology, developed by Spider Project Team, which describes how scheduling-related project management is done. Other project management software tools can use SDPM methods by adjusting the method to match that tool's functions.

Spider Project Team promotes project management in general, as well as PMBOK Guide specifically in Russia.

Features

Resource Leveling

Resource leveling is emphasized in most of publication about Spider Project. Though no academic-level report is available with comparison of the resource leveling algorithms of different project management tools, Spider Project has shown the best results among other tools compared in limited tests conducted by members of the professional Planning. Planet forum (tests were conducted based on library of Resource-Constrained Project Scheduling Problems (RCPSP), made available by Technical University of Munchen).

Resource Productivity

Spider supports activities with type "productivity". When specific activity is marked to be a productivity type, user needs to specify productivities of resources, assigned to this activity. Duration on such activity will then be calculated by Spider and will depend on the combined productivity of resources, assigned to this activity.

Skill Scheduling

In addition to conventional assignment of resources to activities, Spider supports assignment of resource Skills. In this situation user has to create table with relation between resources and skills. One resource can have one or more skills, equally every skill, can have one or more resources assigned to them. During project scheduling Spider automatically selects the actual resource, which will be assigned to activity. The decision which resource to assigned will be based on resource skills, productivities, costs and user defined priorities.

Variable Resource Assignment

In addition to conventional assignment of resources, when user specifies a fixed amount of resources assigned to a specific activity (e.g. Brick Layer [500%]), Spider supports situation, when user specifies a range (minimum and maximum amount of resources) required for activity. In this situation activity will be ongoing if minimum amount of resources is available, and if and when more resources become available, they will also be assigned to this activity.

Architecture

Though used for multi-user portfolio management, Spider does not have a server. It manages portfolios using the same software that manages individual projects. It does this with a distributed architecture, through software features and organisational procedures. This includes:

- Consolidating individual projects over a computer network into a portfolio, followed by redistributing projects, in case information in them has changed. This procedure must be executed regularly, following a schedule update cycle.
- Keeping information in "Corporate Reference Books, " which must be identical for all projects of the portfolio (e.g., resource information, resource calendars etc.). Corporate Reference Books should be protected by file system access control. If Corporate Reference Books are updated, those working on individual projects must synchronize them with their schedules (e.g., to use new resources, etc).

Software Versions

Spider project is available in four versions, which differ in functionality and price:

- Professional.
- Desktop Plus.

- Desktop Lite.
- Lite.

The Professional and Lite versions are also available in demo versions. The demo versions provide most program features and have no expiration time, but have a limit of 40 activities (though any number of project phases).

A Spider Project licence lets users access and distribute to any number of other users a Spider Project Viewer. Spider Project Viewer can open and analyse Spider Project files and generate reports, but not modify the project file.

Time-tracking Software

Time-tracking software is a category of computer software that allows its employees to record time spent on tasks or projects. The software is used in many industries, including those who employee freelancers and hourly workers. It is also used by professionals who bill their customers by the hour. These include lawyers, freelancers and accountants. The tool could be used stand-alone or be integrated with other applications like project management software, customer support and accounting to name just a few. Time tracking software is the electronic version of the traditional paper timesheet. Tracking time can increase productivity, as businesses can track time spent on tasks and get a better understanding of what practices causes the employees to waste time. Time tracking software enhances accountability, by documenting the time it takes to finish given tasks. The data is collected in database and could be used for data analysis by the human resources departments. Features offered by time-tracking software include:

- Automatic generation of invoices to the professional's clients or customers based on the time spent.
- Tracking of cost overruns for fixed cost projects.
- Workforce management packages which track attendance, employee absences, human resources issues, payroll, talent management, and labor analytics.

Types of Time-tracking Software

Timesheet

Allows users to manually enter time spent on tasks.

Time-tracking/Recording

Automatically records activities performed on a computer.

Time-tracking software can be:

- Standalone: Used only to record timesheets and generate reports.
- Integrated as part of:
    - Accounting systems, e.g. timesheet data fed directly to company accounts.
    - Billing systems, e.g. to generate invoices, especially for contractors, lawyers, etc.
    - Project management systems, e.g. timesheet data used by project management software to visualize the effort being spent on projects or tasks.
    - Payroll systems, e.g. to pay employees based on time worked.
    - Resource scheduling, e.g. bi-directional integration allows schedulers to schedule staff to tasks, which, once complete, can be confirmed and converted to timesheets.

Timesheet Software

Timesheet software is software used to maintain timesheets. It was popularized when computers were first introduced to the office environment with the goal of automating heavy paperwork for big organizations. Timesheet software allows entering time spent performing different tasks.

When used within companies, employees enter the time they've spent on tasks into electronic timesheets. These timesheets can then be approved or rejected by supervisors or project managers.

Since 2006, timesheet software has been moving to mobile platforms (smartphones, tablets, smart watches, etc.) enabling better tracking of employees whose work involves multiple locations.

Time-tracking/Recording Software

Time-tracking/recording software automates the time-tracking process by recording the activities performed on a computer and the time spent on each of them. This software is intended to be an improvement over timesheet software. Its goal is to offer a general picture of computer usage. Automatic time-tracking/recording software records and shows the usage of applications, documents, games, websites, etc.

When used within companies, this software allows monitoring the productivity of employees by recording the tasks they perform on their computers. It can be used to help filling out timesheets.

When used by freelancers, this software helps to create reports for clients (e.g. timesheets and invoices) or to prove work that was done.

Time-tracking Methods

There are several ways companies track employee time using time tracking software:

- Durational: Employees enter the duration of the task but not the times when it was performed.
- Chronological: Employees enter start and end times for the task.
- Automatic: The system automatically calculates time spent on tasks or whole projects, using a connected device or a personal computer, and user input using start and stop buttons. Users can retrieve logged tasks and view the duration, or the start and stop times.
- Exception-based: The system automatically records standard working hours except for approved time off or LOA.
- Clock-in Clock-out: Employees manually record arrival and departure times.
- Monitoring: The system records active and idle time of employees. It might also record screen captures.
- Location-based: The system determines the working status of employees based on their location.
    - Resource-scheduling: By scheduling resources in advance, employees schedules can be easily converted to timesheets.

Onepager Pro

OnePager Pro is a project management software package published by Chronicle Graphics, Inc., based in Denver, Colorado. OnePager Pro is primarily designed as a project presentation and reporting tool, creating Gantt charts, timelines, and schedule summaries based on data from other project management software such as Microsoft Project. In 2012, the company trademarked the term "Gantt Art" to describe the visuals that OnePager Pro creates.

Features

- Creating presentation-ready Gantt charts.
- Conditional formatting of Microsoft Project schedules.
- Summarizing one or multiple project plans.
- Dynamically grouping and sorting tasks in a project schedules.

- Tracking project changes over time with versioned snapshots.
- Showing dependencies between project tasks and milestones.

Teamwork

Twproject is a web-based project and groupware management tool developed by Open Lab, an Italian software house founded in 2001. It won the 17th Jolt Productivity Award in 2007 in the project management category. It has widespread use in universities as a teaching tool in project management courses. It is used by Canonical Ltd., Oracle Corporation, General Electric and many other companies from corporations to small start-ups.

Features

- Project management (with Microsoft Project import/export), and JSON format.
- Gantt editor: Uses jQuery Gantt components.
- Time tracking: Several entry points: dashboard, weekly view, issues, start/stop buttons.
- Resource planning with weekly/monthly view, work load overview, unavailability from agenda.
- Issue tracking (with Kanban), e-mail integration, task dedicated inboxes.
- Dashboard configuration, with customizable portlets and layout.
- Message boards.
- Scrum module.
- Meeting and minute management, attached documents.
- Agenda (Integrates with iCal, Microsoft Outlook, Microsoft Entourage, and Google Calendar).
- Document management, remote file systems link with NTFS, FTP, SVN, S3 (Dropbox, Google drive).
- Mobile application for iPhone, iPad, Android, Blackberry, Windows phone.

Integration

The database structure and the relative Java sources are available from Sourceforge in

GPL. A basic JSON API is available for a simple integration. The applications runs in Java JDK 6 on the Hibernate object/relational mapping.

The standard distribution uses Apache Tomcat 6, but can run on any J2EE application server. Twproject is tested on these DB servers: MySQL, Oracle, SQL Server, PostgreSql, HSQLDB, but as uses Hibernate can run on many others. There is simple graphical step-by-step installer for Windows, Mac, Linux both 32 or 64 bit processors or .zip/.tar.gz/.rpm packages.

Smartsheet

Smartsheet is a software as a service (SaaS) offering for collaboration and work management, developed and marketed by Smartsheet Inc. It is used to assign tasks, track project progress, manage calendars, share documents, and manage other work, using a tabular user interface.

Features

Smartsheet is used to collaborate on project timelines, documents, calendars, tasks, and other works. According to IDG, it is "part office productivity, part project management, part document sharing. It is trying to be the central hub for how people work." Smartsheet competes with Microsoft Project. It combines some of the functionality of Microsoft Project, Excel, Access and SharePoint.

According to *Forbes*, Smartsheet has "a relatively simple" user interface. The interface centers on "smartsheets," which are similar to spreadsheets typically found in Microsoft Excel. Each smartsheet can have its rows expanded or collapsed to see individual tasks or large-scale project progress respectively. Tasks can be sorted by deadline, priority or the person assigned to them. If a spreadsheet contains dates, Smartsheet creates a calendar view.

Each row in a smartsheet may have files attached to it, emails stored within it, and a discussion board associated with it. When a new smartsheet is created, notifications are pushed out to staff to populate its rows and columns. As information is updated, other smartsheets tracking the same task, project or data-point are updated automatically. The service also has alerts for when a task deadline is coming up, and keeps track of document versions.

Smartsheet can import data from Microsoft Office or Google applications. It integrates with Salesforce.com, Dropbox and Amazon Web Services. There is also a Smartsheet mobile app for Android and iOS operating systems. The service is offered on a subscription basis with no free tiers.

Employee Scheduling Software

Employee scheduling software automates the process of creating and maintaining a schedule. Automating the scheduling of employees increases productivity and allows organizations with hourly workforces to re-allocate resources to non-scheduling activities. Such software will usually track vacation time, sick time, compensation time, and alert when there are conflicts. As scheduling data is accumulated over time, it may be extracted for payroll or to analyze past activity. Although employee scheduling software may or may not make optimization decisions, it does manage and coordinate the tasks. Today's employee scheduling software often includes mobile applications. Mobile scheduling further increased scheduling productivity and eliminated inefficient scheduling steps. It may also include functionality including applicant tracking and on-boarding, time and attendance, and automatic limits on overtime. Such functionality can help organizations with issues like employee retention, compliance with labor laws, and other workforce management challenges.

Purpose

A theoretical underpinning of an employee scheduling problem can be represented as the Nurse scheduling problem, which is NP-hard. The theoretical complexity of the problem is a significant factor in the development of various software solutions. This is because systems must take into account many different forms of schedules that could be worked, and allocate employees to the correct schedule. Ultimately, optimization of scheduling is to minimize costs, but also often requires a reciprocal approach from management instead of complete reliance on software.

Punch Cards

The earliest form of automated employee scheduling and managing of employee hours was the Punch Card. The idea first created by Basile Bouchon developed the control of a loom by punched holes in paper tape in 1725. Herman Hollerith improved the design. IBM manufactured and marketed a variety of unit record machines for creating, sorting, and tabulating punched cards, even after expanding into electronic computers in the late 1950s. IBM developed punched card technology into a powerful tool for business data-processing and produced an extensive line of general purpose unit record machines.

Magnetic Tape

During the 1960s, the punched card was gradually replaced as the primary means for data storage by magnetic tape, as better, more capable computers became available. Mohawk Data Sciences introduced a magnetic tape encoder in 1965, a system marketed as a keypunch replacement which was somewhat successful, but punched cards were still commonly used for data entry and programming until the mid-1980s when the combination of lower cost magnetic disk storage, and affordable interactive terminals on less expensive minicomputers made punched cards obsolete for this role as well. However, their influence lives on through many standard conventions and file formats.

Auto-scheduling and Intelligent Rostering

In the 2010s, the wide adoption of mobile devices and the rise of 3G, 4G, and 5G networks worldwide has made it possible to approach the task of scheduling differently. In the last decade, many software solutions have sprung up to make the lives of business owners and managers easier and less burdensome.

The first wave of solutions helped small business owners to schedule, manage, and communicate with their employees in a more streamlined way. The newer way of solutions go a step further, leveraging machine learning and are being built on even newer cloud technologies. The need for automation and intelligent rostering in workforce management will continue to grow as society's heads into a gig economy.

Complexity

Algorithms are used within the employee scheduling software in order to determine not only who is working, but also the specific jobs and tasks required of the workers. The system still must be monitored, and any further issues with assigning of specifics is done manually. Within the context of roster problems and models, there are three main factors to work out the differences: the integration of days off scheduling with line of work construction and task assignment, roster construction, and demand type. These complexities thusly require that each and every workplace must optimize employee scheduling software based off their own unique set of rules, issues and needs. Additionally, it is difficult to determine optimal solution that minimize costs, meet employee preferences, distribute shifts equitably among employees and satisfy all the workplace constraints. In many organizations, the people involved in developing rosters need decisions support tools to help provide the right employees at the right time and the right cost while achieving a high level of employee satisfaction. Due to constant change within work environments, new models and algorithms must be created in order to allow for flexibility as needs and demands arise. For example, when a large number of new employees are hired, as in the total workforce is increased, the scheduling software likely will need to be updated in order to allow for such a change.

Features

Although employee scheduling software won't necessarily improve business practices by itself, it does automate typically tedious business administration. It can also have positive effects on aspects of the business indirectly, including employee engagement, employee retention, and lowered labor costs. By providing management with large amounts of data, this software can assist management in making decisions and automatically create a work schedule that fits as many constraints as possible. Also, the software may be a part of an ERP package or other human resource management system.

Features vary depending on software vendor, but some typical features include:

- Gantt chart or calendar view of the schedule.
- Approve employee requests for time off.
- Reduce unproductive workforce due to over scheduling.
- Use weather forecasts to predict staffing needs.
- Days off scheduling.
- Allow employees to swap shifts.
- Templates to roll out shift plans over medium term.
- Interface to payroll and/or management accounting software.
- Ability to easily identify unassigned shifts.
- Ability to create reports for invoicing and payroll.
- Manage the task of automation and data collection.
- Workplace analysis.
- Mobile application integration.
- Interface agents.

Rational Plan

Rational Plan is a project management platform that puts the emphasis on improving productivity, simplified use and fast learning. It was developed to address various types of users, ranging from novice project managers, users that require an environment to manage multiple projects and up to enterprises that are in need of a distributed solution with concurrent access. With RationalPlan, project managers and team members will find it easy to build project plans that are consistent with their requirements and end goals, effectively manage resources and evaluate workload, monitor project progress, estimate expenditures, and track and manage budget.

Choosing Rational Plan entails a string of advantages for project managers, team members, and companies alike. Among the benefits Rational Plan presents include:

- Effortless management and monitoring of projects, budget, and resources.
- Quickly identify issues and potential problems that might hamper a project's progress.
- Monitor and follow project progress in terms of completion, schedule, and expenses.
- Undo or redo steps on multiple levels.
- Build and implement project plans immediately and plan schedules.

Rational Plan puts the accent on productivity and tries to be as easy to use as possible: straightforward and intuitive.

Compared with other products, Rational Plan has the same power but is more affordable to users. If you compare, for example, the Rational Plan Single product with Microsoft Project standard version you get 80% of the functionality at 20% of the price. The vendor states that a particular customer, after buying Rational Plan, wanted a refund because could not find certain features that were available in MS Project. After explaining to him where he can find that functionality, the vendor also recommended to keep the product. A few days later, the vendor received this answer: "Now that I get to know Rational Plan better, I wouldn't want to miss it anymore. You helped me save a lot of money by preventing me from buying MS-Project."

Embedded Project Guide

Project management applications tend to be a little bit more complicated and require some training for users to understand how to use them. There are special terms and notions that need additional explanations to understand them. Rational Plan offers an embedded project guide that takes users step by step through the whole process of initiating, planning and controlling a project. It is great for a novice or accidental project manager and also has the power and the tools to assist an experienced one. Once users get used to the software they can hide the project guide, increase the workspace area and create their own pattern in using the product.

Works Every Where

Rational Plan was developed to work on any operating system: Windows, Mac OS X, different Linux flavors. Even more with the cloud service module it can run directly within the browser no matter what the underlying operating system is.

References

- Project-management-software, definition-13132: techopedia.com, Retrieved 13 August, 2020
- Fasttrack-schedule-concurrent, project-management-software: aecsoftware.com, Retrieved 12 January, 2020
- Goff, Stacy A. (2009). "9. Visions For the Project Management Software Industry" (PDF). Project Management Circa 2025. Project Management Institute, Inc. ISBN 978-1-933890-96-8
- Rationalplan: reviews.financesonline.com, Retrieved 28 February, 2020
- Glover, Fred; McMillan, Claude; Glover, Randy (1984-02-01). "A heuristic programming ap-proach to the employee scheduling problem and some thoughts on "managerial robots"". Journal of Operations Management. 4 (2): 113–128. doi:10.1016/0272-6963(84)90027-5

PERMISSIONS

All chapters in this book are published with permission under the Creative Commons Attribution Share Alike License or equivalent. Every chapter published in this book has been scrutinized by our experts. Their significance has been extensively debated. The topics covered herein carry significant information for a comprehensive understanding. They may even be implemented as practical applications or may be referred to as a beginning point for further studies.

We would like to thank the editorial team for lending their expertise to make the book truly unique. They have played a crucial role in the development of this book. Without their invaluable contributions this book wouldn't have been possible. They have made vital efforts to compile up to date information on the varied aspects of this subject to make this book a valuable addition to the collection of many professionals and students.

This book was conceptualized with the vision of imparting up-to-date and integrated information in this field. To ensure the same, a matchless editorial board was set up. Every individual on the board went through rigorous rounds of assessment to prove their worth. After which they invested a large part of their time researching and compiling the most relevant data for our readers.

The editorial board has been involved in producing this book since its inception. They have spent rigorous hours researching and exploring the diverse topics which have resulted in the successful publishing of this book. They have passed on their knowledge of decades through this book. To expedite this challenging task, the publisher supported the team at every step. A small team of assistant editors was also appointed to further simplify the editing procedure and attain best results for the readers.

Apart from the editorial board, the designing team has also invested a significant amount of their time in understanding the subject and creating the most relevant covers. They scrutinized every image to scout for the most suitable representation of the subject and create an appropriate cover for the book.

The publishing team has been an ardent support to the editorial, designing and production team. Their endless efforts to recruit the best for this project, has resulted in the accomplishment of this book. They are a veteran in the field of academics and their pool of knowledge is as vast as their experience in printing. Their expertise and guidance has proved useful at every step. Their uncompromising quality standards have made this book an exceptional effort. Their encouragement from time to time has been an inspiration for everyone.

The publisher and the editorial board hope that this book will prove to be a valuable piece of knowledge for students, practitioners and scholars across the globe.

INDEX

CPSIA information can be obtained
at www.ICGtesting.com
Printed in the USA
LVHW060907030122
707669LV00002B/385

9 781639 894468